W9-BQS-830

Drinking
Water

Drinking Water

A HISTORY

James Salzman

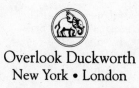

Overlook Duckworth
New York • London

This edition first published in paperback in the United States and the United
Kingdom in 2013 by Overlook Duckworth, Peter Mayer Publishers, Inc.

NEW YORK
141 Wooster Street
New York, NY 10012
www.overlookpress.com
For bulk and special sales, please contact sales@overlookny.com,
or write us at the above address.

LONDON
30 Calvin Street
London E1 6NW
info@duckworth-publishers.co.uk
www.ducknet.co.uk

Copyright © 2012 by James Salzman

All rights reserved. No part of this publication may be reproduced
or transmitted in any form or by any means, electronic or mechanical,
including photocopy, recording, or any information storage and
retrieval system now known or to be invented, without permission
in writing from the publisher, except by a reviewer who wishes to
quote brief passages in connection with a review written
for inclusion in a magazine, newspaper, or broadcast.

Cataloging-in-Publication Data is available from the Library of Congress
A catalogue record for this book is available from the British Library

Book design and typeformatting by Bernard Schleifer
Manufactured in the United States of America
1 3 5 7 9 10 8 6 4 2
ISBN US: 978-1-4683-0711-5
ISBN UK: 978-0-7156-4728-8

To Heather

Contents

Preface

THE COVER OF THE AUGUST 2011 ISSUE OF *Reader's Digest* features a picture of a glass of water with a question superimposed in bold type: "How Safe Is Our Water?" To make sure the interested reader is left in no doubt, an arrow connects a product warning in bright red type to the glass. The warning says, "MAY CONTAIN: ROCKET FUEL, BIRTH CONTROL PILLS, ARSENIC, AND MORE SHOCKING INGREDIENTS."

The same month's cover of the trendy magazine *Fast Company* features a head shot of the movie star Matt Damon. No mention is made of his current starring role or love life. Instead, the attention-grabbing title reads, "Matt Damon and His Global War for Water."

Water has become big news, and not just in corporate boardrooms or city halls. There is likely little overlap in the audiences of *Reader's Digest* and *Fast Company* (indeed, it would be hard to come up with two titles less likely to be bought by the same person), but editors of both clearly think that their readers care about drinking water. At the mention of drinking water people immediately become engaged. Is it safe to drink tap water? Should we feel guilty buying bottled water? Is our water vulnerable to terrorist attacks? The issues surrounding drinking water speak to a remarkably broad community, and they always have.

The term "drinking water" is a wonderfully ambiguous pairing of words. "Drinking" can be an adjective, describing the many natures of this clear liquid. This water has special, vital qualities. It's not ocean water, not dish water, not swamp water. It is potable water—safe enough to consume without getting sick. A rare liquid, one that will become less and less taken for granted in the future.

Or "drinking" can connote an action—a specific intent to drink water rather than freeze water, sell water, wash with water. And if the water is for the act of drinking, then who gets to drink, when can they drink, and where can they drink?

Such ambiguity is entirely appropriate for one of the few human actions and conditions that are truly universal. Some people choose to eat red meat; some eat only fish; some eat no meat at all. But everyone drinks water. And, though a clear liquid, it contains many meanings. While nothing could seem simpler than a clear glass of water, it is difficult to find a more complex or fascinating topic. After all, drinking water is the story of empire. Since prehistoric times, human settlements have been located near safe drinking water. The great capital cities of the world—Machu Picchu, Rome, London, New York—all developed new technologies to ensure safe water for their citizens. A scarce resource, access to water is power. Who gets to drink and who doesn't? Bloody conflicts over the control of drinking water sources go as far back as the Bible yet are featured on the front page of today's *New York Times*.

It is bound up in myth, both good and evil. Natural waters have long been viewed as special, with similar tales across distant cultures of eternal youth, passages to the afterlife, miraculous cures, and mystical wisdom. The mythmaking continues today, implicit in the marketing campaigns of many bottled water companies. And it is a central concern of science and medicine. The fields of epidemiology and public health developed specifically to manage the health threats posed by unsafe water. Even today, there is much we do not know about how much arsenic or other contaminants are safe in our drinking water.

Drinking water is the stuff of commerce. There basically was no commercial market for bottled water forty years ago but today bottled water rivals soft drinks for dominance in the multibillion-dollar beverage sector. And drinking water is the story of humanity's future. The greatest threat to human well-being in the world today is not climate change, AIDS, or warfare. Unsafe drinking water is the single largest killer in the world. Roughly half of the developing world suffers from illnesses caused by contaminated water supplies.

No surprise, then, that the history of drinking water highlights the most pressing issues of our time—from globalization, social justice, and commerce to terrorism, national security, and technology.

THE ORIGINS OF THIS PROJECT GO BACK TO 2004, WHEN I WAS TEACHing a class on the Clean Water Act. As I mused aloud how amazing it was that water treatment technologies now allow more Americans to receive safe drinking water through the tap than ever before, I was caught by surprise. Looking around the room, more than half the students had bottles of water sitting on their desks. *If tap water is safer than ever before*, I thought, *then why is bottled water so popular? What do they think they're buying?*

A fan of Mark Kurlansky's books *Cod* and *Salt* and other works that tell the history of the world through the prism of a commodity, I searched local bookstores for a popular history of drinking water but found nothing. More than half a dozen books have recently been published about bottled water, inefficient use of water, conflicts over water, or the challenges we face from running out of water, but the drivers for these issues are large-scale water uses such as agriculture, industry, and municipalities. This is the first book to take a broad look at drinking water, how we and past societies have thought about and managed this most vital of all resources.

This book would not be possible without the assistance of many others. I have been greatly helped by many student researchers since 2004: Justin Becker, Ryan Crosswell, Jill Falor, James Gillenwater, Michael Hiatt, Kelcey Patrick-Ferree, Jena Reger, Jonathan Williams, and Gray Wilson. I am grateful for the assistance from Duke's law library and support staff, in particular Jane Bahnson, Jennifer Behrens, Molly Brownfield, Kelly Leong, Michael Hannon, Carla Reyes, Laura Scott, Katherine Topulos, Sheilah Villalobos, and a special thanks to Dawn Cronce. Duke Law School has been most generous in supporting my research for this book.

I am grateful to many colleagues for brainstorming over the past few years. Those who commented included Jamie Boyle, Andrea Cast, Don Elliott, Dan Esty, Rob Fischman, Victor Flatt, Rob Glicksman, Bruce Hay, Eleanor Johnstone, Susan Keefe, Dan and Betty Ann Kevles, Doug Kysar, Richard Lazarus, Joan Magat, Tracy Mehan, Eric Muller, Alex Pfaff, Sandra Postel, Jed Purdy, Carol Rose, J. B. Ruhl, David Smith, Heather Stanford, Jonathan Wiener, and Mike Young. I apologize if have inadvertently left out others. I also received extremely valuable comments from law school workshops at Brooklyn, South Carolina, Duke, UC Irvine, Georgetown, Tel Aviv University, Minnesota, Arizona, Brigham Young, and Yale as well as the Woods Institute at Stanford.

My literary agents, Doris Michaels and Delia Berrigan Fakis, have been most helpful in guiding me through the publications process, as has my editor, Dan Crissman. A final thanks is due to John and Elaine Elkington and to Michael Heller for helping prompt an initial musing into a published book.

The book is dedicated to Heather Stanford and was written in memory of my late father, Edwin W. Salzman, and my late brother, David Brook Salzman, both of whom always took a delighted interest and pride in this project and so many others.

Drinking
Water

Introduction:
Mother McCloud

Nestled between Dogwood Butte and Thimbleberry Ridge, the Northern California town of McCloud is a simple place: a population of thirteen hundred, no stoplights, one grocery store, and one roadside hotel. It's also breathtakingly beautiful, surrounded by fir tree forests, some of the country's best trout-fishing streams, and Mount Shasta looming above it all. For most of the past century, the town has had one and only one business: logging. For all intents, the McCloud River Lumber Company, or "Mother McCloud," as it was affectionately called, *was* the town. The company owned the grocery store, the hotel, even the houses.

Mother McCloud was a doting parent. The mill supplied electricity for the town, and when a kitchen faucet was leaking or the lights didn't work, it took no more than a phone call for a crew from Mother McCloud to arrive and set things right. Every Thanksgiving, workers' families were given free turkeys. At the Christmas party, the curtain was raised at the local theater to reveal a huge mound of presents, one wrapped for each and every child. Life was good.

In the 1960s, the company's fortunes started to turn, and with that began the town's slow decline. Homes were sold. Local businesses folded. People moved away. The mill shut its doors in 2002, and former middle-class loggers had to make do with menial jobs and food stamps. The high school, which had once held one hundred fifty students, now counted fewer than a dozen. The school had not been able to field a football team for years. The huge letters on the side of the gym spelling out "HOME OF THE LOGGERS" seemed a cruel joke. McCloud was dying.

Desperate for new sources of jobs, a few members of McCloud's local government started looking beyond lumber. In what must have seemed a leap of faith, they placed their hope for the town's future in another plentiful local resource: its water.

Much of the glacial melt from Mount Shasta flows underground and reemerges down the slope. These springs gurgle out clear, bracingly cold water that's clean enough to drink. Locals have joked that their surprisingly young appearances are due to McCloud's fountains of youth. New Age voyagers think something is special about the water, too. Some come from as far as Japan to meditate at what they consider a spiritual vortex.

Doris Dragseth ran the local auto parts shop with her husband before retiring. To her and the other members on McCloud's district board, the idea of water replacing timber must have seemed an odd choice. Spring water had always been free for the taking. Locals just walked up and filled a gallon jug. But times were clearly changing. As soft drink vending machines and supermarket shelves made clear, the bottled water business around the country was booming. In 2011, Americans drank more than nine billion gallons of bottled water—roughly 312 single-serve bottles per man, woman, and child. And the numbers keep climbing. Bottled water is now poised to become the nation's dominant beverage, surpassing even soft drinks.

To Dragseth, this was clearly a market they should be in. After all, McCloud's spring water was as good as anything sold in bottles, probably better. The McCloud River Lumber Company was gone for good, but maybe a new Mother McCloud could be found to harvest the local waters. It seemed a long shot at the time, but so did the future of the town.

During the late 1990s, McCloud's district board tried to woo water companies to build a bottling plant. They had no luck until Nestlé Waters North America, a subsidiary of the giant Swiss food and beverage company, took an interest. Nestlé, the largest bottled water company in America, already controlled nearly one-third of the market with popular brands such as Perrier, Poland Spring, and San Pellegrino. Nestlé liked what it saw. Large sources of unpolluted spring water with few dissolved minerals—the flat, clean taste that American consumers prefer—have become increasingly hard to find. Some of California's best groundwater, for example, around Lake Tahoe in the Sierra Nevada mountains, is contaminated with MTBE, an additive that makes gas burn cleaner but is also a human carcinogen.

McCloud's district board was so broke it couldn't afford a lawyer, so Nestlé paid for the legal fees, outside consultants, and permitting fees. The proposed deal was more than McCloud boosters could have hoped for: a one-million-square-foot bottling plant located on the old lumber mill site, big enough to enclose all the houses in town; a contract to bottle the town's waters for fifty years with an option for fifty more; annual payments to the town; and the lure of steady jobs. To Dragseth, the choice was simple: "I couldn't imagine why anyone in the world would be against this. We need the jobs, we need the money."

On September 29, 2004, about one hundred McCloud residents showed up at a public meeting to hear about the proposal. Nestlé showed a corporate video and some PowerPoint presentations. The five district board members all voted to approve the proposal. No discussion. Deal done.

Richard McFarland, a local business owner, sat stunned in the audience. This was the first he had heard of the agreement. He'd expected to talk over the pros and cons, not mutely watch a vote. As he learned of the details over the next few days, he got angry. This was a *big* operation. Nestlé would withdraw up to 520 million gallons of water annually from local springs, pack it as Arrowhead brand water, and load up to six hundred semitrailers a day full of bottles.

From McFarland's perspective, Nestlé was threatening to suck the aquifer dry, harm the ecology of the local streams, and clog McCloud with truck traffic, noise, and pollution. In exchange, it was paying McCloud virtually nothing—just one penny for every seventeen gallons that Nestlé bottled and then sold retail for forty-five dollars or more. As McFarland saw it, "the contract read like nobody on the services district knew what they were doing. It read like Nestlé's lawyers wrote it."

Nor was McFarland alone. Local gallery owner Janet Connaughton despaired: "We feel mugged. This town shouldn't sell its birthright for a few dollars." Curtis Knight, manager for a fishery conservation group, worried about the environmental impacts of the water Nestlé would pump out of the aquifers. What if the river levels fell? "The McCloud River is sacred water," he said. "It's one of the most treasured and popular trout fishing streams in the country and has a reputation throughout the world." With these supporters and others, the McCloud Watershed Council was formed, its sole mission to oppose the plant. It has fought Nestlé in court and in the media.

The well-meaning effort to save this close-knit town changed it, and for the worse, with residents taking sides in an increasingly bitter conflict. Many of the longtime locals resent opponents to the plan, mocking recent residents from other parts of California as "Flatlanders." As former mill worker Ron Berryman complained, "These sorts of people did their level best to put the timber industry out of business. Now they're asking us to reject a bottled water plant. How much cleaner can you get? Bottled air?"

Debra Anderson's family goes back four generations in McCloud. A vocal opponent of the agreement, she has seen her car tires slashed. Things could get more violent. In a similar conflict in Michigan, four incendiary devices were found in a pumping station for a Nestlé bottling plant. The bombs didn't go off, but the Earth Liberation Front claimed responsibility. Its members left a note with a clear warning: "We will no longer stand idly by while corporations profit at the expense of all others. To this end, we have taken action against one of the pumping stations that Perrier uses to steal water. . . . Clean water is one of the most fundamental necessities and no one can be allowed to privatize it, commodify it, and try and sell it back to us."

Five years after the September 2004 public meeting, the plant still had not been built.

THE STORY OF MCCLOUD IS ABOUT WATER AND A TOWN DOWN ON its luck, bitterly divided over what type of future it wants. Over what type of future it needs. But it's about far more than that. Similar stories could be told about conflicts in Fryeburg, Maine, or Mecosta County, Michigan, or Groveland, Florida; or about battles overseas in Cochabamba, Bolivia, or Kerala, India, or on the West Bank and Gaza Strip. Fights over drinking water are on the rise around the country and around the globe, and not only at the community level.

These conflicts may be over a simple and abundant substance, but the nature of the conflicts is anything but simple. The history of drinking water is fraught with legend and strife, science and religion, ethics and business. It should come as no surprise that the story of McCloud reflects these themes, for it is drawn from the pages of a much larger, much older story.

For more than three thousand years, understanding and management of drinking water have dictated the growth and health of human settlements. The situation is no different today. Look to current debates ranging from globalization to community rights, conspicuous consumption to poverty, terrorism to public health, and environmental protection to economic growth. Concerns over drinking water figure large in them all. If you doubt this, consider some of the larger themes described below.

McCloud locals may joke about their fountain of youth, but there is no question that drinking water holds a special place deep within our collective consciousness. We surely need to drink water, and obviously want to ensure that quenching our thirst does not make us sick. But since time immemorial, long before Perrier's chic green bottles, long before Ponce de León's futile quest for the Fountain of Youth, long before tales of Jesus offering his followers "living water," we have sought more from drinking water than simple hydration.

Drinking water is infused with symbolism and myth around the globe. There's a reason that New Age voyagers are willing to flock to McCloud, that the McCloud River is said to flow with sacred water. Early Christian missionaries were entranced, as well. Soon after arriving in a new territory, they would rename the local pagan well after a Christian saint, often inventing a vivid story of a miracle to persuade doubters. What is it that leads people from vastly different cultures to view drinking water as special, with strikingly similar tales of water providing eternal youth, passages to the after-life, miraculous cures, and mystical wisdom?

In all of these stories, the physical act of drinking these special waters creates a medium to the supernatural, a means of connecting the physical and the metaphysical. And the mythmaking continues today, implicit in the marketing campaigns of many large bottled water companies.

Of course, part of the attraction of bottled water is its perceived purity. Aquafina is the leading brand in the country. This Pepsi product is essentially municipal tap water that has been highly filtered, which may lead one to wonder why its label prominently features mountain peaks. The product's slogan, spelled out in big letters, suggests why—"Pure Water. Perfect Taste." A big part of the bottled water boom is due to concerns over health and the safety of tap water. But is bottled water really healthier than tap water? For that matter, how do we know that water, bottled or tap, is safe to drink in the first place?

This proves to be a surprisingly difficult question to answer. Part of ensuring safety lies in engineering—from the protection of source waters through to final consumption. Our technical fixes range from Roman aqueducts and the unlikely market success of Dixie Cups a century ago to fluoridation battles in the 1950s and efforts since the attacks of 9/11 to protect our water supplies from terrorists. The more difficult part of ensuring safety lies, ironically, in simply deciding what it means to be safe. There is no life without water. Indeed, we use its presence as an indicator for the possibility of life beyond the earth. But drinking water can kill, and always has.

The basic problem is that, apart from distilled water, no water source can ever be completely risk-free, whether from the tap or bottle. The water we drink contains a lot more than just two parts hydrogen and one part oxygen. Microbes and minerals have always been in our water and always will be. So how do we decide what is "safe enough"? The answer is as much cultural as scientific, depending on whether the drinker is in America or Bangladesh, and raises some thorny ethical issues in the process.

In the world of 2030, the UN estimates that more than half the world's population will live in water-scarce areas. This number could be even higher, depending on how climate change worsens droughts, reducing already scarce freshwater supplies. Today, where communal or free water sources are too far away or contaminated, the poor purchase their water from private providers—street vendors or tanker trucks. These prices are always higher than the price of water from municipal supply systems, often twelve times as much, with the tragic irony of the poorest in society paying the most for their water. Where safe water cannot be had at any price, it can kill. Unsafe drinking water is the single leading source of mortality in the developing world, exacting its greatest toll on children.

The scarcity of safe drinking water has subtler consequences, though equally dire. In many developing countries, women and girls spend a large part of their day collecting domestic water. This squeezes out their opportunities for employment or education, perpetuating gender inequality and poverty. It is no exaggeration to say that providing drinking water to poor communities can transform lives, with social benefits equal to or greater than the health benefits. But in these communities, as McCloud witnessed, the search for private capital to provide local water has unleashed furious globalization battles, where proponents of privatization clash against claims for a human right to water.

At a basic level, these debates concern the nature of drinking water, whether it should be managed as a commodity for sale or a public good. In 1776, the same year that the American colonies declared independence from Britain, Adam Smith, the father of economics sought to explain a paradox: Why are diamonds more valuable than water? Water is essential for life while diamonds are a fashion bauble, yet diamonds demand a much higher market price. Shouldn't the opposite be true?

In *The Wealth of Nations*, Adam Smith explained that the answer lay in supply and demand. Both diamonds and water are desired, but diamonds are scarce while drinking water is plentiful. Hence one commands high prices and the other is almost free for the taking. We have taken drinking water for granted. What held true in 1776, however, is no longer true in many parts of the world, and will certainly be wrong in the future. We have reached the tipping point where abundant, safe drinking water cannot be assumed. As a result, while some argue that there is a human right to water, many others contend that, if anything, water is far too cheap and should be even more of a market commodity. Whether we admit it or not, drinking water has become too valuable to take for granted.

There is serious money at stake. No surprise, then, that venture capitalists and entrepreneurs have already decided that "blue is the new green." The Earth Liberation Front sees the matter far differently, and while its violent method is widely condemned, its opposition to bottled water companies is shared by many. Criticism of corporate ownership of water has become a mainstay of the antiglobalization movement. The popular mantra is that drinking water is a public good, not a bar-coded product. Human need should take precedence over corporate greed. Water is for life, not profit.

These make for great protest signs, but once one moves beyond facile slogans the issues become a good deal trickier. The real question is how society should best manage a scarce resource among conflicting demands. McCloud's prior lifeblood, trees and timber, relied on the market. Wood is sold as a commodity, even when logged from national forests that belong to the public, and we seem to like it that way. Water is different, one might say, because it is necessary for survival. But it's not so simple. People also need food to survive, but no one complains about farmers and companies charging for corn or beans. So what's wrong with doing the same for water, even with a bar code?

Who really owns the water, anyway? Should McCloud's district board be able to sell the glacial melt filtered under Mount Shasta? Should Nestlé be able to buy it? These conflicts pit conservation and the duty not to harm your neighbor against the strong tradition of private property rights and the freedom to use the resources on and under your land as you see fit. The ethos of "Don't Tread on Me!" and the allure of local jobs are on a collision course with concerns over depleting local groundwater and harming the fish and plants that depend on those waters.

The ultimate privatization of water, of course, comes in the sale of disposable, personal containers of water. While we think of bottled water as a recent development, its sources run deep. The medieval market for holy waters provided the original template for the commercial branding of waters, satisfying the demands of the pilgrimage trade. In the eighteenth and nineteenth centuries, this developed into the practice of "taking the waters" at upscale spas such as Vichy in France, Baden-Baden in Germany, Bath in England, and Montecatini in Italy—towns that owed their economic existence to their spring waters. Thanks to developments in bottling technology in the late 1800s, people were able to take the waters *from* the spa, and the bottled water market took off.

The introduction of chlorination in municipal water in the early 1900s led to the near collapse of the bottled water industry in America. The nationwide bottled water market did not *exist* four decades ago. In the 1960s, the idea of selling bottled water in a convenience store would have sounded as ludicrous as the suggestion that we sell bottled air. Now, though, the assumption has reversed, with the expectation that you shouldn't get water for free. When was the last time you saw a public water fountain? Cafeterias and stadiums without free water are increasingly common. One gets the sense that drinking fountains are following the path of public phones, more a historic curiosity than a given.

Water is now widely viewed as much as a commodity as a public good. The highest-margin product in restaurants and convenience stores, twenty ounces of bottled water sells, at more that $8 per gallon, for far more than gasoline, yet it costs a fraction to produce.

No wonder Nestlé is so interested in McCloud. But how to explain the paradox that in the United States today, at a time when we are delivering more clean tap water to more people than ever before, sales of bottled water are gushing through the roof? In the face of this growth, environmentalists, church groups, and local governments have turned their sights on bottled water, denouncing the packaging waste and transport impacts.

THE LARGER THEMES OF MCCLOUD, THEN, SUGGEST MUCH BUT LEAVE even more unanswered. Where did bottled water come from and why has it become so popular? Why is the opposition so intense? Have natural waters always held such a powerful allure? Is our water safe to drink? What can be done for the billions of people who do not have access to safe drinking water? Will the combined threats of climate change and pollution soon make safe drinking water a scarce resource in America? And, as safe drinking water becomes increasingly scarce, who should own it? In answering these questions, the stories recounted in this book will feature different actors, different regions, and different eras, but all will be concerned with fundamentally the same issue: our relationship with drinking water.

"Relationship" may seem a strange word to use for a glass of water, but it is apt. This book argues that how we conceive of drinking water has always been fundamental to our relationship with the liquid. And the relationship is ever evolving. Drinking water has long been the source of both conflict and veneration, of healing and sickness, and it has always been central to our sense of well-being.

From ancient societies to the present, our conceptions of how this resource should be understood and managed—as sacred or market commodity, safe or unhealthy—have changed dramatically. In the chapters that follow, we will chart the course of that evolution.

1

The Fountain of Youth

I N THE WINTER OF 1512, JUAN PONCE DE LEÓN HAD IT ALL. Two decades earlier, he had set off for the New World as a raw seventeen-year old deckhand on Christopher Columbus's second voyage. When Columbus returned home, Ponce de León chose to stay on and seek his fortune. As his biographer later described, Ponce de León was a fierce fighter, hard and ambitious: "a man spirited, sagacious and diligent in all warlike matters." These were valuable qualities in Spain's emerging empire, where fabulous wealth was waiting to be taken, and they assured his rapid advance. He led the conquest of Puerto Rico, claiming the island for Spain, and was appointed governor in 1509. With lands and wealth to his name, he had officially arrived.

Life at the top, though, was unsatisfying. Official duties and managing territories for the Crown were not the life for a conquistador. He wanted more. Seeking new adventures, he set out again, but this time in search of far more than the riches of land and gold. He had heard stories from local Indians of a truly remarkable place. As Washington Irving, the famed short story writer, later described:

> [This place] promised, not merely to satisfy the cravings of his ambition, but to realize the fondest dreams of the poets. They assured him that, far to the north, there existed a land abounding in gold and in all manner of delights; but, above all, possessing a river of

such wonderful virtue, that whoever bathed in it would be restored to youth!

Here was the dream of the alchemist realized! One had but to find this gifted land, and revel in the enjoyment of boundless riches and perennial youth! Nay, some of the ancient Indians declared that it was not necessary to go so far in quest of these rejuvenating waters, for that, in a certain island of the Bahama group, called Bimini, which lay far out in the ocean, there was a fountain possessing the same marvelous and inestimable qualities.

Juan Ponce de León listened to these tales with fond credulity. He was advancing in life, and the ordinary term of existence seemed insufficient for his mighty plans. Could he but plunge into this marvelous fountain or gifted river, and come out with his battered war-worn body restored to the strength and freshness and suppleness of youth, and his head still retaining the wisdom and knowledge of age, what enterprises might he not accomplish in the additional course of vigorous years insured to him!

Entranced, Ponce de León sought a charter from Spain's King Ferdinand II for profits from any lands he might discover. The king granted his wish, and in March 1513, Ponce de León set out with three ships and sixty-five men. His pursuit of these magical waters took him throughout the Caribbean. He discovered the Gulf Stream, so critical to later navigators, and came upon a new land on Easter Sunday that he called Pascua de Florida—"flowers of Easter." It was he, not Columbus, who found his way to the American continent. His discovery of Florida opened the way to future European settlement in North America. By most measures, his career should have been a great success.

Ponce de León failed, however, in his overriding quest. On his second voyage, he was wounded by an Indian attack in Florida. He died from his wounds in Havana, Cuba, in 1521. The intrepid explorer, who did so much to chart the seas and lands of the Caribbean, never set eyes on the Fountain of Youth he sought so obsessively. Ironically, while Ponce de León was unable to drink the fabled elixir, his search has gained an immortality of its own.

Juan Ponce de León, 1474–1521

His quest for the mythical Fountain of Youth has become one of the most famous of all adventure tales.

Sadly, though, little of the story is true.

Ponce de León did sail with Columbus; he was governor of Puerto Rico; he set sail on expeditions with royal blessing in 1513 and again in 1521; and he did discover the Gulf Stream and Florida. Washington Irving's riveting account of his search for the Fountain, though, has more in common with Irving's other classic fables, "The Legend of Sleepy Hollow" and "Rip Van Winkle," than the actual voyage.

Like his contemporaries and other successful men throughout history who have it all yet still want more, Ponce de León sought gold and new lands where he might be appointed governor. There is no evidence that he ever looked for or even knew about a Fountain of Youth. That romantic search was apparently fabricated by the Spanish court's historian, Gonzalo Fernández de Oviedo, writing fourteen years after Ponce de León's death. Spicing up the story, Oviedo even claimed that the explorer had sought the Fountain to cure his sexual impotence (*el enflaquecimiento del sexo*). Oviedo's failure to mention that Ponce de León took his mistress with him on the voyage, or that he was the father of four children, suggests he may have held a somewhat poor view of the conquistador. But why let facts get in the way of a good story?

Subsequent historians took the search for the Fountain as given, some imputing the powers from drinking the waters, others from bathing in them. The myth is alive and well today. St. Augustine, Florida, boasts the Fountain of Youth Archaeological Park, where, according to its website, you can "Drink from the Legendary Fountain!"

If the search for the Fountain of Youth was made up, then why has the story stuck around for so long? What is it about Juan Ponce de León's mythical quest that has struck such a popular chord in successive generations for almost five hundred years?

In part, the legend speaks to our shared longing for eternal youth, to our fear of aging and inevitable loss. How else to explain the attraction of cosmetics and plastic surgery to those approaching the far side of middle age? But the Fountain of Youth story resonates deeply within us for another reason. It draws from far older legends—stories of eternal youth, passages to the afterlife, miraculous cures, and mystical wisdom. In fact, drinking water myths appear in every culture, though with different meanings and in different contexts. These special waters serve as a medium to the supernatural, a means of connecting the physical and the metaphysical.

This chapter explores our deepest relationships with drinking water—those of myths and legends from around the world—from Babylon, Greece, and China to Ireland and India. In recounting these stories we learn not only about past cultures but something of how our current drinking water myths define visions of ourselves. For, to be sure, the mythmaking continues today. Just look at the market power of "natural" bottled waters, or at the millions of pilgrims who voyage to Lourdes, France, every year to take its holy waters.

PONCE DE LEÓN'S QUEST FOR THE FOUNTAIN OF YOUTH IS HARDLY the only legend of a special substance that renews youth. The first volume of the amazingly successful Harry Potter series follows the attempt by Lord Voldemort to seize the regenerative powers of the Sorceror's Stone. Many of the eternal youth legends turn on drinking special waters as the means of renewal. These tales go back well before the time of Hogwarts or even the discovery of the New World. In fact, the earliest version goes back at least five thousand years to ancient Mesopotamia and the journey of Ishtar to the Underworld, one of the very oldest of recorded legends.

Ishtar, the goddess of fertility, is grief-stricken over the death of her lover, Tammuz. Descending into the Underworld, she hopes to find Tammuz, resurrect him with the Water of Life, and return with him to the world of the living. During her descent, however, Ishtar must pass through seven gates. At the first gate, the guard demands she give up her crown; at the second gate, her earrings; at the third, her necklace, and so on until, upon passing the seventh gate, she stands naked. Ereshkigal, goddess of the Underworld, insulted by Ishtar's willful descent into her domain, then afflicts her with all manners of disease. Thus is Ishtar gradually stripped of her clothing, flesh, and ultimately her life. With her death, fertility on earth ceases. No calves are born; no harvests are gathered. Only upon the entreaties of the other gods does Ereshkigal provide Ishtar the Water of Life and allow her to return, alone.

A Fountain of Youth legend developed later in the Muslim world, with the tale of Alexander the Great and his vizier Khidr. The legend commences with Alexander's fortunate discovery of Adam's will (perhaps this makes law the world's oldest profession). The will relates that God had created a spring beyond the mountains surrounding the world, in the Land of Darkness. The water of this spring was unique—"whiter than milk, colder than ice, sweeter than honey, softer than butter, and sweeter smelling than musk." Those who drank from it would be granted eternal life. Khidr set off to find this distant place. Enduring terrible hardships, he traveled through the Land of Darkness where he found the spring, bathed, and drank its sweet waters. He became immortal. Upon returning to show Alexander its location, however, he could not find the spring again.

Tales of life-renewing water were by no means entirely situated in ancient times. The English knight Sir John Mandeville provided an eyewitness account little more than a hundred fifty years before Ponce de León's supposed quest. Mandeville's travel memoir was hugely popular. Translated into every major European language by the year 1400, it was one of the books that Leonardo da Vinci brought with him to Milan. Columbus used it to plan his voyage to China. Mandeville wrote of a forest near the city of Polumbum, India:

> Beside it is a mountain, from which the city takes its name, for the mountain is called Polumbum. At the foot of the mountain is a noble and beautiful well, whose water has a sweet taste and smell, as if of different kind of spices. Each hour of the day the water changes its smell and taste. And whoever drinks three times of that well on an empty stomach will be healed of whatever malady he has. And therefore those who live near that well drink of it very often. I, John Mandeville, saw this well, and drank of it three times, and so did my companions. Ever since that time I have felt the better and healthier. . . . Some men call that well the *fons iuuentuitis*, that is, the Well of Youth; for he who drinks of it seems always young. They say this water comes from the Earthly Paradise, it is so full of goodness.

Mandeville paints a fantastic scene, and one wonders what else he might have been drinking. Who would not want to discover such a magical place? The famed sixteenth-century German painter Lucas Cranach's vision of the Fountain is shown on the facing page.

The Fountain of Youth *by Lucas Cranach the Elder*

Special waters can do more than restore health or reverse aging. In Norse and Irish mythology, drinking water provides wisdom. The Norse god Odin, for example, sought to drink from the sacred spring that flowed beneath the roots of the world tree, Yggdrasil. So eager was he for just one sip, he offered to sacrifice an eye to the giant guard Mimir. The exchange made good, with one gulp Odin gained eternal wisdom. Finn, the hero of Irish legend, gained his wisdom from water, as well. Rather than drink the water, though, he ate the Salmon of Knowledge, which had gained its wisdom from swimming in the waters of a magic well.

There is a Chinese variant of this tale involving the noted philosopher Huai-nan Tzu. It is said that in 122 BC he discovered how to distill the elixir of life. Upon drinking it, he was carried up to heaven. While ascending, he dropped his flask and spilled the waters. When his curious dogs and chickens drank from the magical puddle, they ascended to heaven as well.

These legends of magical waters that bestow eternal life, youth, or wisdom can have religious overtones, often related as allegory. Indeed, water carries great symbolism throughout the Judeo-Christian tradition. Consider, for example, the story of the woman at the well in the Gospel of John. On a trip to Galilee, Jesus passed through Samaria. Tired from his journey, he sat to rest beside Jacob's Well. A Samaritan woman came to draw water and Jesus asked her for a drink. She replied,

"You are a Jew and I am a Samaritan woman. How can you ask me for a drink?" (For Jews do not associate with Samaritans.)

Jesus answered her, "If you knew the gift of God and who it is that asks you for a drink, you would have asked him and he would have given you living water."

"Sir," the woman said, "you have nothing to draw with and the well is deep. Where can you get this living water? Are you greater than our father Jacob, who gave us the well and drank from it himself, as did also his sons and his flocks and herds?"

Jesus answered, "Everyone who drinks this water will be thirsty again, but whoever drinks the water I give him will never thirst. Indeed, the water I give him will become in him a spring of water welling up to eternal life."

The woman said to him, "Sir, give me this water so that I won't get thirsty and have to keep coming here to draw water."

On its face, Jesus is promising the same gift of eternal life as that sought by Ponce de León, the vizier Khidr, and the philosopher Huai-nan Tzu, but here the rebirth is spiritual, not physical. Simply drinking the well's water will not save the woman or quench her thirst. She is not even thirsty. It is her soul's thirst that Jesus offers to quench. Only full acceptance of his teachings, drinking the full glass of "living water," will satisfy her spiritual needs. There is more than just intellectual understanding going on here. By taking the water Jesus offers into her body, her acceptance becomes visceral. Water thus becomes a source not of physical but metaphysical life. The symbol of living water is repeated any number of times in the Gospels. Later in the Book of John, Jesus stands before a crowd and declares, "If any man thirst, let him come unto me, and drink. He that believeth in me, as the scripture hath said, out of his belly shall flow rivers of living water." The symbolism appears in the Old Testament as well. In the book of Jeremiah, the prophet cries, "My people have committed two evils: They have forsaken Me, the fountain of living waters, to hew for themselves cisterns, broken cisterns that can hold no water."

In each of these cases, by drinking the water, by taking the holy message within themselves, the drinkers become infused with the Holy Spirit and are, themselves, physically connected to the divine by their deliberate acts. Such a spiritual transformation through taking a symbol of divinity within oneself is not, of course, limited to water. Communion at Mass describes the same infusion of divinity into the supplicant through the forms of wine and a wafer, which represent the blood and body of Jesus.

Spiritual purification generally involves bathing or washing, rather than drinking, since this act symbolically cleanses the body of impurities. Christians do just this in the sacrament of baptism, which Jesus commanded his disciples to carry out following his resurrection. The significance of baptism varies among Christian denominations. In many, it serves the dual purpose of symbolizing both death and rebirth. Immersion in the baptismal font can represent the death of the past life of sins and birth into the Kingdom of God, hence the practice of baptizing adult born-again Christians. In Islam, too, water is used for spiritual purification. Many mosques have a clear pool of water just outside the walls, where ablution is required before praying. One can find similar practices among the ancient Greeks and the followers of Zoroastrianism.

In ancient Rome, sacred wells and springs also symbolized spiritual purification. They were cared for by priests and the vestal virgins. The virgins' chastity obviously symbolized purity, but so did their connection with the spring waters. The vestal virgins were not allowed to drink water that had passed through the Roman water system. They only drank water from a marble tank situated in their temple that was filled daily from a sacred water source.

These chaste priestesses performed a ritual every year during the ides of May, at the full moon, intended to beseech the gods for the continuous flow of sacred spring waters. Their symbolic purity was complete—no contamination from sexual activities or waters entered their bodies.

Interestingly, many cultures have a strong mythic tradition that presents the very opposite of the Fountain of Youth and spiritual rebirth. Rather than drinking water to provide eternal life, water now provides the means and a balm for death.

Rivers serve as the crossing point between life and afterlife in many cultures. In Greek mythology, for example, the spirits of the recently deceased must cross five rivers. The River Styx is the first boundary between earth and Hades, the domain of the Underworld. It was guarded by Phlegyas, and gods made oaths upon its waters. Gods that broke such oaths had to drink the river's water, making them mute for nine years. The next crossing was the River Phlegethon, eternally burning. The River Acheron followed. Placing a coin under the tongue of corpses ensured the spirits could pay their deathly toll to the famed ferryman, Charon, for transport across the Acheron. Those who arrived without a coin were refused passage, and had to wander the river's banks one hundred years before they could cross.

Approaching the end of their journey, souls then crossed the River Cocytus, the river of wailing. The final river, less well known in popular tales of the Greek Underworld, is the River Lethe, also known as the River of Oblivion or the River of Forgetfulness. Drinking its waters caused spirits to forget their life on earth. This amnesiac draught broke the spirits' ties to the past and eased the transition to their new immortal existence.

Similar tales of amnesiac drinks to ease the passage of the dead are found in Nordic, Hindu, and other cultures. In Fiji, for example, the dead spirit must stop at a spring as he makes his way to the other world. Upon tasting the water, he forgets his lost life and friends, and stops weeping. This drink is called Wai-ni-dula, or the Water of Solace.

Drinking special waters eases the passage of those who remain to mourn on earth, as well. The Tring Dayak people in Borneo cannot drink ordinary water when in mourning. Instead, they drink only "soul water" that has been gathered from the leaves of vines. Presumably this pure liquid, untouched by the soil, is a lingering connection with the pure realm the recently departed have now entered. In northern India, following a funeral, the elder Kacharis of Assam pass out *santi jal*, the Water of Peace. Drinking this terminates the mourning period. After a funeral, the Chaco Indians of the American Southwest drank hot water.

Burials in the famed Indian River Ganges make quite physical the role of drinking water and passage from this life. According to tradition, the dead person's family carries the body to the banks of the river. Here, water from the Ganges is poured into the corpse's mouth. Only at this point is he laid upon the death pyre and the structure lit. His ashes are then scattered in the river, taking his spirit to rejoin the cycle of reincarnation.

Just as drinking the water of oblivion eases passage into the world of darkness, the inability of the dead to drink water can make the passage a torment. This is clearest in the Greek myth of Tantalus. One legend recounts that Tantalus was honored by an invitation to dine with the gods on Mount Olympus. He stole ambrosia and nectar, however, and shared it with other mortals. Another version recounts that he invited the gods to dine and served them a stew of his own son Pelops. Demeter, mother of Persephone, was the only one hungry enough to eat the meat, which turned out to be Pelops's shoulder. When Pelops was restored to life, part of his shoulder was replaced by ivory crafted by Hephaestus, surely one of the earliest examples of joint replacement surgery.

Whichever tale one relies on, Tantalus made the gods angry, which is never a good idea. As punishment, upon his death, Tantalus was imprisoned chest deep in a lake in Tartarus, the deepest region of the Underworld, condemned to suffer from eternal hunger and thirst. Just in front of his mouth hung a tree branch heavy with luscious fruit, but every time he tried to eat, the branch would pull away. Every time he tried to drink the lapping water just beneath his parched lips, the waters would recede before him. This was his cursed fate for all eternity, providing us the word for unsatisfied desire: "tantalizing."

THE TALES OF THE FOUNTAIN OF YOUTH, THE RIVER LETHE, AND THE spring beneath Yggdrasil all involve mythical waters that do not exist, or at least have not yet been found. But many legends of drinking water are tied to local wells and fountains, places that actually do exist and can be visited. Stories from around the world speak of specific wells with healing powers that can cure the sick and restore movement to the lame, eyesight to the blind, and fertility to the barren. These are holy wells, and they marry the myth to the real.

There are few universals in the human condition, but sacred wells may be one of the rare constants. They have been found in virtually every culture around the world and in virtually every era. From earliest times, natural water sources have been linked with mystical healing and powers. An archeological site in Wales, for example, uncovered a vast temple complex extending across more than eighty-five acres. More than thirty times bigger than Stonehenge, the oval site is one and a half miles long and once featured 1,400 massive oak pillars, each towering twenty-three feet high, with a pristine natural spring at its center. Researchers say it had been in continuous use for 4,700 years before it was overrun by the Romans. Archeological digs in Europe have uncovered evidence of religious worship at springs since the Neolithic Period.

One can understand why a natural spring would appear miraculous to premodern people. How the water came to the surface could not be easily explained. The minerals, carbonation, heat, and smells coming from springs would have been mysteries. Surely these had mystic origins, but special origins were rarely enough. Those special wells also held special powers. Particular springs offered particular benefits. Below are some of the most notable examples compiled by a chronicler of sacred wells.

- Insanity was cured at St. Maelrubha's Well on an island in Loch Maree, Scotland. Reportedly, the "patient" was dragged behind a boat and rowed twice around the island, then plunged into the well and made to drink the water—all of which produced the cure. However, drinking from Borgie Well near Cambusland, Scotland, produced insanity.

- Those seeking relief from toothaches would go to a healing well on the Scottish island North Uist. They were required by tradition to remain silent and not to eat or drink until they reached the well, where they then drank three handfuls of the healing water and said, "The Father, the Son, and the Holy Ghost."

- Additional holy wells known for their gifts of fertility can be found on the Isle of Skye. One ensured the birth of twins, while another ensured the fertility of cattle.

- The Northern Pomo (Indians living in modern-day Northern California) used a spring that they called "child water" to facilitate pregnancy. It was thought that if a married woman desired a child, she should drink from this spring.

- The holy well at Sommested in Iceland offered healing but would lose its powers if a horse washed in the well.

- At the aptly named Holywell in Wales, those seeking a cure would enter the bath waters three times while saying the Rosary.

The list of sacred wells and how to obtain their specific benefits could go on for pages. In a sort of hypochondriac's fantasy, one can find wells that cure the full spectrum of maladies, from blindness and soreness of the eyes to rickets, lameness, whooping cough, leprosy, paralysis, and an assortment of other ailments. Some of these cures defy modern medical explanations and seem downright silly to a modern reader. A placebo effect may exist, but surely mental illness cannot be caused or cured by drinking from a well, can it?

As with many enduring legends, there is a kernel of truth here. Natural spring waters often have high mineral content that do provide therapeutic value. Lithium dissolved in spring waters, for example, can treat mental illness. While modern medicine may help explain the curative powers of sacred springs, the more interesting question is how ancient people explained the waters' powers prior to chemical analysis of their contents, indeed how they explained the very presence of the waters. In a society with no understanding of modern disease, there had to be another explanation.

The waters come from places we cannot venture, are transported by forces we cannot see, and cure through means we cannot understand. How did these waters become sacred? Even today, with medical discoveries seemingly an everyday event, many people still attribute special powers to holy waters. Where do their special powers come from?

From the earliest wells until recent times, the answer has been found in divine origins. Some stories attribute the waters' existence to gods demonstrating their power or bestowing gifts on their followers. In the earliest of Greek legends, it was thought that rainwater came from Zeus while spring water issued from the female earth goddess Gaia. Thus spring water was used for rituals because it was imbued with sacred properties. In another Greek myth, Poseidon, god of the sea, challenged Athena over who would become the patron god of Athens. Striking his staff on the ground, Poseidon created a spring. In response, Athena created an olive tree. Poseidon's spring, however, poured out useless salt water and the Athenians chose the goddess of wisdom.

As religions and local gods changed, the mythic nature of the wells endured. As R. J. Stewart has written about Celtic traditions: "The therapeutic power of wells remained into historical Christian times, with saints taking over but never quite disguising pagan functions. Rituals were preserved in folklore deriving from pagan worship; these include processing around wells, making offerings . . . and ceremonies involving drinking from skulls."

On the other side of the world, an ancient Hawaiian legend speaks of Ka-ne, the "water finder." Like Poseidon, he struck his staff against the ground. The crushed lava rocks revealed a large pool of pure water. The natural springs around the islands were called Ka-Wai-a-ke-Akua, "the water provided by a god." In other stories, divinities act through chosen people, such as when Moses strikes the rock at Horeb. God commands Moses to "strike the rock, and water will come out of it for the people to drink."

Bernadette Soubirous, 1844–1879

These are all ancient stories. But the allure of holy wells and their sacred waters remains strong today, exercising a powerful attraction on believers. And nowhere is this clearer than in Lourdes, France.

Lying in the foothills of the Pyrenees in southwestern France, Lourdes was, for centuries, merely a small market town. Dominated by the fortified castle rising in its midst, the town's population counted a modest four thousand people through the middle of the nineteenth century. On February 11, 1858, though, this all changed. A poor fourteen-year-old girl, Bernadette Soubirous, was walking through the town's untended outskirts, looking for firewood and bones within an area commonly used as a garbage dump. Pausing to cross a stream beside a small cave known as the grotto of Massabielle, she had a vision of a dazzling light and a beautiful woman. Her companions saw nothing.

Returning to the grotto a few days later, she had another vision. In all, Soubirous experienced eighteen visions of the white-veiled lady, who later described herself as the Immaculate Conception. This figure was interpreted by the villagers as the Virgin Mary.

The mystic lady's messages were different each time, calling for penance, for a chapel to be built on the site, and, later, for Bernadette "to drink of the water of the Spring, to wash in it, and to eat of the herb that grew there." This seemed impossible, since the only water to be found in the grotto was in the moist mud. Following instructions only she could hear, Bernadette clawed in the mud and tried to drink the dirt-filled water. She seemed crazy. The next day, however, it was reported that clear water flowed from the grotto. This spring later became the source of the famed water of Lourdes, drastically changing the town's future.

Needless to say, there were many skeptics at the time of Bernadette's claims and since then. She was first denounced as deranged or a fraud, but after multiple interviews church officials became convinced, finding her story credible both because of her unwavering conviction and because they concluded the poor, uneducated girl could never have known about the theology of the Immaculate Conception.

Soubirous died in 1879 and following her death the fame of her story only continued to grow. A group of admirers soon began to push for her canonization as a saint. Her body was exhumed three times to seek evidence for sainthood, and each time it showed remarkably little decomposition, seen as proof of her incorruptibility. Having satisfied the Church's requirement for three miracles, she was officially declared Saint Bernadette by Pope Pius XI in 1933. Her body has been on constant display in a glass coffin in the Sisters of Charity Convent in Nevers, France, since 1925.

Visitors started coming to Lourdes for its waters shortly after Bernadette's claims. Some come in the hope that the waters will cure an ailment, others just for the chance to bathe in or drink such holy waters. The town now hosts roughly five million visitors a year with seven churches and upward of 270 hotels—incredibly, the greatest concentration of hotel rooms in France outside of Paris. Streets are filled with shops catering to the trade, with all manner of Lourdes-emblazoned statuettes, jewelry, and bottles of water. It's estimated that pilgrims contribute up to $300 million to the local

Holy water bottles on sale in Lourdes, France

economy. The holy and mercantile exist alongside one another in an uneasy pairing. The English journalist Malcolm Muggeridge derided the commerce as "tawdry relics, the bric-a-brac of piety."

Nor is the commerce limited to purchases on site. The website directfromlourdes.com, for example, offers a range of Lourdes bottled water to those who cannot make the journey. The marketing pitch takes in both holy and practical concerns: "We are one of the only stores to sell bottles containing *fresh* water from the spring. Be aware that when you buy from other Stores that have imported the water, you may be buying stale water, that has been sat in storage for days, weeks or even months this water may not be fit to drink." My personal favorite is the Lourdes bottled water key ring with a screw top, so you can have easy access to the holy waters while stuck in traffic.

The "pilgrimage season" runs from Easter through October. Upon arriving, pilgrims are met by volunteers who guide them to the grotto and nearby baths, one for men and one for women. Volunteers assist bathers by helping those who come for healing submerge up to their chins in the water. If a person is unable to walk, a volunteer will carry him or her. In addition to the baths, pilgrims may also visit the actual spring, in order to fill containers to take the water home. The spring is covered in glass with spigots leading out of it. In 1990, due to heavy consumption, authorities had to ration Lourdes water.

Unlike the holy wells described earlier, where news of legendary cures was passed on by word of mouth, the Catholic Church has meticulously documented miracles at sites around the globe. Indeed, in 1883, the Church created a formal system to confirm miracles at Lourdes. Known as the Bureau des Constatations Médicales (Medical Verification Agency), the Bureau has reviewed a staggering 6,700 claimed cures and deemed 66 officially "miraculous."

To obtain miracle status, the illness and cure must meet certain criteria set out in a rigorous, multistep review process. Pope Benedict XIV established these standards in the eighteenth century. An article in *The Economist* explains the core requirements:

> The original disease must be incapacitating, with a sure and precise diagnosis. Any organic or physical ailment qualifies, but psychiatric conditions are, for the moment, excluded since diagnoses are too uncertain and recoveries too hard to assess. The cure, which should be sudden, instantaneous and without convalescence, must not result from medical treatment; and recovery must permanently restore the normal function to the beneficiary.

When a pilgrim initially claims a miracle, a doctor will consult with the patient and the patient's doctors and write up a case history. Assuming the cure has lasted, the patient then returns a year later with the relevant medical records. For a further three years, up to 250 doctors making pilgrimage to the site review the record. If the case makes it past this comprehensive review, it is submitted to an international medical committee, comprised of twenty experts (not all of the Catholic faith), that votes on recommending miracle status to the bishop of the patient's diocese. A two-thirds majority vote is necessary to confirm that the case cannot be accounted for by medical understanding. With increased understanding of disease, it may not be surprising that there has been a significant decline in the number of documented Lourdes miracles, with only eight declared cures since 1956.

While impressive in its rigor, such a detailed administrative process seems strangely at odds with the very idea of holy waters. Religious belief, after all, is often described as the ultimate leap of faith. This does not sit well with a rigorous examination to ensure objective verification of inexplicable events. Indeed, in 2008, the international medical panel of doctors, appointed by the Roman Catholic Church, stated that it no longer will approve miracles, leaving that decision to the Church officials.

The intense interest of Catholics in Lourdes and its waters makes clear that the allure of holy waters is alive and well. This remains true in other cultures today. Consider this assessment in a multivolume history of water:

> People come from all over the world to drink and collect the water [at Lourdes], just like the Hindus, who over thousands of years have carried water from the Ganges across the Indian subcontinent. Or like the Muslims, who for hundreds of years have carried water from Mecca on their pilgrimages across the African savannah to Mali and Mauritania. Millions believe that this water can work wonders, that its miraculous properties can heal the sick, cleanse the soul, and ensure longer life.

And, while perhaps not as obvious, we see the veneration of drinking water in our own lives. Think of the New Age appeal of the town of McCloud's water, attracting people from around the globe to meditate at the waters' spiritual vortex. Or consider the mass marketing of bottled water. The "natural origins" of bottled water feature prominently in the marketing for some of the most important bottled water brands. Part of this is surely meant to demonstrate the purity of the water and the implication that it is safer to drink than tap water. But it may be getting at something deeper, as well—that drinking this water brings you closer to Mother Nature, to a purer place. As the historian William Cronon observed, nature "has become a secular deity in this post-romantic age." Our relationships with drinking water have long been told through spiritual, sanctified stories, and they continue today.

SHOULD WE DRINK EIGHT GLASSES OF WATER A DAY?

We have all heard this at some point: To stay healthy, you should drink eight eight-ounce glasses of water every day. Not juice, not beer, and definitely not coffee. Water. While omnipresent advice, this turns out to be an urban myth. As a comprehensive 2008 review in the *Journal of the American Society of Nephrology* concluded, "There is no clear evidence of benefit from drinking increased amounts of water."

No one seems to know for sure where this maxim originated. A 1945 report from the U.S. government's Food and Nutrition Board recommended that people consume a milliliter of water for every calorie of food. This would work out roughly to sixty-four ounces for a day's eating. The problem, though, is that this neglects to make clear an important point: much of the water we consume is not drunk. It's in the foods we eat such as fruits, ice cream, and vegetables. The amount of water we should drink depends on how much water we also have eaten, not to mention how hot it is, activity levels, etc. And even if a standard rule did make sense, eight glasses a day is likely too many. Jurgen Schnermann, a kidney specialist at the National Institutes of Health, recommends half that amount, about a liter of water, to satisfy the body's daily needs.

What about beauty? Over one-quarter of bottled water drinkers believe it improves the appearance of their hair or skin. Despite lots of websites claiming that drinking lots of water will make your skin smoother and more youthful, there is no evidence that drinking water offers dermatological benefits or prevents wrinkling.

And weight loss? We often hear that drinking throughout the day will make us feel less hungry. If you drink regularly, the pounds will melt away. If only . . .

In fact, as Pennsylvania State University nutritionist Barbara Rolls explains, "hunger and thirst are controlled by separate systems in the body. People are unlikely to mistake thirst for hunger." Filling your belly with water, in other words, doesn't make you less hungry. Nor, she found, does drinking water before or during a meal affect appetite. Eating water-rich foods, however, does make a difference. Subjects who ate soups were less hungry and consumed fewer calories. Better to eat chicken soup than chicken casserole and a glass of water.

But does it have to be water? Doesn't drinking some liquids, like soda or coffee, cause us to lose more in urine than we take in? Some beverages are diuretics, but only alcohol comes close to being a net loss in hydration and that's if you consume several servings. Researchers have found that the body retains about two-thirds of a cup of coffee if you're not a regular java junkie. If your body is accustomed to caffeine, though, then your body retains almost all of what you drink.

Nutritionists counsel that thirst is one of the body's strongest signals. If you are from Maine and hiking in the Arizona desert, of course, you may not recognize the symptoms of dehydration. For everyday living, though, if you are thirsty, your body will let you know it.

2

Who Gets to Drink?

THE EPIC 1962 MOVIE *Lawrence of Arabia* DOMINATED THAT year's Academy Awards, winning Best Picture and six other Oscars. One classic scene features Lawrence (played by Peter O'Toole) first meeting his future Arab brother-in-arms, Ali ibn el Kharish (played by Omar Sharif). Lawrence, parched after his travels through the desert, has reached an oasis and is greedily drinking from the well with his guide, who is from the Hazimi tribe. His guide tells Lawrence they are drinking from a well belonging to the Harif tribe, a "dirty" people. From the distance, slowly becoming visible in the shimmering waves of the desert sun, approaches the armed and dangerous-looking Ali ibn el Kharish. Panicking, Lawrence's guide pulls a gun but is shot down by Ali ibn el Karish. A wonderfully terse dialogue follows.

ALI IBN EL KHARISH:	What is your name?
LAWRENCE:	My name is for my friends. None of my friends is a murderer.
ALI IBN EL KHARISH:	You are angry, English. He was nothing. The well is everything. The Hazimi may not drink at our wells. He knew that. Salaam.

As a scarce resource, safe drinking water has been governed by rules from the earliest times. Indeed, rules establishing access to water in arid regions may very well have predated property rules for land. As the shooting from *Lawrence of Arabia* amply demonstrates, in the desert, control of an oasis is far more important than control of the dry desert around it.

Water is one of the few essential requirements for life. Without water, plants wilt, shrivel, and die. Even viruses, which may not even be alive, go dormant and "turn off" without water. Throughout history, societies have been predicated on ready access to sources of drinking water, whether in the cisterns of Masada high above the Dead Sea, the graceful aqueducts carrying water into Rome, or the sacred Aboriginal water holes in Australia's outback. While not an obvious issue to us in twenty-first-century America, management of drinking water as a resource—who gets it, when they get it, and how much they get—has been a life-and-death matter for much of human history.

While we tend not to think much about who gets to drink, drinking water is a dauntingly complex resource to manage. For millennia, human societies have faced the challenge of supplying adequate quality and quantities of drinking water. Whether limited by arid environments or urbanization, provision of clean drinking water is a prerequisite of any enduring society, but it is a multifaceted task, in large part because water is a multifaceted resource.

Drinking water is most obviously a *physical resource*, one of the few truly essential requirements for life. Regardless of the god you worship or the color of your skin, if you go without water for three days in an arid environment your life is in danger. And water's physical characteristics confound easy management. Water is heavy— it is difficult to move uphill. Water is unwieldy—it cannot be packed or contained easily. And drinking water is fragile—it easily becomes contaminated and unfit for consumption. That much seems obvious.

Less apparent, though, is that drinking water can also be regarded as a *cultural resource*, of religious significance in many societies. It can also be a *social resource*, for in some societies access to water reveals much about relative status, and a *political resource*, as the provision of water to citizens can help justify a regime. And finally, when scarce, water can become an *economic resource*. Taking these facets together, one can ask how different societies, from ancient times to the present, have thought about drinking water, and how they have determined access. These questions are, of course, interrelated. How we think of water, whether as a sacred gift or a good for sale, both influences and is influenced by how we manage access to drinking water.

On July 28, 2010, for example, the General Assembly of the United Nations passed a resolution proclaiming a human right to "safe and clean drinking water." Maude Barlow, a famed international campaigner on this issue, declared that "when the 1948 Universal Declaration on Human Rights was written, no one could foresee a day when water would be a contested area. But in 2010, it is not an exaggeration to say that the lack of access to clean water is the greatest human rights violation in the world." And making this struggle harder, she argued, has been the commodification of water: "Instead of allowing this vital resource to become a commodity sold to the highest bidder, we believe that access to clean water for basic needs is a fundamental human right." The public interest group Food & Water Watch describes the conflict more starkly: "Around the world, multinational corporations are seizing control of public water resources and prioritizing profits for their stockholders and executives over the needs of the communities they serve." Should water be a basic right or a marketable good?

As we shall see later in this book, this conflict is right now playing out in stark and often violent encounters in water privatization debates around the world. While much ink and, unfortunately, blood, has been shed over this debate, it has been remarkably lacking in any sense of history or what we have learned over time. After all, it's not as if access to water is somehow a new issue or concern.

An age-old concern, the story of how societies have managed the complex resource of drinking water goes back well over five thousand years. Through a voyage across ancient cultures in the Middle East, Europe, Australia, and Asia, we will find that a society's management of something as seemingly simple as drinking water is actually no simple matter.

GIVEN THE CRITICAL IMPORTANCE OF DRINKING WATER TO SURVIVAL, it should come as no surprise that human settlements have always depended on ready access to sources of drinking water. As societies developed from hunter-gatherer economies to more advanced grazing and agriculture, the need for secure, abundant supplies of water became even more important. Archaeological excavations have found that settlements since the Neolithic time go hand in hand with water engineering. As settled populations grew, access to and control over water sources needed to grow at the same time. Cisterns and wells carved from rock have been found in excavations at Ebla, in Syria, dating from 2350 BC. Even earlier water storage sites have been found in northeastern Jordan, dating from the fourth millennium BC. Though half a world away, water storage basins with storage capacities of 10,000 to 25,000 gallons of water have been excavated in the Mesa Verde region of the American Southwest, and large collection and storage structures have been uncovered throughout the Maya lowlands.

The Minoan civilization in Crete had flushing toilets and domestic water as early as 1700 BC, while tunnels directing water from reservoirs and plumbing have been identified at ancient sites in Iran, Palestine, and Greece. Perhaps the most impressive ancient water engineering in the Americas was constructed at Machu Picchu by the Incas, who faced the challenge of moving water from a distant spring to their capital, located at an elevation of more than seven thousand feet. Sloping canals delivered water through agricultural terraces to the emperor's residence and then, through a series of sixteen fountains, down the mountain slope to the city's residents.

The Old Testament is filled with references to springs and wells, their importance clearly evident from the fact that each was given a special name. A desert people, the ancient Jews understood all too well the importance of access to water. As the Book of Jeremiah plaintively recounts, failure to bring water was calamitous.

The word of the Lord that came to Jeremiah concerning the drought: "Judah mourns, and her gates languish; her people lament on the ground, and the cry of Jerusalem goes up. Her nobles send their servants for water; they come to the cisterns; they find no water; they return with their vessels empty; they are ashamed and confounded and cover their heads."

When water was scarce, who had access to it, and how was this determined? Jewish law regarding drinking water has been traced as far back as 3000 BC, when Semitic tribes settled in Ur in the land of Mesopotamia. The basic rule was one of common property. As reflected in the later writings of the Talmud: "Rivers and streams forming springs, these belong to every man." Because water from natural sources was provided by God, sale of these waters would be tantamount to desecration—selling divine gifts.

Not all sources of water were natural, however. Many important sources of water came from wells, where human labor was necessary to gain access to the groundwater. In these cases, drinking water was managed as a community resource, though not free for the taking. Within each community, Jewish law prioritized access according to use, with high priority given to drinking water, followed by irrigation and grazing. Importantly, however, the highest priority for access was granted to those in need, regardless of whether or not they belonged to the well's community of owners.

In practice, this amounted to a Right of Thirst, and this type of rule makes perfect sense. Any traveler in an arid region could foresee a situation where he or she might need water from strangers for survival. A rule that gave water to those in need might very well one day benefit them or their tribal members.

Islamic water law is quite similar to Jewish water law in both substance and significance. Indeed, the Arabic word for Islamic law, "Sharia," literally means "the way to water." Priority was given for drinking, then domestic needs, then agriculture and grazing, favoring needs in the community over outside users. There was also a Right of Thirst. The Koran clearly instructs, "Anyone who gives water to a living creature will be rewarded. . . . To the man who refuses his surplus water, Allah will say: 'Today I refuse thee my favor, just as thou refused the surplus of something that thou hadst not made thyself.'" Since water is a gift from God to all people, sharing water was regarded as a holy duty. Access to water for basic survival was a right common to those inside and outside the community.

Islamic water law was largely adopted into the legal code of the Ottoman Empire, the vast kingdom spanning much of southern Europe and northern Africa. It is still followed by the Bedouin in the Negev and the Berbers in Morocco. As a scholar of the region has described, drinking water is "sacrosanct and neither may be denied anyone for any reason at any time." While it makes for riveting cinema, the scene at the well in *Lawrence of Arabia* was likely the invention of the British screenwriter. It certainly does not reflect the Right of Thirst.

In Australia, the driest inhabited continent, the need for rules over access to drinking water is self-evident. Given the scarcity of water, all uses are carefully managed and Aborigines draw no distinction between water for drinking and other purposes. Most water sources are sacred parts of the landscape, and knowledge of their location is vital to a group's survival (a truly critical example of intellectual property). Given the variability of rainfall, sharing has played a key role in water management. Researchers have described the system as "always ask." While water is a closely protected community resource, in practice those requesting water are given permission to drink. As with the Bedouin and Berbers, it is widely understood that those with water today may find themselves needing water in the future. The golden rule applies: give and you shall receive.

In rural Africa, too, one can find clear parallels to the Right of Thirst. A study of communal lands in Zimbabwe, for example, reported that private wells and boreholes are still made available for communal drinking. The authors concluded that "cutting across all the different tenurial systems is the notion that no one should be denied access to safe drinking water." This is not to say, however, that it is free for the taking. In times of scarcity, communities may restrict the amount of water gathered, banning, for example, the filling of large drums. Moreover, people must ask permission from the owner prior to using the well. As one person described, "You go to someone you are in good books with." If someone gathers too much water, uses it for a different purpose than requested, or is unhygienic near the well, then his access rights are limited or even denied.

Studies of the Bihar, thousands of miles away in the northeast region of India, also reveal a Right of Thirst. Because of the complex social hierarchy, priority of access and management is carefully proscribed along social caste lines. Water is seen as capable of transmitting both physical *and* metaphysical pollution. Thus upper castes maintain distinct water sources from lower castes to avoid the risk of aqueous contact with "polluted" individuals. The rule of sharing, however, is widely observed, and those in need must be given access to water. At times of water scarcity, even access to an upper caste well is allowed.

This brief survey suggests three important points. First, while traditional rules governing drinking water management vary from culture to culture, there seems to be a common theme. Whether expressed through the Right of Thirst in Jewish and Islamic law, as sharing norms in India and Africa, or as "always ask" in Australia, access to drinking water in times of need seems to be a basic right in a wide range of societies. Aspects of this right can even be found in the United States today, where public utilities are required to provide service to all customers in their area. Second, these cases provide clear examples of how drinking water can be managed as a physical resource (through rules over how water sources are maintained), a social resource (rules governing which castes and communities may use particular sources), and a cultural resource (with water sharing regarded as a religious duty).

Third, drinking water in traditional communities has not been viewed primarily as a priced good with allocation determined by market forces. Perhaps it is too important a resource, too connected with divine beneficence and social identity, to be treated as a fungible item for sale or barter. Drinking water clearly is a commercial good in many societies today, though, so how did the transition to commodification occur? There is no better place to look for clues than ancient Rome.

ROME IS THE FIRST GREAT CITY DEFINED BY ITS MANAGEMENT OF drinking water. The graceful aqueducts that carried clean water to Roman cities were among the most magnificent structures of the ancient world, and some stand intact even today. The water fountains that continue to define the splendor of Rome were important parts of the city's drinking water provision more than two thousand years ago. Rome is also the first major city that managed drinking water as a priced resource.

While aqueducts play a critical part in the story of Roman drinking water, that was not their original purpose. Because of Rome's high water table, there was plentiful water available from local wells and springs. The main reason for construction of the aqueducts was not hygienic but social. Bathhouses were an integral part of Roman society, and they required large volumes of clean water. Over time, however, as the city's population grew, the water of the Tiber became increasingly polluted. The ready availability of a reliable source of clean water from the aqueducts spurred

The famed Pont du Gard in France, still structurally intact two millennia after its construction, is a prime example of the Roman Empire's water engineering marvels.

demands for its water to be used for drinking, fountains, gardens, and even public toilets.

Rome's first aqueduct, the Appia, was built in 312 BC, later joined by ten others over the next five centuries. Some spanned more than fifty miles, providing more than thirty million gallons of water daily to the empire's capital. The skill needed to construct these aqueducts from stone and cement impresses even today. Always maintaining a downward slope for the water to flow, the aqueducts forded rivers, crossed ravines, even ran beneath the earth. Built to last, many of these tributes to engineering acumen still stand across the former empire, witness to the Romans' mastery of water, stone, and cement.

The Marcia was the third Roman aqueduct. Built in 144 BC, it was much larger than its predecessors and intended for a special purpose. Brought into the city at a great height, the Marcia's waters were distributed throughout the city by gravity and primarily used for drinking. Almost half of the Marcia aqueduct's prized water went to private use, and roughly a quarter went to the city's public basins, known as *lacus*.

The *lacus* were used by citizens for gathering water for domestic use. Most residents of Rome collected their water in this way, and the *lacus* provided communal meeting places, much as wells continue to serve as a focus for public life in many rural societies. Excavations in Pompeii have uncovered their spacing about 150 feet from one another throughout the city.

Notably, the water in the *lacus* was free for the taking. Not everyone chose to collect their water from public sources, however, and the economics of Roman water supply depended on this demand for private water. Indeed, it is estimated that 40 percent of all the water delivered within Rome went to private buildings, and not all of this was for baths. A special water tax, known as a *vectigal*, was charged for people who had pipes running from the main system to their houses or baths. Because the aqueduct was free-flowing and the distribution system worked by gravity, the water was always running. Thus the tax was assessed by the size of the supply pipe nozzle rather than the amount consumed. And this was a lot of

The historic postcard above shows a lacus *on a street in Pompeii. It is located on the right side of the picture, jutting out from the sidewalk.*

water. The daily water delivered to a Roman household has been estimated as the equivalent of a modern household's use over two months.

Piped delivery of water to a private residence was a status symbol of wealth, and a common luxury of senators. We know that piped water was highly valued because a major black market arose in what a Roman engineer at the time, Frontinus, called "puncturing"—attaching secret pipes to main lines in order to draw water illicitly into private residences. This became such a problem that a punishment was dedicated specifically to this type of offense. The Roman legal code made puncturing subject to a fine of 100,000 sesterces, roughly $500 of purchasing power today.

Beyond the engineering challenge, simply building the aqueducts required thousands of laborers, stone masons, surveyors, potters, metal workers (to shape the lead piping), and other skilled craftsmen. A massive public undertaking, construction was funded primarily by the emperor and private donations. Wealthy patrons would enjoy the reflected glory of their beneficence, perhaps not too different from the naming rights we see today for professional sports stadiums, such as Coors Field in Denver or Heinz Field in Pittsburgh. The funds raised by the *vectigal*, by contrast, were used to cover the costs of system maintenance.

This water-financing scheme gave Roman drinking water a dual nature. To the wealthy Roman, water in the house—whether for drinking, an ornamental fountain, or domestic uses—effectively was a priced good. The water itself was free, but charging for the service of water delivery made it a commodity. To the average Roman resident, however, water in the city was available by right, as free for the taking as water from the Tiber River.

Each source relied on different allocation strategies for a scarce resource—use of *lacus* water was limited by the physical effort of carrying water from the basin to the home; use of water piped into the home was limited by the cost of paying the *vectigal*. *Lacus* water was, in modern parlance, a completely subsidized municipal service, but it was perceived as much more than that, for water supply had an implicitly political message.

Consider that, in the time of Emperor Augustus, the number of *lacus* increased dramatically, from ninety-one to almost six hundred. And many of these were magnificently decorated, with bronze and marble statues surrounded by columns. These ornate water masterpieces strengthened the tradition of majestic fountains we still associate with Rome. But why were they built?

Classical scholars suggest these impressive public works were intended, first and foremost, as political statements. Augustus was the first Roman emperor, seizing the reins of power after the struggle following the murder of Julius Caesar on the Ides of March. Romans still remembered the more democratic Republic. Augustus, it has been suggested, sought to remind the common people that they received their water from imperial beneficence in the name of their ruler. As historian Matthew Malott has written:

> By totally revamping the water system and making it more conspicu-
> ous and lavishly decorated, Augustus, and then Claudius after him,
> wanted to make the people forget that the older aqueducts survived
> from a time when the Emperor had no power. He wanted to erase the

history of the aqueducts before him and suggest that they were his personal possession, and that although they were a free public service, the people still received their water by his generosity and permission.

These beautiful fountains and basins provided a clear justification of regime change. The Romans' right to water was acknowledged, ensured, and enhanced as *Aqua Nomine Caesaris*—water in the name of Caesar.

The practice of free drinking water provided in the name of Caesar has endured throughout Italy to modern times. The journal of Rutilius Namatianus, a thirsty traveler in western Italy in 416 AD, contains an outraged passage recounting how he was required to pay for drinking water from a spring near Populonia. A marble wellhead from the ninth century in Rome's San Marco church carries an inscription cursing anyone who dares to sell the well's water. Even today, many Italian towns and villages still maintain public water fountains where locals come to fill their jugs to drink at home. Venice, in particular, has one in virtually every piazza.

The story of Rome, then, provides within the same city fundamentally different conceptions of drinking water—as a public good provided by right through imperial beneficence, on the one hand, and as a private good for domestic consumption, on the other. Yet the two depended upon one another, for it was the treatment of drinking water as a priced good that enabled cross-subsidization to ensure its public nature. This model worked well for more than five centuries, but how did it evolve with the rise of modern industrial cities? New York provides the next stop in our story.

EVER SINCE PETER MINUIT'S CELEBRATED PURCHASE OF MANHATTAN from the natives for beads and trinkets in 1626, the island has faced challenges of ensuring adequate drinking water. While New York City is obviously surrounded by large rivers, they open on the ocean and are too salty for drinking. The first Europeans to live in Manhattan, the Dutch settlers of New Amsterdam, collected rainwater in cisterns and shallow wells. Most of the settlement's water came from a deep spring-fed, freshwater pond known as the Kalch-Hook, covering seventy acres in lower Manhattan (just east of where Broadway now cuts between Chambers and Canal streets).

The wells in New Amsterdam were private, and none too attractive. As Dr. Benjamin Bullivant described at the time, "[there are] many publique wells enclosed & Covered in ye Streetes . . . [which are] Nasty & unregarded." Although there had been plans in 1660 to build a public well, the famed regional governor, Peter Stuyvesant, refused to approve the funding. This proved remarkably shortsighted, however, when British warships sailed up the Hudson in 1664. The Dutch defense was brief and feeble. Besieged in a fort, the Dutch realized to their chagrin that the fort had no wells and therefore no water sources. Following a quick surrender, which kept the town's commercial prospects intact, Stuyvesant justified the loss to his employers as not a particularly serious matter since the lack of freshwater on the island made it impossible to defend and easy to regain.

No surprise, then, that one of the first acts of the new British masters, after renaming the city New York, was construction of public wells in the city. Begun in 1667, these would remain a primary source of water for New Yorkers well into the nineteenth century. While the wells were regarded as public works projects, few public monies were actually spent at first. People living on the street where a well had been sited were told to undertake construction on their own. This approach went nowhere, though, with only one brackish well completed. Finally, in 1686, construction of eight wells got underway through a combination of public funding and assessments of families who would be serviced. People refusing to pay the assessment were threatened with forced sales of goods to make up the shortfall. Local residents were charged with ensuring proper maintenance; indeed, some of the wells later became known by the names of these overseers. By the 1700s, this had developed into a common practice in which a local group would petition the authorities to dig a public well or install a pump at a convenient place. In exchange, the costs of construction would be charged to the local residents.

Most New Yorkers relied on these wells and the "Collect" (the anglicized pronunciation of the Kalch-Hook) for free drinking water. During this period, however, urbanization continued and further industrial and population growth were clearly in store. Sanitation, an ever-present problem in British cities, was becoming unmanageable. Peter Kalm, a Swedish botanist visiting New York in 1748, observed, in a remark Rodney Dangerfield would have loved, that the well water was so terrible horses from out of town refused to drink it. The Collect, once the best source of drinking water on Manhattan, had become polluted by the tanneries and slaughterhouses on its banks. As the *Commercial Advertiser* reported in 1798:

> [The Collect] is a shocking hole, where all impure things center together and engender the worst of unwholesome productions; foul with excrement, frogspawn, and reptiles, that delicate pump is supplied. The water has grown worse manifestly within a few years. It is time to look out some other supply, and discontinue with use of a water growing less and less wholesome every day. . . . Can you bear to drink it on Sundays in the Summer time? It is so bad before Monday morning as to be very sickly and nauseating; and the larger the city grows the worse this evil will be.

To those with an entrepreneurial spirit, the poor maintenance of the public wells and the increasingly disgusting state of the Collect posed not a problem but a business opportunity. People with means began to purchase water from springs outside of town and from deeper wells. The best known of these wells, located near the main settlement, became a popular source of water for tea and other kitchen uses. In a foreshadowing of bottled water's future marketing of brands, different water pumps were favored over others. Indeed, a cottage industry developed around a pump operated by the Hardenbrook family, popularly known as the Tea Water Pump, which apparently was the Perrier of its time. With attractive landscaped gardens around the well, the Tea Water Pump became a popular attraction.

The real value, though, came in water distribution. Water sold from the pump and other sources became generically known as Tea Water. "Tea Water Men" purchased water directly from pump owners and carted it throughout the city for sale in buckets and barrels at a healthy profit. By the middle of the eighteenth century, sale of Tea Water had become the best and dominant source of New York drinking water. As the *American Gazetteer* described at the time:

> Most of the people are supplied every day with fresh water, conveyed to their doors in casks, from a pump near the head of Queen street, which receives it from a spring almost a mile from the centre of the city. This well is about 20 feet deep and four feet diameter. The average quantity drawn daily from this remarkable well, is 110 hogheads of 130 gallons each.

Twenty-four wholly separate distributers carted the water around the city. Purchasing a hogshead of water for six cents and selling bucketfuls at one cent a gallon, distributors had a profit margin of 2170 percent, an early example of just how much money could be made selling drinking water to individuals.

The limitations of public wells and the Collect in providing clean water, growing dependence on Tea Water sales, and general concern over the availability of water to fight fires made clear the need for a serious rethinking of New York's water supply. Thus, in 1774, the city approved an ambitious plan for a steam engine–powered waterworks that would pump water throughout the city in aqueducts similar to those of Rome. To fund the public works, the city issued £11,400 of "Water Works Money." Notes were printed with the text "payable on DEMAND, by the MAYOR, ALDERMEN, and COMMONALTY of the City of *New-York*, at the Office of Chamberlain of the said City."

Construction commenced, but the timing could not have been worse. As the colonies descended into the Revolutionary War, the British occupied the city and promptly destroyed the waterworks construction. Following the Revolutionary War, the newly inde-

Water Works notes were the first paper money issued by an American city.

pendent government stumbled along for more than fifteen years trying to solve the water supply issues. Plans were proposed for public waterworks and carefully studied, but none were funded. Water from the Tea Water Pump grew increasingly poor in quality and increasingly high in price. Nor did public wells provide a more attractive option.

New York was not alone in its troubles. The challenge of providing safe drinking water confronted all of the new nation's cities in the years following the Revolution. In 1793, a yellow fever epidemic shut down Philadelphia. Highly infectious, yellow fever was a death sentence in the eighteenth and nineteenth centuries, its victims suffering from fever, nausea, and jaundice from liver failure (hence the yellow appearance of the body and the name of the fever) before eventual death. For three months, the country's capital and busiest shipping port was paralyzed. Almost half of the city, more than twenty thousand people, fled to escape the contagion. Imagine, for a moment, the hysteria that would ensue today if half of a major city's population hurriedly left to avoid a rampant disease.

Benjamin Franklin had already foreseen this danger. His last will and testament, read at the Philadelphia City Hall in 1790, had contained the following instructions of how his £100,000 bequest to the city should be spent.

And having considered that the covering of the ground-plot of the city with buildings and pavements, which carry off most of the rain, and prevents its soaking into the Earth and renewing and purifying the Springs, whence the water of wells must gradually grow worse, and in time be unfit for use, as I find has happened in all old cities, I recommend that at the end of the first hundred years, if not done before, the corporation of the city Employ a part of the hundred thousand pounds in bringing by pipes, the water of the Wissahickon Creek into the town, so as to supply the inhabitants, which I apprehend may be done without great difficulty, the level of that creek being much above that of the city and may be made higher by a dam.

While the city fathers initially ignored this prescient advice, the yellow fever epidemic shocked them into action. Philadelphia's water system was completed in 1801, and its residents enjoyed reliable public water supply with streets washed down daily. Thanks to this bold public investment, Philadelphia avoided many of the terrible epidemics that afflicted other American cities in the following decades.

New York had been badly hit by yellow fever in 1795, and many blamed the disease on the city's foul water and fouler streets. With citizens and business leaders alike demanding action, the city council directed that the state legislature in Albany pass a bill providing the city with the power to tax goods sold at auction and use these proceeds to build the necessary water infrastructure. These were, by no coincidence, the same powers that the Philadelphia City Council had requested from the Pennsylvania state legislature in its push for civic improvement.

However, affairs in Albany took a decidedly different turn in an alliance that would seem unthinkable years later. Assemblyman Aaron Burr teamed with Alexander Hamilton, recently retired as the nation's first Secretary of the Treasury, to transform the city's request for public financing powers into a private project. This is the same Aaron Burr who, nine years later as vice president, shot and killed Hamilton in a duel over insults supposedly made by Hamilton about Burr's candidacy for governor in New York.

In the portraits above, Burr is on the left and Hamilton, the face on the $10 bill, on the right.

In an argument that would echo two centuries later through privatization debates in Cochabamba, Bolivia, and other cities around the world, Hamilton persuaded the New York state legislature that privatization was preferable to public financing because the service provider would be able to raise the necessary capital and save the city the politically difficult task of raising money through loans and taxes. Nor was this an unreasonable argument. While Philadelphia's waterworks had been provided by the municipality, this was uncommon. Through the eighteenth and early nineteenth century, urban water projects were generally provided by private enterprise. Municipal authorities were often politically weak and, daunted by the high capital costs and maintenance expenses, city councils were much more comfortable relying on private capital to provide a public service. The corporation's shareholders might reap the profit, but they also bore the risk.

Burr hurried a bill through in just three days. Authorized by the New York state legislature, the Manhattan Company, as the new organization would be called, was limited to $2 million in capital but granted broad-ranging powers. With the power of eminent domain, it was free to select whatever land it thought necessary for construction and any waters it deemed appropriate. If the parties could not agree on the proper compensation for private property taken by the company, a three-person body appointed by the New York Supreme Court would arbitrate. In stark contrast to other charters creating water companies during this period, the Manhattan Company had no obligation to repair city streets torn up placing pipes, provide free water for fighting fires, seek approval for water rates, or open its books for official inspection. Indeed, the only constraint was that, within ten years of its creation, the Manhattan Company shall "furnish and continue a supply of pure and wholesome water sufficient for the use of all such citizens dwelling in the said city as shall agree to take it on the terms to be demanded by the said company." If this condition were not met, the company would lose its charter.

This was a sweeping range of powers for a water company, but Aaron Burr had more than water supply on his mind. Near the end of the company's charter, a short paragraph revealed the real game afoot.

> And be it further enacted, That it shall and may be lawful for the said company to employ all such surplus capital as may belong or accrue to the said company in the purchase of public or other stock, or in any other monied transactions not inconsistent with the constitution and laws of this state or of the United States, for the sole benefit of the said company.

Burr didn't care about providing water. He wanted a bank charter, and one with far fewer constraints than other banks of the day. In short order, the company directed only 10 percent of the Manhattan Company's $2 million toward investments in waterworks. The other money was profitably invested in the banking business. The bank could not ignore water completely, for its existence depended upon satisfying the charter's requirement to furnish and supply "pure and wholesome water." Just how pure and wholesome, though, was a matter of dispute.

The lawmakers' assumption seems to have been that water would be piped in from the Bronx River, since the water sources on Manhattan Island had come to be regarded as undrinkable. But the Manhattan Company waterworks drew most of its water from the closer, cheaper, more revolting Collect. Doing the bare minimum to maintain its charter, the company laid only twenty-three miles of pipe in its first thirty-two years. Centuries before the invention of water meters, the company charged customers based on the number of fireplaces. Houses with fewer than five fireplaces paid $5 annually, with a charge of $1.25 for each additional fireplace and a maximum charge of $20. There were bitter complaints over the quality of the water. A letter in the *New York Evening Journal* angrily asserted:

> I have no doubt that one cause of the numerous stomach affections so common in this city is the impure, I may say poisonous nature of the pernicious Manhattan water which thousands of us daily and constantly use. It is true the unpalatableness of this abominable fluid prevents almost every person from using it as a beverage at the table, but you will know that all the cooking of a very large portion of this community is done through the agency of this common nuisance. Our tea and coffee are made of it, our bread is mixed with it, and our meat and vegetables are boiled in it. Our linen happily escapes the contamination of its touch, "for no two things hold more antipathy" than soap and this vile water.

A letter in the *New York Commercial Advertiser* described the company as "the most outrageous insult ever offended to an afflicted city." Despite unhappy water customers, the company defended its monopoly power over water provision and helped drive Tea Water pumps out of business. New Yorkers were thus forced to rely on the increasingly noxious Collect pond and local wells. People with money turned to imported soda water and well water mixed with liquor. As a historian of the era has described, "As for New Yorkers, drinking no more Tea Water and scant Manhattan, it was once again back to street wells and carted spring water. New York had entered the first American century with less good water than the Dutch had bequeathed to the English."

Over time, this water company gave up all pretense and developed into the powerful Chase Manhattan Bank (now known as JP Morgan Chase), undoubtedly the first commercial bank that owes its origins to drinking water. In homage to its origins, the corporate logo of Chase Manhattan is a stylized cross section of a wooden water pipe. Ironically, Burr, the mastermind of the enterprise, ran into financial difficulties, sold his stock in the company, and was forced off the board in 1802.

By the first decades of the nineteenth century, the citizens of Philadelphia enjoyed ample supplies of clean water for drinking, cooking, battling fires, cleaning, and washing down the streets. Boston and Baltimore were in the process of building public waterworks based on Philadelphia's model. But following the debacle of the Manhattan Company, New York did nothing. In 1828 a large fire caused extensive property damage, and in 1832 a severe cholera epidemic killed 3,500 people. Philadelphia, by contrast, had lost just 900 lives during the same scourge. A water commission appointed by the New York City Council had to admit the obvious in its 1835 report: New York suffered by comparison with its rival City of Brotherly Love.

> No disagreeable odor assails the persons who pass through the streets of that city [Philadelphia]; everything calculated to annoy the senses is swept away by the running stream; but in New-York a person coming in the city from the pure air of the country, is compelled to hold his breath, or make use of some perfume to break off the disagreeable smell arising from the streets. . . . The only way we can account for this difference in the health of the two cities is, that Philadelphia is supplied with abundance of pure and wholesome water, not only for drinking and culinary purposes, but for bathing, and for washing the streets of the whole city, while New-York is entirely destitute of the means for effecting any of these purposes.

The need for new infrastructure to store and distribute water was clear. The key question was how to pay for it—whether to rely on public or private financing, municipal funds or private capital. Philadelphia's experience certainly showed that public funding could be successful. London, however, was the capital of the world's greatest empire, and it relied on private means.

Through the Middle Ages, Londoners had gathered drinking water from local springs, wells, and the Thames River (the Romans never built aqueducts for London). In the thirteenth century, a connection known as the Great Conduit was built from springs near Tybburn to cisterns in the city and provided a source of clean drinking water, which apparently was sold by leasing official tankards to people for drawing water. The poor relied on the unsanitary and foul-smelling Thames, and some merchants even tried to charge for that. A 1417 city ordinance forbade owners of wharves and stairs on the Thames from charging for access to the river.

During the sixteenth century, with the rise of England's first industrial revolution, the city was unwilling to spend money on public works and relied instead on private commerce for water supply. As early as 1609, an open canal nearly forty miles north of London had been dug. It was known as the New River, and its management was granted to a private company. In 1721, the Chelsea Waterworks Company was founded, followed by six more private water companies over the next century. In all, eight companies provided more than twenty-eight million gallons of water from various sources in and around London. Supporters of privatization pointed to the might of the British Empire and urged New York to follow the privatization path of London.

Yet the same story could just as easily provide the opposite conclusion. Much of the water was taken from the River Thames, the receiving body for the city's sewers. Terrible cholera outbreaks were quite common but shrugged off as an unpleasant fact of urban living. The different water companies did not compete. Far from it. Following a model familiar to crime bosses, they realized far better profits by dividing the territory into separate monopolies where they each set their own rates as they saw fit.

In the end, chastened by the Manhattan Company debacle and envious of rival Philadelphia's success, New York's water commission strongly recommended public financing for construction. A permanent Board of Water Commissioners was created and authorized to raise infrastructure capital and condemn land in order to supply water to the city. Surprising even today, the condemnation authority extended beyond the boundaries of the city, for the water source lay upstream of New York in the town of Croton. By 1838, condemnation of thirty-five acres of land in the Croton watershed had been completed.

The Croton Reservoir was a massive project, piping ninety-five million gallons daily through forty-one miles of pipe to a reservoir located in Central Park, lavishly decorated with Egyptian designs. The civic pride in the completion of the new water system is hard to imagine. The four days of inauguration ceremonies in October 1842 put a modern-day ticker-tape parade to shame. As Mayor Philip Hone wrote in his diary at the time, "Nothing is talked of or thought of in New York but Croton water; fountains, aqueducts, hydrants, and hose attract our attention and impede our progress through the streets. Political spouting has given place to water spouts, and the free current of water has diverted the attention of the people from the vexed questions of the confused state of the national currency."

Commencing the festivities, amid one hundred firing cannons and ringing church bells, a five-mile parade snaked through the city. City Hall Park featured a fifty-foot fountain, and a hymn, "The Croton Ode," written specially for the occasion, was performed by the New York Sacred Music Society.

Croton water, however, satisfied the city's needs for only a few decades. The city then looked farther north, to the Catskills and Delaware watersheds some 125 miles from the city. In an even more impressive feat of engineering, more than six thousand miles of tunnels, aqueducts, and distribution mains carried 1.2 billion gallons a day. In all, twenty-two upstate farming communities were moved in New York City's quest to secure freshwater, their towns drowned beneath the massive new reservoirs.

Construction of the reservoir in Croton marked the end of significant private provision of drinking water for New Yorkers, displacing the Manhattan Company. Interestingly, however, it did not mark the end of water as an unpriced good, for with construction

of the Croton Reservoir and the Croton Aqueduct came the installation in New York of so-called Croton Hydrants. Following the
lead of Philadelphia, these fire and street hydrants provided water
free of charge and proved very popular.

The net result bore a fascinatingly strong resemblance to the
Roman system of cross-subsidization from private pipes to *lacus* at
the time of Caesar. Water from hydrants and fountains was free for
the taking. Indeed, most New York homeowners felt no need to install piping or pay for the water service. It took several decades after
introduction of the Croton Aqueduct for piped water to become
dominant. The greatest attraction for piping water into the home
was not drinking water but, rather, the convenience of domestic uses
such as toilets (aptly named "water closets"), washing, and bathing.

AT THE BEGINNING OF THIS CHAPTER, MAUDE BARLOW ARGUED FOR
access to drinking water as a human right granted by the state rather
than a commodity furnished by markets. This remains a harshly
fought controversy, with strident advocates on both sides of the
issue. If our survey of drinking water management in different societies has shown anything, though, it is that markets and rights to
water have often existed alongside one another.

A rights-based water management regime is clearly not a new
idea. Not only have markets and rights to water coexisted, they
have openly depended upon each other through cross-subsidization.
In Rome, the private *vectigal* tax largely funded the *lacus* public
wells. Though different in detail, a strikingly similar arrangement
of private and public drinking water reappeared two millennia later
in the form of the Croton Hydrants in New York and open hydrants
in Philadelphia. From a historic vantage, the cases of Rome and
New York show that markets can actually be used to *ensure* fulfill-
ment of rights. Whether we can achieve the same result in the
twenty-first century remains an open question, one that we will
return to later in the book. First, though, we need to consider
whether the water provided, by right or market, is safe to drink.

Did lead pipes contribute to the fall of the Roman Empire?

The behavior of many of the Roman emperors during its decline has always seemed bizarre, to say the least. Claudius slobbered when talking and suffered from tremors and inappropriate giggling. The brutal Caligula declared himself a god and appointed his horse a priest. There are plenty of other examples of mad behavior, starting with the infamous Nero who allegedly fiddled while Rome burned. Classicists have long wondered why there were so many crazy emperors.

In 1909, the German pharmacologist Rudolf Kobert proposed an explanation that has remained popular today. Kobert argued that the emperors' aberrant behavior was the result of lead poisoning from drinking water that had passed through lead pipes.

The theory seems more than plausible on its face. Lead was readily available, had a low melting point, and was easy to work into sheets and pipes. Indeed, the name for lead craftsmen was "*plumbarii*," the origin for our word "plumbers." Lead pipes were in common use both in aqueducts and street connections to houses. There is also clear evidence that Romans ingested large amounts of lead, more than enough to cause lead poisoning and perhaps some of the strange behavior so common among the emperors.

Interestingly, the Romans knew about the dangers of lead poisoning. The father of medicine, Hippocrates, clearly described the symptoms of lead poisoning as early as the fourth century BC. The great chronicler of Roman engineering, Vitruvius, advised that "water conducted through earthen pipes is much more healthy than that through lead; indeed that conveyed in the lead must be injurious, because from it white lead [often used for facial cosmetics] is obtained, and this is said to be injurious to the human body. . . . Water should therefore on no account be conducted in leaden pipes if we are desirous that it should be wholesome." Despite Vitruvius's warnings, lead pipe remained in common use.

The lead pipe theory sounds reasonable, but was drinking water the primary source of lead found in the Roman bodies? Probably not, for two reasons. First, the aqueducts were constantly flowing. Water fees, the *vectigal*, were based on the size of the nozzle, not how much water was actually consumed, so there was no reason to collect and store water. As one archeologist has written, "you could no more turn off a Roman aqueduct than you can turn off a river." The water would not have the chance to settle and stay in contact with lead for very long. More important, the geology around Rome is dominated by limestone. This makes the water "hard," which leads to scaling inside pipes. We know from Frontinus's accounts that "the accumulation of deposit, which sometimes hardens into a crust, contracts the channel of the water." Analysis of aqueduct pipes today shows just such an incrustation. This layer of calcium carbonate would effectively have created a second, inner pipe, insulating the water from contact with the lead pipes and, as a result, prevented lead from dissolving into the water.

So what was the source of lead? The most likely culprit was the Romans' diet. Sugar was not an ingredient in Rome. Instead, cooks would boil down fermented grape juice, reducing it to a thick syrup known as *sapa*. This was widely used in sauces and mixed with wine and fruits to preserve and enhance their flavor. The *sapa*, unfortunately, was generally produced by boiling the mixture in lead pots or lead-lined copper kettles. Lead would leach into the acidic liquid, resulting in a sweet but poisonous elixir. Studies of *sapa* suggest that just one teaspoon of the syrup ingested once a day would have caused chronic lead poisoning over time. Modern analysis of the lead content in the bones of exhumed skeletons show much higher lead levels in the aristocrats than slaves, supporting the *sapa* theory since only the wealthy could afford a diet with *sapa*. It may well be that the fall of Rome was due in part to the Roman sweet tooth.

3

Is It Safe to Drink
the Water?

IF YOU BOARD A FERRY IN BUSTLING HONG KONG, CROSS TO Lantau Island, and get on a local bus, the forests of cranes atop new buildings soon give way to forested hills too steep for the construction boom to reach. An hour's ride up the spine of the mountain range brings you to Po Lin Monastery. Towering above the temple buildings sits Tian Tan Buddha, a bronze statue of Buddha sitting cross-legged. The statue is massive, one of the largest seated bronze statue of Buddha in the world. Lantau Island is hot and humid, even in the hills, and you get thirsty climbing the many ceremonial steps up to the statue. A decade ago, amid the monastery buildings, stood a public fountain. Chained to the fountain was a bamboo ladle, thoughtfully provided for the thirsty visitor. And there was a small line of tourists patiently waiting to drink from it.

Such communal drinking cups have been common in many parts of Asia. They used to be widespread in the United States. A century ago, though, this practice started to change due to safety concerns. In 1908, for example, *Technical World Magazine* featured an article by a Lafayette College biology professor with the ominous title "Death in School Drinking Cups." Newspapers and public health boards took up the cause as well, with dire warnings and grim illustrations of this dangerous practice.

A 1910 pamphlet titled "The Cup-Campaigner" made its views on the dangers of common drinking cups gruesomely clear.

In 1909, Kansas became the first state to ban communal cups in public places, and others soon followed. Indeed, the success of the paper Dixie Cup was largely due to the new demand for cheap, disposable drinking cups for use at public fountains.

At the turn of the twentieth century, shared water cups in American public places came to be regarded not only as unsafe but illegal. Even today, some American and British churches now advise against taking Communion from a common chalice during flu season. Yet shared cups remain commonplace in many parts of the world. While you didn't find many Western tourists drinking from the Tian Tan Buddha fountain, there was a line. For most of the visitors, it obviously seemed safe to drink the water. From the perspective of this American visitor, though, one could not help but find the practice gross. *Yuck,* I thought to myself as I watched them take turns drinking from the cup. *Don't they know that's unsafe?*

All successful societies throughout history have depended on reliable access to drinking water, whether through natural sources such as rivers and oases or built structures such as wells and reservoirs. We explored in the last chapter who gets access to water, but access is not enough. The water has to be safe to drink. And this presupposes a deceptively simple question: *How do we know what "safe" water is?*

In twenty-first-century America, the answer seems simple—government experts and scientists tell us. We take for granted that our tap water is treated to exacting chemical and biological analyses. The name of the relevant federal law says it all: the Safe Drinking Water Act. This law requires the Environmental Protection Agency to set maximum contaminant levels for copper, lead, and more than eighty other compounds. Our water is regularly tested by local officials, and if the standards are violated, we expect to find out and have something done about it. It is not as if the water we drink from the tap is pure, distilled H_2O, of course. There are plenty of minerals and bacteria in our tap water and, indeed, in the bottled water we buy at stores and restaurants, but it is considered safe enough to drink.

This seems a commonsense, perhaps obvious approach. Yet, in historical terms, the very idea of the need to conduct detailed chemical and biological analyses, much less care about drinking water's invisible contents, is still stunningly novel. The germ theory of disease has only existed for about 150 years, a recent development compared to the history of human settlement. And even this approach has shortcomings. Legitimate questions are still being asked about our drinking water. Are the standards stringent enough? Can the infrastructure treating our water meet these standards? How can we be sure that we are even regulating the right substances?

Our technical understanding of water safety is more sophisticated than ever before, but a society's regulation of drinking water has never been a purely technical matter. While the Safe Drinking Water Act may look dramatically different than the laws and practices relied on by other societies and in other times, they share far more similarities than differences. The fundamental problem, as we shall see, is that no source of water can ever be totally safe, completely risk-free, either today or two hundred years from now.

The conception of safety evolves over time and across cultures, informed by a society's understanding of disease, technological capability, and aversion to risk. Popular perceptions shape our management of safe drinking water just as surely as do chemical assays. Because of the universality of this challenge, because safety is a timeless moving target, one can take valuable lessons for today from the historical record.

The next three chapters explore this broad topic. In chapter four, we will explore nonliving, chemical dangers such as arsenic and modern challenges such as pharmaceutical residues and persistent organic pollutants in our water sources. Then, we turn to terrorism and the dangers we face from enemies intent on poisoning the water we drink. But first, in the pages that follow, let's consider how societies have dealt with waterborne diseases and the immediate dangers they present.

DESPITE THE ENTICING IMAGES ON BOTTLED WATER LABELS OF GUSHing mounting streams and burbling springs, the simple fact is that freshwater is just not very clean. Water is a great solvent, but many things in nature that are water-soluble are not good for us. Teeming numbers of microorganisms live in water. In fact, natural selection has ensured that many of these microorganisms can *only* live in water. As hydrologist Francis Chapelle has memorably described:

> These bacteria, algae, fungi, and viruses—often as many as 100 million *per milliliter*—can live in water that is hot or cold, clear or muddy, rapidly flowing or stagnant. They can live in desert pools where water temperature exceeds 140° F, or on frozen tundras where temperatures dip below -50° F. We like to think that water drawn from unpolluted rivers, streams, and lakes is naturally pure and fit for human consumption. Sometimes it is, but this is not common. Water, by its very nature, is often very dirty.

And this is water from natural surroundings. Once water in wells, rivers, or lakes comes into contact with the garbage and animal and human waste we inevitably produce in towns and cities, things only get worse.

Travel books to distant places have long held warnings not to drink the water. Martin Lister warned seventeenth-century visitors to Paris that drinking the water caused "looseness, and sometimes dysenteries." Euphemistic phrases for travelers' upset stomachs range from "Montezuma's Revenge" in Mexico and "Delhi Belly" in India to "Mummy Tummy" in Egypt and the "Karachi Crouch" in Pakistan. While the names may be lighthearted, the condition is not. The Centers for Disease Control estimate that 20 to 50 percent of international travelers suffer from diarrhea and abdominal cramping every year. These generally strike within a week of arriving. The main causes of these scourges are bacteria such as E. coli and shigella, with protozoa such as giardia afflicting in some regions, as well.

The frustrating question posed by such omnipresent travelers' woes is why travelers get sick drinking the same water that locals drink with apparently no problems at all. The answer is immunity. The local citizens have spent their lives with these microorganisms in their water, and their bodies' immune systems have developed antibodies to counter many of the specific pathogens that afflict visitors. This is not true for all microorganisms, of course, which is why some waterborne diseases, such as cholera, remain such widespread problems in developing countries.

Asking whether it is safe to drink the water remains an important question, both in the United States and abroad. But how to consider such a broad-ranging question? The basic task of providing safe water has remained the same for as long as we have had human settlements, and it can be broken into four separate challenges.

- SOURCE IDENTIFICATION—how to find drinking water
- SOURCE PROTECTION—what to do around the source to keep the water uncontaminated
- TREATMENT—how to make the water safe for drinking
- DISTRIBUTION—how to get water from the source to the final point of consumption, and keep it clean during the journey

To protect against waterborne diseases, every one of these tasks must be effectively managed, and each presents its own set of quite difficult technical, policy, and legal challenges.

Source Identification

Everyone needs to know how to find a reliable source of drinking water. For some of us, this involves no more than going to the sink or pulling a bottle of water from the refrigerator. For early explorers of unknown lands and mariners in uncharted seas, however, death from thirst was a very real threat. They all faced the same terrible fear of running out of water before chancing upon a new source. A person can go three weeks or more without food. The body starts consuming its own fat and muscle. But we can only go a few days without water, and it is a terrible way to suffer.

In 1906, Pablo Valencia wandered for eight days in the Sonoran Desert outside Tucson, Arizona. When found by the rescue party, he was described by his rescuer in gripping detail.

> Pablo was stark naked; his formerly full-muscled legs and arms were shrunken and scrawny; his ribs ridged out like those of a [starving] horse; his habitually plethoric abdomen was drawn in almost against his vertebral column; his lips had disappeared as if amputated, leaving low edges of blackened tissue; his teeth and gums projected like those of a skinned animal, but the flesh was black and dry as a hank of jerky; his nose was withered and shrunken to half its length, the nostril-lining showing black; his eyes were set in a winkless stare, with surrounding skin so contracted as to expose the conjunctiva, itself black as the gums; his joints and bones stood out like those of a wasted sickling, though the skin clung to them in a way suggesting shrunken rawhide used in repairing a broken wheel.

This was no less terrifying for ancient nomadic peoples in arid lands. Discussions of springs and wells are found throughout the Old Testament, their importance clear because each had its own name. Indeed, it may be the earliest example of critical intellectual property. Knowledge of water sources has always been vital to a group's survival.

As the journalist Elizabeth Royte has described, "From the beginning of human time, access to sufficient clean water was the *sine qua non* for establishment of a settlement. Lack of good water cramped expansion, and the search for new sources drew civilization's map." Archaeological excavations from the Neolithic Period onward have found a striking correspondence between settlements and reliable sources of nearby drinking water, whether wells, springs, streams, or lakes. Storage of drinking water was often necessary to urban planning, as well. Thus one can find examples of sophisticated water management in virtually every archaeological excavation of ancient civilizations—from complex drains in Machu Picchu high atop the Andes, to intricate systems of canals in Egypt, to the Romans' towering aqueducts that remain standing today. Indeed, the historian Karl Wittfogel invented the term "hydraulic civilization" to describe those societies that maintained power by control over water resources.

The need to identify safe sources of water is as crucial for mobile settlements as permanent ones, and nowhere has this been more true than during times of war. As the Roman general Vegetius observed, "An army must not use bad or marshy water: for the drinking of bad water is like poison and causes plagues among those who drink it." Napoleon was only half right when he said that an army marches on its stomach. It also needs to slake its thirst. Consider that in the Napoleonic Wars, disease killed eight times more soldiers than battle injuries. In the American Civil War, diarrhea and dysentery claimed more lives than the battlefield. And during the pivotal battle of El Alamein during World War II, as many as 50 percent of the German and Italian troops suffered from waterborne diseases. The German general commanding the North African theater, Erwin Rommel, is said to have claimed that his defeat was due to dysentery, not Field Marshal Montgomery's Eighth Army.

Nor was dangerous water only in army camps. In many cultures, the most effective strategy to avoid unsafe drinking water has been to *avoid water* altogether. Part of this aversion was for safety's sake, but there was a snobbish motive, as well. As a classical scholar has described, the Roman elite regarded water as "the characteristic drink of the subaltern classes, the cheapest and most easily available drink, fit for children, slaves, and the women who had been forbidden from drinking wine very early in the Republic."

This aversion to water carried into the Middle Ages. In the time of Charlemagne, high-ranking military officers were punished for drunkenness by the humiliation of being forced to drink water. In the fifteenth century, Sir John Fortescue observed that the English "drink no water unless it be . . . for devotion." The sixteenth-century English doctor William Bullein warned that "to drinke colde water is euyll [evil]" and causes melancholy. His contemporary Andrew Boorde claimed that "water is not holsome soole by it self; for an Englysshe man . . . [because] water is colde, slowe, and slack of dygestyon." Presumably, water interfered with digestion by cooling the stomach and its furnace-like operation.

The eighth-century author Paul the Deacon recounts a wonderful anecdote showing the relative prestige of wine and water. A nobleman's enemies planned to kill him and chose the method of poisoning his wine chalice. As dinnertime approached, they eagerly waited for him to raise the poisoned goblet to his lips. The canny nobleman, however, had suspicions about the wine and foiled the plot by surprising everyone. Instead of drinking wine with his meal, as everyone had expected, he drank water, a liquid so common and beneath his standing that no one had even considered poisoning it. Stooping beneath his station to drink water instead of wine saved the canny nobleman's life.

The aversion to water carried over to the New World, as well. As Francis Chapelle has described, despite readily available water in New England, the Pilgrims sought other drinks.

> Drinking water—any water—was a sign of desperation, an admission of abject poverty, a last resort. Like all Europeans of the seventeenth century, the Pilgrims disliked, distrusted, and despised drinking water. Only truly poor people, who had absolutely no choice, drank water. There is one thing all Europeans agreed on: drinking water was bad— very bad—for your health.

If not water, then what did people drink? The answer in ancient times often was alcohol. The drink of choice in Egypt was beer, and in ancient Greece wine. It may not be surprising that one of the very first buildings constructed in Plymouth Plantation was a brewhouse.

More common, though, was a mixture of water with another substance. Sometimes this was alcohol. The fifth-century Hippocratic treatise "Airs, Waters, Places" recommended adding wine to even the finest water. Beer was routinely added to water (called "small beer") in the Middle Ages. Water was also commonly mixed with vinegar, ice, honey, parsley seed, and other spices. This both improved the taste and served as a status symbol. The mixtures elevated the status of what otherwise would have been a common drink. After the discovery of the East Indies, mixing hot water with coffee and tea became popular.

It is interesting to note that none of these mixing practices was consciously intended to make the water safer to drink, though this often may have been the result. Alcohol added to water retarded and even killed microbes. While India Pale Ale may now be all the rage in microbreweries, the addition of hops was originally intended to preserve ale in the hot colonial outposts of India (unbeknownst to the brewers, it slowed bacterial growth). Boiling water for tea and coffee would have had a similar effect.

Despite the preference for alcohol over water, water was always drunk, sometimes as plain water but often in the cuisine. Soups, stews, and dried foods were commonly prepared in water. Indeed, in the Middle Ages, more water may have been consumed in a household through prepared foods than drunk. So the question remains, how did those searching for drinking water know the source was safe? Long before recognizing the role or even the existence of microorganisms, people have understood that they need to be careful about what they drink. Over time, different groups' collective experience of identifying safe water has developed into unwritten rules, oral versions of a safe drinking water act. Importantly, however, these practices focused primarily on the *source* of the water because that was all they could observe.

The ancient Greek father of medicine, Hippocrates, for example, wrote that water from rock springs was "bad since it is hard, heating in its effect, difficult to pass, and causes constipation. The best water comes from high ground and hills covered with earth." Perhaps the greatest water engineers of all, the Romans, designed their aqueducts to segregate drinking water from other uses. The chroniclers of the time debated over which waters should be most prized. Pliny the Elder favored well water, while Columella preferred spring water. Disparaging the choice of the very wealthy, Macrobius counseled against drinking melted snow because it no longer contained water's healthy vapors.

Europeans recognized, as well, that certain water sources should be avoided. William Bullein warned in the sixteenth century, for example, that "standing waters and water running neare unto cities and townes, or marish ground, wodes, & fennes be euer ful of corruption, because there is so much filthe in them of carions & rotten dunge, &c."

Nor are such practices purely historical. A recent study of villages in Yorubaland, a region in southwestern Nigeria, examined how safe water is identified in traditional African communities today. Just as the Romans and Europeans developed rules to identify safe water, the Yoruba believe that when water comes from the mountains it has a sacred origin and, therefore, it has many qualities that other streams lack. Because a rock represents a mountain, also any water springing under a rock of these streams is believed to be safe. Similarly, rainwater is always regarded as safe because it comes directly from heaven. The local people give movements of flowing water a strong emphasis. They say that it is easy to *see* if the water is clean and good for human consumption. Flowing water is regarded safe, as the movements will take dirt away.

In fact, all societies have such rules and practices to identify safe water sources, though they may look very different. In a number of cultures, for example, drinking water is as much a spiritual as a physical resource—water can transmit both physical *and* metaphysical contaminants. As a result, there are specific rules to prevent spiritual pollution of drinking water. Traditional Hindus in India, for example, maintain a complex social hierarchy among separate castes. Reinforcing this order, upper and lower castes actually draw their water from distinct sources. If sources were shared, there would be a risk of the lower caste transmitting their social pollution from the impure to the pure. This extends to food preparation. A Brahman should not even touch food that has been prepared with water by a non-Brahman.

In the United States this practice should look familiar. Less than fifty years ago, resource segregation was commonplace in many parts of the South. Drinking fountains were separated by law, with one for "White" and one for "Colored." This was accepted as entirely justified under the law. While half a world away, was the anxiety some whites felt over drinking from a fountain that had been used by blacks all that different from the Hindi concern of higher castes drinking from the same sources as lower castes?

*A drinking fountain on the Halifax County courthouse lawn
in North Carolina, 1938*

Most of these rules intuitively seem to make sense. We can see if water comes from fast-flowing waters and appreciate why it would be safer to drink than water from a stagnant pool. By contrast, the Safe Drinking Water Act seems light-years from these sorts of norms. The EPA is currently assessing the adverse health effects of the microbe *Helicobacter pylori* and the chemical 1,2,4-trimethyl-benzene. This hyper-technical approach could not seem more distant from checking whether water emerges from under a rock or whether the person who used the well before you was an Untouchable. Yet these sets of rules all seek the very same end—safe drinking water from a trusted source, whether faucet or stream—and they all make sense to their respective societies. Such norms are essential and they are effective, to a point. Indeed, if such rules have endured over long periods of time, almost by definition they have to work; otherwise, the society that followed them would have been incapacitated by waterborne diseases. The Yoruba preference for clear, flowing water makes some sense in a modern light. It avoids the higher microbial activity in warmer, stagnant water.

Assessing *how well* such rules work, though, is a complicated matter. To assess that, we need to understand how popular conceptions of disease influence our perceptions of water quality. If water from a particular source is regarded as unsafe, locals have clearly made the connection between drinking the water and some bad result—such as spiritual impurity, blindness, or stomach cramps. But there must also be a causal mechanism lurking beneath this judgment. Today, one might say that people get typhoid because they drink water with *typhoid bacteria*, of course. But before the microscope revealed an entirely new world beyond our eyes, for most of human history physicians grappled with the problem of people getting sick without any physical contact at all with ill people.

With our modern understanding of disease, we may look patronizingly on earlier practices of bloodletting or of locating latrines next to wells, but before the era of the germ theory, these seemed entirely reasonable in their respective societies. In fact, cultural understandings of what causes disease, whether physical or spiritual, underpin the rules for drinking water.

An eighteenth-century French illustration by Johann Lavater shows how these humors were expressed in physical features: phlegmatic in the upper left, then, moving clockwise, choleric, melancholy, and sanguine.

At the time of the Greeks and Romans, for example, physicians believed that the health of the body depended upon the balance of four humors: black bile, yellow bile, phlegm, and blood. Each humor was linked to specific physical qualities. Blood was warm and moist, while black bile was cold and dry. Hence Bullein's admonition that drinking cold water was evil. Its chill risked slowing the flow of humors and could cause melancholy. Indeed the name of one particularly virulent waterborne disease, cholera, comes from the term for yellow bile, "choler." "Sanguine," equally, came from the humor of blood ("sang" in French), and "phlegmatic" from the humor of phlegm. The task of the physician was to diagnose the illness and deduce the surplus or deficit of each humor causing the ailment. He could then nurse the patient back to proper balance and health. Thus the common practices of bleeding a person or using emetics were both intended to remove surplus humors.

This conception was eventually supplanted by the miasmatic theory of disease. This theory held that diseases were caused by breathing contaminated air. The general concept was that an airborne mist containing poisonous "miasma" served as the agent of disease and could often be identified by its foul odor. Hence the name for malaria, which means "bad air." This theory explained how people could quickly infect one another without physical contact, as well as the awful stench surrounding diseased flesh. Although an inaccurate explanation, the miasma theory was effective. Its immediate policy implication—improved cleanliness—no doubt reduced the spread of pathogens.

A moment's reflection makes clear the consequences of the miasmatic theory of disease for how people thought about drinking water. If the most threatening diseases—epidemics such as bubonic plague, cholera, and typhoid—were airborne, then drinking water was unlikely to be a serious cause of concern. This is not to say, of course, that people were ignorant of the link between drinking water and disease. People obviously could get sick from drinking certain types of water, but not from the most feared epidemics. The drinking water was safe enough, just not risk-free, to use modern parlance.

Source Protection

Once one has identified a reliable and safe source for drinking water, it is essential to protect the source from harms, both seen and unseen. Most obviously, and particularly in arid regions, one must protect against physical appropriation. Where water is scarce, clear property regimes emerge with effective sanctions. As described previously, despite the widespread norm of a Right of Thirst, outsiders still need to ask permission to drink from a well in southern Zimbabwe or a spring in central Australia.

The most common approach for source protection has been through rules restricting activities that may cause pollution. Biblical text from Deuteronomy, for example, requires that waste be disposed of far away from areas of human habitation. The Babylonian Talmud similarly forbade throwing waste into wells. Nor could tanneries, slaughterhouses, cemeteries, or furnaces operate within twenty-five meters of a well. Some of the earliest environmental laws and policies in England concerned source protection. Building owners were required to keep their street frontages clean. People were paid to collect "night soil" and other waste from streets and cesspits. Dung was collected, transported in boats to the middle of the Thames, and dumped where the current ran strongest.

Half a world away, Australian aboriginal groups have had clear source protection rules as well. Defecating and starting a fire near a waterhole were vitally serious offenses, giving those responsible for the water the right to punish these transgressions by death. Among the Yoruba in Africa, the head of the community establishes rules for source protection. Bathing and clothes washing are prohibited near drinking water sources, nor are small children or anyone with a disease permitted to walk in nearby streams. Those caught washing clothes near a drinking water source are reported to the King and punished.

In addition to regulating behavior, societies have long relied on engineering to protect sources. The Book of Genesis describes how the shepherdess Rachel kept her well covered with a rock to keep the water clean. As with all things hydrological, though, for impressive technology, one inevitably looks to Rome. The Romans made the critical realization that water for flushing wastes out of the city was just as important as the clean water piped into the city. While the aqueducts are justly renowned, equally impressive was the Cloaca Maxima, Rome's sewer system. Constructed in the sixth century BC, the connected pipes and ditches drained the filth of the city's public toilets, bathhouses, buildings, and streets into the Tiber, which carried it safely away downstream.

With the fall of the Roman Empire, however, the engineering approach to source protection in Europe largely fell away. Almost no major works were built to address sanitation until well into the nineteenth century, in part perhaps because there was no money to be made, and in part because the connection had not yet been made between sanitation and source protection. For the most part, filth flowed out windows, down the streets, and into the same streams, rivers, and lakes where the city's inhabitants drew their water. As a result, cities stank to high heaven.

This state of affairs only became worse as cities grew in population through the Middle Ages. As late as 1854, journalist George Goodwin graphically described London as a "cesspool city. The entire excrementation of the Metropolis shall sooner or later be mingled in the stream of the river, there to be rolled backward and forward around the population." The Thames grew so polluted in an 1858 episode, dubbed "The Great Stink" by the *Times*, that the overpowering stench forced Parliament to adjourn until the odors subsided. In a desperate attempt to make the Houses of Parliament bearable, curtains in the chambers were soaked in chloride of lime. Indeed, one historian has claimed that "the Dark Ages for water were the nineteenth century, when increasing industrialization, urbanization, inadequate hygiene, and inadequate knowledge made drinking water dangerous."

By the end of the nineteenth century, however, London's drinking water and sanitation had improved dramatically, and this was the case in many other European and North American cities. The cause for this sea change was twofold: the development of the germ theory of disease and the "Great Sanitation Awakening." These came together in the classic story of John Snow and the famed Broad Street Pump.

Beginning on August 30, 1854, an outbreak of cholera in the Soho area of London resulted in more than five hundred deaths in just ten days. There was nothing particularly notable about this. Cholera and typhoid outbreaks in urban areas were common throughout the nineteenth century. Long known as "the poor man's plague" because of its prevalence in poor, crowded urban areas, cholera killed remarkably quickly. A victim could feel healthy in the morning and be dead by that evening, felled by painful cramps, vomiting and diarrhea. The disease seemed to be gaining ground, and not just in poor quarters. A cholera outbreak in New York City had killed 3,500 people in 1832, and typhoid had killed more than 50,000 Britons a year earlier. But since common wisdom held that these diseases spread in miasmic air, most precautions taken by the

John Snow, 1813–1858

authorities did little to solve the underlying problem. John Snow, though, suspected that miasma was missing the mark. A self-made man, Snow had become an influential London physician, personally chosen to administer chloroform to Queen Victoria during the birth of her son Prince Leopold—the first royal to give birth under anesthesia.

Snow was a fanatic about clean water. Soon after moving to London, he had already constructed a distillation apparatus in his lodgings so that he could boil and purify his water before drinking it. He had been fascinated by cholera epidemics for much of his career, and the miasmatic explanation struck him as inadequate. If cholera passed through the air, how to explain the fact that some members of a family would become ill while others did not, all living under the same roof and breathing the same air? How to explain that workers surrounded by the foulest of odors—"nightsoil handlers" and "flushermen" working with human waste—were not more susceptible to cholera than others? Snow suspected that cholera "poisons" passed through water contaminated with human waste and had published a pamphlet arguing this in 1849. He did not know how to demonstrate conclusively the disease's cause, however, and the medical establishment's confidence in the miasma theory remained unshaken.

The Soho deaths caught Snow's attention, and he took advantage of the available data. In 1836, Parliament had passed the Registration Act, for the first time requiring personal records to be kept of the recently deceased, including the cause of death. Snow grew increasingly encouraged as he checked the records of the Soho cholera outbreak. He found that every cholera victim had lived within a quarter-mile of the popular Broad Street Pump, a fifteen-foot-deep well known for its clear drinking water. Snow's theory, though, faced a major obstacle. A widow, Susannah Eley, had died of cholera during the outbreak but lived in Hampstead, nowhere near Soho; another woman had died in Islington, even farther away. If cholera had been transmitted through drinking water at the Broad Street Pump, how had it infected these women so many miles away?

Unwilling to discard his theory, Snow visited the widow's son to see if there might be some unknown connection with the Broad Street Pump. As Snow heard the story of her death, he grew increasingly intrigued. While the widow had not visited Soho prior to her death, she had previously lived in the area. She so enjoyed the water from the Broad Street Pump that she regularly sent her servant to fill water bottles there. Indeed, she had done so days before her death. The son of the recently deceased widow went on to sadly relate that he had also recently lost a cousin. Had the cousin visited his mother? Snow eagerly inquired. Oh yes, the son replied. In fact, she had drunk the same Soho bottled water as his mother before returning to her home in Islington and dying the next day.

The famed "Ghost Map" from a report written by Snow in 1855 shows the incidences of cholera around the pump. Armed with this conclusive information, Snow persuaded the Soho Parish leaders to remove the pump handle at Broad Street, and the outbreak stopped soon after. This marked both the first time a government had sought to stop the outbreak of a waterborne disease and the birth of the modern field of epidemiology—the study of disease in

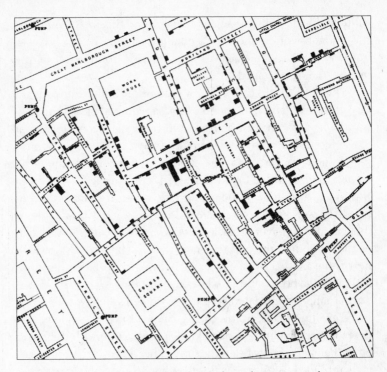

*John Snow's map of cholera cases shows clustering around
the Broad Street Pump*

populations. To honor Snow's achievements, the International Epidemiology Association boasted a pump handle as its symbol (not to mention the pub, The John Snow, which is located right in front of where the pump used to stand).

While rightly celebrated as real-life medical sleuthing that puts *CSI* and its innumerable spin-offs to shame, Snow's detective work proved particularly persuasive to the Soho Parish leaders because it coincided with scientific developments playing out at the same time. While Antoni van Leeuwenhoek had seen and described the newly discovered world of microorganisms to the British Royal Society in the late 1600s, no connection had been made at the time between disease and these newest known additions to the living world. The hold of the miasmatic theory of disease was slowly loosening its grip through the nineteenth century, though, thanks to developments in the field of microbiology by Louis Pasteur, Robert Koch, Joseph Lister, and others.

The germ theory of disease was premised on two hypotheses: first, that specific diseases are caused by specific microorganisms that live in air and water, and second, that the same germs reproduce from bearers of the same disease, meaning that microorganisms and other life are not created by spontaneous generation. This was still highly controversial in Victorian England, however, and strong opposition arose to Snow's explanation for the spread of cholera. The *London Medical Gazette*, a leading journal of the day, dismissed his arguments as "an entire failure of proof that the occurrence of any one case could be clearly and unambiguously assigned to the use of the water. . . . Foul effluvia from the state of the drains [i.e., an airborne miasma from the sewers] afford a more satisfactory explanation of the diffusion of the disease."

Snow's findings supported the germ theory, as did the later realization that the mother of an infant suffering from cholera had disposed of the child's soiled diaper in a cesspit directly adjacent to the Broad Street Pump just days before the cholera outbreak. While the germ theory of disease remained controversial throughout the 1800s, its increasing credibility was crucial in shifting popular attitudes toward the prevalence of waterborne diseases.

The Soho Parish leaders were also well aware of the raging debate at the time over public sanitation. Championed by Edwin Chadwick, the Victorian crusade for improving the sanitary conditions of the urban poor centered on the idea that disease could be prevented. Trained as a lawyer, Chadwick was relentless, leading John Stuart Mill to praise him as the most effective politician of his time. Chadwick accepted the miasmatic theory of disease but opposed common wisdom by arguing that closer attention to drainage, clean drinking water, and removal of waste would greatly improve the well-being of the city's poor.

In 1832, Chadwick was appointed as a member of the Royal Commission into the Operation of the Poor Laws and served as its secretary. The commission's work led to reform in how aid was pro-

Edwin Chadwick, 1800–1890

vided to the poor in Britain and resulted in a standing body, the Poor Law Commission, to oversee implementation of the new law. Chadwick served on the commission and used its platform to promote his agenda.

In 1842, he set forth his views in the commission's 457-page Report of the Sanitary Condition of the Labouring Population of Great Britain. In denouncing the state of affairs, Chadwick's prose reads powerfully even today. Indeed, it was so incendiary that his fellow commission members refused to place their names on the report, leaving Chadwick as the sole author. In bold statements, he concluded that:

> The various forms of epidemic, endemic, and other disease caused, or aggravated, or propagated chiefly amongst the labouring classes by atmospheric impurities produced by decomposing animal and vegetable substances, by damp and filth, and close and overcrowded

dwellings prevail amongst the population in every part of the kingdom, whether dwelling in separate houses, in rural villages, in small towns, in the larger towns—as they have been found to prevail in the lowest districts of the metropolis.

Such disease, wherever its attacks are frequent, is always found in connexion with the physical circumstances above specified, and that where those circumstances are removed by drainage, proper cleansing, better ventilation, and other means of diminishing atmospheric impurity, the frequency and intensity of such disease is abated; and where the removal of the noxious agencies appears to be complete, such disease almost entirely disappears.

The formation of all habits of cleanliness is obstructed by defective supplies of water.

The population so exposed is less susceptible of moral influences, and the effects of education are more transient than with a healthy population.

These adverse circumstances tend to produce an adult population short-lived, improvident, reckless, and intemperate, and with habitual avidity for sensual gratifications.

The report was a sensation, its sale of ten thousand copies far exceeding sales of previous government publications. Beyond Chadwick's clear indictment of dirty water and unsanitary surroundings as a prime cause of disease, it is worth taking a closer look at his prose, for Chadwick was concerned not only with the physical consequences of polluted water but the moral consequences, as well. Hence his warnings about those who drank defective supplies of water becoming "less susceptible of moral influences," "reckless, and intemperate." To Chadwick's eyes, poor sanitation fostered immorality just as surely as it did physical disease.

Indeed, the direct connections Chadwick drew between sanitation and moral health are a significant part of the story. Chadwick's and others' calls for improved sanitation were reinforced by moral crusaders, evangelicals who sought to remedy society's evils by physical as well as spiritual cleansing. The notion that "cleanliness is next to godliness" took root during this era, and made the religious community a powerful ally for sanitation reform. Chadwick and Charles Kingsley, another great reformer, often described sanitary reform as the "Will of God."

The ranks of "sanitarians" swelled with the great and the good, including such luminaries of the age as Charles Dickens, Benjamin Disraeli, and Florence Nightingale. Their efforts, and those of their religious and morality allies, led to pioneering legislation such as the Sanitary Acts, Water Acts, and Public Health Acts, all of which laid the legal foundation for improved source protection. In a matter of decades, centuries-old habits were formally challenged and rejected.

The great wealth flowing from the four corners of the British Empire provided the means for major infrastructure projects. A firm believer in the miasmatic theory of disease, Chadwick contended that "all smell is disease." The answer to the wastes creating the poisonous miasmas was, he argued, water flowing through sewers, which would wash away the sewage and, with it, the source of the city's ills. This was a novel idea, long forgotten since the Romans. Prior to Chadwick's time, sewers had been designed to drain rain from the streets; in fact, the term "sewage" did not even exist until 1849. It is interesting to note that John Snow and Edwin Chadwick, who agreed on most issues, strongly differed over the outflow of the sewers. Guided by the miasma theory of disease, Chadwick argued that the sewers should flow directly into the Thames. Snow, by contrast, realized that this would pollute the drinking water for many Londoners.

Improved sanitation and the provision of readily available safe drinking water both gradually became explicit government priorities, and the results proved impressive. In 1852, the average age of death in the English town of Dudley had been a shocking seventeen years old. Twenty years after sewers were constructed there, life expectancy had almost doubled. Similarly, from 1850 to 1900, life expectancy in French cities improved from thirty-two to forty-five years old. Medical advances clearly contributed to this increased longevity, but the Great Sanitation Awakening seems an apt title for such striking results.

London was not alone in these leaps forward. One could tell similar stories for Chicago, Philadelphia, or other cities. Similar to Edwin Chadwick, Noah Webster, author of the famed dictionary, urged his fellow Americans to recognize and improve the state of urban sanitation. Until this happened, he moralized, the poor "will still wallow in filth; croud their cities with low dirty houses and narrow streets; neglect the use of bathing and washing; and live like savages, devouring, in hot seasons, undue quantities of animal food at their tables, and reeling home after midnight debauches." The Quakers of Philadelphia took the lead in this regard, mandating in 1794 that the streets be watered down for cleansing daily.

As described previously, New York's strategy had focused on a massive engineering project to pipe water from the pristine Catskills-Delaware watershed, more than 120 miles northwest of the city, to a series of local reservoirs. Chicago's efforts at source protection were even more heroic. The city had large sources of water but all were shockingly polluted, even by nineteenth-century standards. In 1860, the city of Chicago hired Ellis Sylvester Chesbrough, who was fresh from designing the water system for Boston. Chesbrough realized, as had Chadwick, that the key to source protection and clean water was removal of wastes. The problem, though, was that Chicago sat in a low swamp, and building a sewer under the city streets would not provide enough elevation for the waste to flow out of town. His solution was as novel as it was ambitious. Needing higher elevation for the waste to flow through the sewers, he laid the sewers on *top* of the streets, covered them, and then built new streets *above* the sewers, raising the buildings in the process, or turning their second stories into ground floors. The source for Chicago's water supply was extended six hundred feet into Lake Michigan and then piped into the city.

Even more ambitiously, the city built the Chicago Sanitary and Ship Canal in 1900. This actually reversed the flow of the fetid Chicago River, sending it into the Mississippi rather than Lake Michigan, the city's source of drinking water. The city's incidence of typhoid fever did, in fact, go down, but the downstream city of St. Louis saw a rise in the disease as Chicago's filth flowed by. The State of Missouri actually sued Illinois for public nuisance, and the case went all the way to the U.S. Supreme Court. Presaging the difficulty of demonstrating causation between pollution and specific illnesses that bedevils today's toxic torts litigation, the Court held for Illinois. St. Louis had not shown a strong enough causal correlation between pollution in Chicago and deaths in St. Louis, three hundred miles down the Mississippi. There were too many potential intervening factors.

Impressive as these engineering feats were, it is important to ask why the same Awakening did not occur in other parts of the world at the same time, particularly in European colonial cities around the globe. This may seem an odd question. After all, the stringent water pollution laws and massive infrastructure in the developed world today stand in glaring contrast to the primitive source protection in much of the developing world. While it has become politically incorrect to use the terms "First World" and "Third World," they have real meaning when discussing drinking water and source protection today.

What may be surprising, though, is that this sanitary divide is a recent distinction. When George Goodwin decried London as a "cesspool city" in the 1850s, he could very well have been saying the same thing for one of the jewels in England's colonial crown, Madras in India. The stark contrast between London and Madras today, where less than a third of the Indian city's population has adequate sanitation, is deceptive. If you had visited both cities a hundred fifty years ago, the similarities would have been more striking than the differences. As Peter Gleick has recounted, "most urban citizens—rich and poor—lived amidst excrement and sewage."

In retrospect, there was a significant fork in the road roughly one hundred fifty years ago, with cities in the global north rapidly improving sanitation and drinking water quality, while those in the global south lagged behind. Indeed, the French term "*cordon sanitaire*" is used today to describe a barrier that prevents disease or other unwanted conditions from spreading. However, it originally referred to the "quarantine line" in colonial cities that quite literally demarcated separate sanitation systems—one for the Europeans and one for the natives.

Marshaling public and private investment for sanitation is a massive undertaking, so daunting that no city was able to create a comparable sewer system to Rome's for almost two millennia. The decision not to invest in sophisticated sanitation infrastructure in colonies at the same time as the Awakening back in the imperial home countries was partly a result of fiscal priorities, partly a result of prejudice. Looking back, though, one thing is clear. Applying separate sanitation standards to the governing and the governed in the Age of Empire had far-reaching consequences for the human miseries from waterborne diseases that continue today.

With the emergence of the germ theory, understanding of the importance of improved sanitation, and acceptance that sanitation infrastructure was first and foremost a government responsibility, by the turn of the twentieth century, source protection had improved dramatically in Europe and North America. This is not to say, however, that drinking water diseases were a thing of the past. Far from it. Typhoid fever still claimed thousands of victims every year, including the famed aviation brother Wilbur Wright, who died in 1912. Indeed, it was just such concerns over drinking water that spurred the trips of wealthy Europeans to spas and the first boom in bottled water sales. Ensuring source protection was a limited solution. To take the next big step in ensuring the safety of drinking water, municipalities turned to an approach that had always been part of the drinking water story: treatment.

Water Treatment

The Old Testament's Book of Kings recounts the story of the prophet Elisha, who followed Elijah. Soon after the death of his predecessor, Elisha traveled to Jericho. There, he was met by the men of the city, who sought his aid.

> The men of the city said to Elisha, "Look, our lord, this town is well situated, as you can see, but the water is bad and the land is unproductive."

> "Bring me a new bowl," he said, "and put salt in it." So they brought it to him.

Then he went out to the spring and threw the salt into it, saying, "This is what the Lord says: 'I have healed this water. Never again will it cause death or make the land unproductive.'" And the water has remained wholesome to this day, according to the word Elisha had spoken.

Once a water source has been identified and protected from pollution, it still may not be clean enough to drink, hence the need for water treatment. While the methods varied, and Elisha's approach was surely unique, treatment of water was commonplace in the ancient world. Sanskrit writings from approximately 2000 BC recommend water purification methods.

In his classic tome written sixty years ago, *The Quest for Pure Water*, M. N. Baker exhaustively sets forth in more than five hundred pages "The History of Water Purification From the Earliest Records to the Twentieth Century." While not a riveting page-turner, the book covers a truly impressive range of treatment technologies, from siphons in ancient Egypt and cloth straining in Persia to techniques of aeration, distillation, flocculation, coagulation, and William Walcot's hopeful patent in 1675 for "making sea water fresh." Interestingly, the most obvious purification method to us—boiling water—was not commonplace. While there are references to boiling water in the Middle Ages, the common practice was light boiling, which would have been only partly effective in purifying the water. Of course, if there is no conception of germs living in water, much less the health threat they might pose, then boiling water seems a waste of time.

At the same time as the Great Sanitation Awakening and the construction of municipal sewage systems, cities started building large-scale treatment works. The most common technology was slow sand filtration, purifying water by passing it through sand. In 1703, the French Academy of Sciences considered a plan that would have provided sand filters for every household, but the first municipal plant was not built until a century later in Paisley, Scotland. By 1827, Glasgow, Scotland, was piping filtered water to its Glaswegian consumers. Even such a simple technology, however, proved controversial, and uptake was slow.

Inscriptions of water treatment devices have even been found in the tombs of the Egyptian pharaohs Amenophis II and Rameses II.

In the late 1890s, for example, Pittsburgh's city government considered plans to pass its water supply through a sand filtration system. This was strongly opposed by Edward Bigelow, director of the city's public works department, who argued that "the city's water did not cause typhoid and warned that impugning its quality would discourage investment in the city." Nor was he alone in his concern about bad press. Philadelphia's city council raised identical concerns over hurting the city's image if its water were filtered.

The most significant development in drinking water treatment occurred at the turn of the twentieth century, with the realization that adding low concentrations of chlorine to water would kill most of the microorganisms. Prior to that time, no municipalities had ever added chemicals to their drinking water supplies. The technical challenge lay in delivery, how best to mix reactive chlorine into large amounts of water. The town of Middelkerke, Belgium, installed the first chlorine disinfection system in 1902. Jersey City took the lead in the United States, providing in 1908 the first chlorination of drinking water for an entire city.

Easy to apply, inexpensive, and persistent in the water, chlorination gradually took hold. The adoption of chlorinated water was accelerated by the U.S. Department of the Treasury, which appointed a commission in 1913 to establish the nation's first drinking water standards. While these standards were binding only on common carriers involved in interstate commerce (particularly trains), they had a widespread and immediate impact. Since water was taken on at local depots along the rail lines, national standards indirectly forced all communities providing water to common carriers to chlorinate their water, as well. By 1941, 85 percent of the country's more than five thousand water treatment systems chlorinated their drinking water.

The widespread adoption of chlorinated drinking water had two immediate effects. The first was in the marketplace, where the bottled water sector collapsed. We tend to think of bottled water as a recent market entry, but it was big business at the turn of the twentieth century. With Philadelphia and other cities' provision of chlorinated public water, however, the prime reason for buying bottled water in the first place—safety—was no longer relevant. And the chic branding that bottled water might have enjoyed was swamped by the appeal of chlorinated water. More than just a novelty, chlorinated water meant that water for an entire city could be made safe because of human ingenuity. In an age of technological optimism, municipal chlorination was a heady achievement. It was trendy, "modern" water. It is hard not to appreciate the irony of how this has reversed today, where tap water is seen as pedestrian and bottled water chic.

The second impact was on public health. The age-old scourges of waterborne disease—typhoid and cholera—had finally been neutered. Both pathogens, deadly and easily spread by water, were acutely vulnerable to low levels of chlorine. Typhoid epidemics were still killing thousands of Americans in the 1920s, but by the 1950s, even individual cases of typhoid had become rare. It has been claimed that chlorination of drinking water saved more lives than any other technological advance in the history of public health.

In retrospect, chlorinating drinking water supplies seems an obvious decision. At the time, though, it was highly controversial. Despite high incidences of waterborne disease, drinking water was still generally regarded as safe. Adding a chemical to water to make it safer had never been done before on a large scale, and it seemed to many *unnatural*—to use a term with particular resonance in the bottled water market today. A pro-chlorine writer in 1918 summarized the many complaints against chlorination:

> The nature of the complaints against chlorinated water is very diversified and includes imparting foreign tastes and odours, causing colic, killing fish and birds, the extraction of abnormal amounts of tannin from tea, the destruction of plants and flowers, the corrosion of water pipes, and that horses and other animals refuse to drink it.

In fact, in 1911, the Jersey City government refused to pay its innovative water supplier, the East Jersey Water Company. The company had signed a contract with the city committing to provide pure and wholesome water. It built a treatment plant for chlorination. Jersey City argued that the water also needed to be free from upstream sewage and therefore filtered. The company responded that its contractual obligation was to provide safe drinking water, which chlorination assured. Expensive filtration was therefore unnecessary. The dispute between old and new visions of water treatment eventually went to court. The judge sided with progress and chlorination, concluding that "the device for removing dangerous germs, now in operation, is effective and capable of rendering the water delivered to Jersey City pure and wholesome for the purposes for which it was intended." The *New York Times* article reporting the decision proved remarkably prophetic, predicting, "So successful has been this experiment that any municipal water plant, no matter how large, can be made as pure as mountain spring water." A century old, its appeal to the purity of natural spring waters almost reads like an ad for bottled water today.

Water can be made safe to drink, but it still needs to be moved to its final point of use. During this journey, water can be contaminated once again, frustrating the earlier efforts. Distribution, then, warrants just as much attention as source protection and treatment.

Water Distribution

In 701 BC, the Assyrian king Sennacherib had assembled a vast army and was imposing his empire's might on the Kingdom of Judah. Judah's fortified cities fell one after the other. Jerusalem was now in the conqueror's sights. Hezekiah, the king of Judah, was determined that his capital would not fall to Sennacherib's assault. While his kingdom's cities were captured and plundered, Hezekiah busily prepared Jerusalem to withstand the coming siege. According to the biblical account, "he took courage, and built up all the wall that was broken down, and raised it up to the towers, and another wall without, and strengthened Millo in the city of David, and made weapons and shields in abundance."

Hezekiah realized, however, that fortifying walls and towers would be futile if the city ran out of water. The problem was that the Gihon Spring, Jerusalem's main source of drinking water, was located in a cave outside the city walls. Without water, a siege of just a few weeks might prove more effective than any armed assault by Sennacherib's forces.

Hezekiah's solution was simple in concept but fiendishly difficult in execution. Working round the clock, workers rushed to dig a tunnel through the local limestone, diverting water from the Gihon Spring to a well within the city walls. If done properly, this would not only provide water to the besieged population but also divert the water from the spring—denying it to the Assyrians.

To ensure completion before the Assyrian army arrived, digging started both near the Gihon Spring and within Jerusalem. The hope was that the two parties of miners would meet halfway along the five hundred meters separating their starting points. The problem, of course, was that both parties were deep underground, encased in rock. There was no obvious way to guide their respective paths, and an error of just a few meters would result in their blindly passing one another, dooming the city. Against all odds, they succeeded in time, solving the problem of water distribution with the sword hanging over their heads. As the Bible recounts:

> And when Hezekiah saw that Sennacherib was come, and that he was purposed to fight against Jerusalem, he took counsel with his princes and his mighty men to stop the waters of the fountains which were without the city; and they helped him. So there was gathered much people together and they stopped all the fountains, and the brook that flowed through the midst of the land, saying: "Why should the kings of Assyria come, and find much water?"

How the two groups of miners met each other remains a subject of archeological debate. Tourists today can slosh through the dark, winding 533-meter path, with dead ends and false starts clearly evident. One possibility is that the tunnel engineers simply widened a natural karst formation—essentially a preexisting fissure running through the rock. Another possible solution is that the tunnelers were guided through acoustic communication from a team on the surface. No one really knows for sure.

Whether Hezekiah's efforts to withstand the siege were successful depends on which history you consult. Hezekiah did pay three hundred talents of silver and thirty talents of gold in tribute to Sennacherib, upon which the Assyrian king reportedly boasted "I ruined the wide province of the land of Judah. On Hezekiah, its king, I imposed my yoke." According to the Hebrew biblical account, however, "the Lord sent an angel, who cut off all the mighty men of valor, and the leaders and captains, in the camp of the king of Assyria. So he returned with shame of face to his own land. And when he was come into the house of his god, they that came forth of his own bowels slew him there with the sword."

The challenge of distribution, of moving safe water from its source of origin to final consumption, is unavoidable. Throughout most of human history and for much of the world today, water distribution has meant manual labor: walking to the water source and filling a gourd, leather sack, clay pot, bucket, or jerry can with water and then carrying it back to the home. Water is heavy—more than eight pounds for a gallon of water—so water that has to be transported a distance exacts a real cost in time and labor.

Piped water largely avoids this problem. We have already discussed the graceful aqueducts of the Roman Empire, many of which stand today, but irrigation channels, canals, and pipes have been the hallmark of most enduring civilizations. Subject to the unyielding force of gravity, engineers have needed to rely on clever solutions that ensure a downward gradient from source to collection.

As cities grew in size, the importance of the distribution system also grew since the nearby water sources became polluted over time. This continued well into the Middle Ages. The Great Conduit of London was built in the thirteenth century between London and the springs at Tyburn. Water was transported to cisterns in the city, and the water then sold by leasing official mugs to people for drawing water. One can find impressive technology in some monasteries as well. Indeed, the cities of Southampton and Bristol contracted with their local monasteries to use their more advanced water systems.

NO DISCUSSION OF MODERN WATER DISTRIBUTION WOULD BE COMPLETE without describing the rise of the drinking fountain. The ancient precursors to the modern drinking fountain were the village wells, *lacus*, or fountains where people would either bring their own containers or share a communal cup to slake their thirst. As cities became more and more crowded and polluted during the industrial revolution, finding safe drinking water became increasingly difficult. As *Punch* magazine explained in its description of the Great Exhibition in 1851, "Whoever can produce in London a glass of water fit to drink will contribute the best and most universally useful article in the whole exhibition."

Given the foul state of easily accessible water, drinks from pubs provided the easiest accessible beverages. Thus it is no coincidence that the Quakers, a Christian denomination that abstained from alcohol, founded in 1859 the Metropolitan Free Drinking Fountain Association—a philanthropic society that built free public fountains around London. The motivation was twofold, in part a public service for those too poor to purchase drinking water, and in large part a strategy of the temperance movement. Many of the fountains were strategically located next to popular pubs, tempting thirsty souls with free, safe, and wholesome water rather than the purchase of sinful beer or spirits.

The Free Drinking Water Association gained immediate support from establishment figures such as Prince Albert and the Archbishop of Canterbury. As the resolution adopted at the inaugural meeting made clear, this was to be a venture dedicated to the common good. The resolution declared:

> That, where the erection of free drinking fountains, yielding pure cold water, would confer a boon on all classes, and especially the poor, an Association be formed for erecting and promoting the erection of such fountains in the Metropolis, to be styled "The Metropolitan Free Drinking Fountain Association", and that contributions be received for the purposes of the Association. That no fountain be erected or promoted by the Association which shall not be so constructed as to ensure by filters, or other suitable means, the perfect purity and coldness of the water.

The association built its first fountain soon after on the wall of St. Sepulchre's church. This was recognized at the time as such a historic event that a banner reading "THE FIRST PUBLIC DRINKING FOUNTAIN" was chiseled into the stone and a celebration was held with formal speeches.

Excitement over the first fountain carried over well into the next decade, with funds pouring in. As noted above, the association sought to provide safe water for free to the poor, and this often competed with pubs. To attract customers, a number of pubs also provided water troughs, enticing people to buy a drink inside while their horses drank outside. Sensitive to the thirst of animals and the temptation of pubs' alcohol, the association changed its name to the Metropolitan Drinking Fountain and Cattle Trough Association. Within eleven years of its founding, there were 140 fountains and 153 cattle troughs available to the public for free use throughout London.

*Commemoration of the drinking fountain adjoining
St. Sepulchre's church, April 30, 1859*

The Victorian period prized charitable works. It also prized ostentatious shows of good works. As a result, many of the drinking fountains were quite ornate and impressive works of architecture in their own right. This extended to a number of public drinking fountains whose pillars, arches, and filigree seemed to hold themselves out as a cathedral to the good works of free drinking water.

The origin of the drinking fountain in America, perhaps not surprisingly, was more commercial. The first bubbler was marketed by the Kohler Company from Wisconsin, whose device sent a stream of water straight up, mimicking the action of a vertical fountain. The invention was a hit and coincided with the popular rejection of communal drinking cups in the early 1900s. Soon the market was dominated by two companies, the Halsey Taylor Company and the Haws Sanitary Drinking Faucet Company.

Both companies' founders were motivated by more than commercial gain. Halsey Willard Taylor's father had died from typhoid fever, contracted from drinking contaminated water. Luther Haws worked as a sanitary inspector for the city of Berkeley, California. Leg-

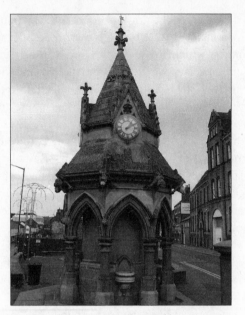

In a Victorian monument from Kidderminster, for example, the drinking fountains seem almost an afterthought to the grandeur of the civic edifice.

end has it that Haws was inspecting a public school and was disturbed by the sight of children sharing a common drinking cup. Both companies' devices employed the same basic design. The building's water supply line was piped directly to the fountain. Pushing the bar or button released a stream of pressurized water at a constant flow. Releasing the bar or button put the seal back in place, stopping the water flow. Taylor soon improved his fountain with a double bubbler design. Twin jets of water were released, intersecting a few inches from the opening. This provided both a larger drink of water and moved the mouth (and any germs it might impart) farther from the fountain itself.

As the popularity of drinking fountains grew, a number of developments were rapidly adopted. The early fountains provided water at room temperature. The demand for chilled water was met by larger units that contained twenty-pound blocks of ice. In time, these were replaced by refrigerated units. The Berkeley school system adopted the first public drinking fountains, and public schools soon became a major market for both companies. Because school halls were narrow with many students passing through, freestanding drinking fountains gave way to wall-mounted fountains. In time, these were replaced by recessed wall fountains that freed up even more space in the halls. Such units also became fixtures at hospitals, factories, and airports.

In recent years, the most significant changes have been in response to the needs of people in wheelchairs. Responding to this market and pushed by the requirements of the Americans with Disabilities Act, drinking fountains are increasingly provided side by side at different levels, offering comfortable sipping heights both for those standing and those seated.

Sadly, the days of easily available public drinking fountains seem to be drawing to a close. As we shall see later, the meteoric rise of bottled water and public acceptance of bottled water as an alternative to drinking fountains have increasingly led to construction of new stadiums, airports, and other public places that hide or even eliminate the presence of drinking fountains. When drinking water is viewed as a commodity, free provision becomes not only unnecessary but anticapitalist. When is the last time you saw a dispenser of free bread, fruit, or vegetables in a public place?

THE BURIED PIPES THAT CHANNEL WATER TO OUR FAUCETS AND carry wastes from our drains form the skeleton of our distribution system. Out of sight, our water and sewage pipes never inspire a second's thought until they fail. This willful ignorance creates a real problem, however, because our nation's water infrastructure has become increasingly enfeebled.

While a rough measure, every two minutes a major water line bursts in the United States. It may be in Topeka, Kansas, or Tucumcari, New Mexico. In our nation's capital, Washington, D.C., the rate is about one pipe break a day. When I lived there, I was shocked to come home one day and see a geyser bubbling in the middle of the road in front of my house. The massive pressure from a burst line had forced water from five feet underground up to the surface, casting aside large slabs of asphalt.

The cause in all these cases is the same: inadequate investment in our pipes and treatment plants. Some of our water and sewer lines date from the Civil War. Many more were built in the 1900s. The massive pipes described in Chapter 2 that supply New York City are leaking thirty-six million gallons per day. Engineers fear that their structural integrity has become so compromised that draining the pipes for repair might cause them to buckle and collapse under the weight of the soil on top. Residents in some areas of Washington, D.C., cannot drink from their taps because of lead in their water, released from the lead soldering used to join the household pipes decades ago. On average, Philadelphia has to deal with more than two breaks in water and sewer lines every day.

Despite the obvious importance, gaining funding to rebuild our water and sewer lines has proven elusive. In recent memory, when hundreds of billions of dollars of TARP money was being disbursed by Congress for "shovel-ready" projects, only $2 billion was dedicated to water projects. People point to the Clean Water Act's tough regulations as the explanation for why our nation's water quality has improved in recent decades. These regulations have been significant, but equally if not more important were the billions of dollars provided to states and municipalities for the construction and enhancement of water treatment and sewage plants.

Perhaps the failure to invest in our water infrastructure should not be surprising. These arteries and veins of our water system are invisible, buried beneath roads, fields, and buildings. The only time we think about them is when they no longer work. And the sums required to remedy the decades of underfunding are massive. The EPA estimates we need $335 billion simply to maintain our drinking water systems. New York alone claims to need $36 billion to maintain its wastewater systems. To be sure, these are large sums, but compared to what? How much would it cost were our water distribution and treatment systems to fail? It is no exaggeration to say that we are playing on borrowed time as our aging water infrastructure continues to give way.

SO HOW ARE WE DOING? FOR THE PAST CENTURY, THE UNITED STATES has paid increasing attention to eliminating the scourge of waterborne contaminants, and the results have been impressive. Most people can drink their tap water, confident in its safety. Most, but not all. Estimates vary, but the *New York Times* reports that roughly nineteen million Americans become sick each year from waterborne parasites, viruses, and bacteria. A study by UNESCO found that *E. coli* and other waterborne pathogens result in about nine hundred deaths of Americans every year. Not all of this is the result of tap water, but safe water is by no means guaranteed, even today.

The single greatest outbreak of waterborne illness in U.S. history occurred just two decades ago, in 1993, when the city of Milwaukee was terrorized by a tiny parasite in the drinking water, *Cryptosporidium parvum*. For two weeks, the city's Howard Avenue treatment plant provided contaminated water to people's faucets. The plant's intake was located at a site in Lake Michigan that directly received the discharge of the Milwaukee River, making the plant's intake susceptible to a recent fecal contamination. More than 400,000 people, roughly one-quarter of the city's population, became ill with stomach cramps, diarrhea, and fever. Those with weak immune systems were most at risk, and sixty-nine people died.

The problem here was not failure to regulate. *Cryptosporidium* is a well-known microbe. Rather, this was a simple case of human error— with tragic results. Just as in ancient Rome and Victorian London, safe drinking water cannot be guaranteed without proper source identification, protection, treatment, and distribution. Breakdowns in any of these areas can lead to disaster, and the sheer scale of modern-day water consumption virtually ensures that some contaminants will eventually make it through. Looking back through history, however, we can take heart that even though the dangers remain very real, we've come a long, long way toward controlling the risks. Of course, it is one thing to combat disease-causing microbes, which generally present obvious symptoms and can be diagnosed quickly. But what if the problem is harder to detect and takes much longer to show its harm?

How did Venice get its drinking water?

Venice is one of the great marvels of the modern world and a most unlikely place. In the 13th and 14th centuries, Venice reigned as the wealthiest city in Europe and arguably in the world. Its fleets dominated trade in the Mediterranean region. Yet it was entirely artificial. Originally a series of settlements on 117 small islands lying across a shallow lagoon, the city we know came into being through ingeniously reclaimed land. Over centuries, thousands of wooden piles were driven into the thick sand and mud until resting on the harder layers of clay below. These provided solid foundations for the sea walls and infill creating the larger islands we admire today, stunningly interlocked by canals and footbridges. Its admirers call Venice "La Serenissima"—The Most Serene.

In terms of drinking water, Venice more resembles a ship than a city, for there are no ready sources of surface water or groundwater. An early observer wrote, "Venice is in the water and has no water." How did one of the most populous cities in the West provide water to its citizens? It looked to the sky.

Rainwater falling from roofs and streets flowed into town squares (*campi*), where it was directed into specially designed cisterns. The cisterns were built by digging a ten foot pit beneath the *campi*, its sides lined with impermeable clay. A hollow cylindrical shaft would be built in the center of the pit, rising to street level and formed by special curved bricks known as *pozzali*. The rest of the hole would then be filled with sand and the pit covered over with stones. Someone strolling along the *campi* would notice a well-head in the center (capping the cylindrical shaft below) and, at each corner, perforated stone slabs through which water could flow into the pit below. Over time, the pit would become saturated with rainwater, purified as it passed through the sand. The water would make its way through the bricks forming the cylindrical shaft and into the well, but the larger sand particles would be filtered out. From the wellhead, water

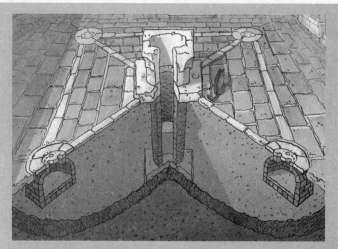

A cross-section of the well shaft and sand drainage in a Venetian square

was free for the taking from the shaft below. Centuries before science knew the first thing about microbes, Venice likely provided the cleanest urban drinking water in the world.

This system served well until the 16th centurye. Venice had stopped reclaiming land so the increasingly dense population needed somewhere to live, making open space scarce. This posed a real problem because the system of cisterns beneath the *campi* required large amounts of unbuilt urban areas to collect rainwater. The Venetians adopted an ingenious new strategy. *Campi* were lost to new construction, but dwellings were now required to build a cistern within their foundations. Rainwater falling on the roof was collected by gutters into clay pipes built into the walls that led directly down to the cistern below the basement. By the middle of the 19th century, there were over 6,000 of these "inside cisterns."

Venice is a city of visual delights, from the sleek black gondolas and graceful bridges to the ornate churches and balconies astride the canal waters. Yet perhaps the most marvelous accomplishment of all, the source of clean water during *La Serenissima's* years of power, lies unseen beneath the plazas and tourists' steps.

4

Death in Small Doses

RSENIC HAS LONG BEEN THE MURDERER'S POISON OF CHOICE. Clear when dissolved, odorless, tasteless, it is almost too easy to slip some of the deadly white powder into an unsuspecting person's food or drink. In cases of quick poisoning, the victim feels cold, clammy, and dizzy with painful stomach cramps. Death follows shortly after. Arsenic's effectiveness and ease in dispatching people was the driver behind the classic play and movie *Arsenic and Old Lace*, where two well-meaning though misguided women eased the passage to the hereafter for lonely widowers enjoying their cookies and poisoned elderberry wine. The most famous historic case of arsenic poisoning may have involved Napoleon, who died on the distant island of St. Helena after his grand attempts of conquering Europe had failed. While the diagnosis at the time of the emperor's death was stomach cancer, modern analysis of his hair suggests arsenic poisoning.

Arsenic is not only lethal when delivered intentionally, however. The compound also occurs naturally in the common mineral arsenopyrite. When these rocks erode, arsenic is released into the soil and groundwater. Even the most reckless person knows that drinking arsenic is a bad idea. Yet, just a decade ago, controversies over how much arsenic people should drink in their water led to public furors in both the world's wealthiest and poorest countries, with very different results.

One of the most densely populated and impoverished countries in the world, Bangladesh sits in the delta of the Ganges and Brahmaputra rivers. Access to freshwater is not a problem—quite the contrary, as the country often suffers from seasonal flooding. Unfortunately, these rivers are heavily polluted as they move downstream and are thus unfit for drinking. Traditionally, Bangladeshis have relied on surface waters from ponds and shallow wells for their domestic water use. Pollution from inadequate (often nonexistent) sewage systems, however, has made high death rates from cholera and diarrhea commonplace, particularly among the young. Seeking to remedy this public health problem, the World Bank and the United Nations Children's Fund (UNICEF) agreed to fund a nationwide program. The ambitious goal was to shift domestic sources from surface water to the country's plentiful groundwater. Groundwater is generally safer than surface sources such as lakes or rivers because the soil filters bacteria and pollution as water percolates down into the aquifer. Literally millions of tubewells—shallow pipes operated by steel hand pumps—were eventually sunk throughout the countryside.

On the surface, this seemed a poster child for what development aid should be all about, providing simple, inexpensive, and effective technology to overcome a terrible public health challenge. Victory was quickly and confidently declared. As researchers later described:

A tubewell became a prized possession: it lessened the burden on women, who no longer had to trek long distances with their pots and pails; it reduced the dependence on better-off neighbors; and most important, it provided pathogen-free water to drink. By the early 1990s ninety-five percent of Bangladesh's population had access to "safe" water, virtually all of it through the country's more than 10 million tubewells—a rare success story in the otherwise impoverished nation.

While the aid groups were congratulating themselves, however, tests of the groundwater revealed a tragedy unfolding. Many of the plentiful freshwater aquifers were located in soils containing arsenic. It had not occurred to any of the engineers to test for naturally occurring arsenic when the wells had been drilled, but it was surely there. Laid down in geologic strata over millions of years, the undetected arsenic had dissolved into the groundwater and was now being pumped up for drinking and domestic use.

The largest public drinking water initiative in the history of Bangladesh had monstrously transformed into the worst case of mass poisoning in the world. Wells in fifty-nine of sixty-four of the country's regions exceed the World Health Organization's guidelines for arsenic in drinking water, and roughly 10 percent of the wells contain more than six times that amount. No one knows just how many people are at risk of arsenic poisoning, but the estimate in 2010 was well over seventy million.

Acute arsenic poisoning can kill within a few hours. Much more common, however, and unlike most waterborne diseases, chronic arsenic poisoning can remain in hiding for up to ten years before revealing itself. The initial symptoms include black spots on the upper body, bronchitis, and loss of sensation. In serious cases, this gives way to swollen legs, cracking palms and soles, and renal malfunction. If the victim survives the likely threats of gangrene and kidney failure, cancer follows. A number of field projects tested wells, painting those with high arsenic levels red and those with low levels green, and this has had some effect. But most wells remain untested, and many people continue to draw their water from red wells.

While Bangladesh and the international development community struggled to respond to their self-inflicted epidemic, halfway across the world, in the world's wealthiest country, concerns over arsenic in drinking water were front page news, as well.

The United States has had an arsenic standard of fifty parts per billion since 1942. Over the past few decades, however, studies in Argentina, Taiwan, and Chile have suggested harmful effects from drinking water with much lower arsenic concentrations. The Environmental Protection Agency and National Research Council started examining the issue and modeling the likely impacts from drinking water with concentrations below 50 parts per billion.

In 2000, shortly before President Clinton left office, his administration proposed a new regulation lowering the legal limit to five parts per billion, comparable to one drop of arsenic in fifty drums of water. Faced with strong complaints by both water system managers and industry over the high costs of compliance and weak scientific case for a five-parts-per-billion standard, the administration doubled the limit to ten parts per billion, the same as that recommended by the World Health Organization. While the new standard would apply to all 54,000 of the country's community water systems, it was estimated that only a small number of water sources, mostly in the West, would be affected. Specifically, regulators estimated that about 5 percent of the systems would need to take action, affecting the water for roughly eleven million people, plus an additional two million people not on community water systems. The rule was scheduled to go into effect in March 2001, two months after George W. Bush took his oath of office.

One of the very first acts of the new Bush administration's EPA, however, was to suspend implementation of the new arsenic drinking water regulations pending further study. The public response was loud and powerful, creating one of the administration's very first controversies. Even the staunchly conservative *Wall Street Journal* thundered, "You may have voted for him, but you didn't vote for this in your water." Representative David Bonior was even more caustic. "If there is one thing we all seem to agree on it is that we do not want arsenic in our drinking water. It is an extremely potent human carcinogen." Stating the obvious, he continued, "It is this simple: arsenic is a killer."

So why did the Bush administration take such a seemingly foolish action? The policy choice was whether to keep the current standard of fifty parts per billion or tighten it to ten parts per billion. It was well understood that the standard would impose significant costs, particularly on small communities. The question was whether it was worth the cost. One might assume it clearly was worth it, given the dangers from arsenic. No one wants to drink poison, even in small amounts, when they turn on their tap.

Is arsenic in the water safe to drink at any level? Perhaps surprisingly, neither Americans nor Bangladeshis have been able to answer that question, but for very different reasons. For the Bangladeshis, the more relevant question is which water source is *less* unsafe to drink? As one researcher described, "It took about twenty years to move everyone from surface water to ground water and then in the 1990s we are suddenly telling people the groundwater can kill you." While some have suggested that people be en-

couraged to go back to surface water, this poses real problems as
well. After all, the harm from microbial diseases is why they
switched to groundwater in the first place.

In a recent study, 29 percent of the water users stopped taking
their water from wells once they were told the water had high levels
of arsenic. But that still leaves more than half of Bangladesh's population exposed. As the researchers concluded, despite identifying
many of the wells as either safe (green) or unsafe (red), "Even with
complete identification of contaminated wells, rural households are
left facing a dilemma: Use river or pond water and face waterborne
disease, or use groundwater, if it is still within reach of hand pumps,
and face slow poisoning from arsenic. Families without alternative
sources of drinking water continue to use arsenic-contaminated
tubewell water, and the response to poisoning has been slow and
incomplete." These same researchers found that where a green
tubewell required a long walk, many families decided to rely on the
nearby polluted water.

In deciding which water is safer to drink, villagers are surely
undertaking some sort of personal risk assessment. On the one side
are the ease and modernity of using tubewell water, which they are
now being told may be dangerous to drink. On the other is surface
water, which they know can lead to cholera and diarrhea. Waterborne diseases in surface water strike quickly, making the connection between disease and water easy to draw. Arsenic is a slow killer,
unseen until it strikes years later.

This type of decision is known as a "risk-risk" choice. Each
option comes with costs. As the saying goes, out of the frying pan
and into the fire. Balancing the trade-offs in this risk-risk dilemma
is complex, and most certainly not a purely technical question.
Time spent going to a more distant green tubewell rather than a
closer red tubewell can impose its own costs in lost time. And
which water you drink can also be a status statement. As one field
worker has described, "In conversations with villagers, we realized
that although they want arsenic-free water, they do not want to feel
that they are going back in time to methods they once discarded.
Tubewells had fitted nicely with their forward-looking aspirations."

Sometimes the devil you know in surface waters is worse than the one you do not know in groundwater. In areas of the country racked with poverty and a low life expectancy, how should people balance uncertain short- and long-term health threats against the convenience, sense of self-worth, and time saved of nearby tubewell water? The situation remains tragic precisely because there are no easy solutions.

And what of arsenic in the United States? Threats facing Americans are very different than those in Bangladesh. Drinking water in the house is never more than a few feet away. Representative Bonior spoke for a lot of people when he said, "It is this simple: arsenic is a killer." Unfortunately, it really isn't this simple.

While everyone wants safe water, the problem is that no one knows just how much more dangerous it is to drink water containing ten parts per billion of arsenic rather than fifty parts per billion. To put this in a different context, the choice is roughly between ten versus fifty pinches of salt in ten tons of potato chips, or ten versus fifty seconds over thirty-two years. To the naked eye, it's not a big difference.

We all know that drinking arsenic isn't good for you. That explains the widespread criticism of the Bush decision to keep the fifty-parts-per-billion standard in place. But what if there isn't much difference to the public health provided by the more stringent standard, and the projected $200 million for compliance costs could be spent on other investments, perhaps additional capacity in the water treatment plant, instead?

The science wasn't very helpful. In the EPA's analysis for the new regulation, the calculated benefits were extremely uncertain, with estimates ranging from six lives saved through the new standards to one hundred and twelve. Spending $10 million to save a life may seem a wise use of public funds. You may feel differently if the cost were closer to $1 billion per life. Cass Sunstein, a professor at Harvard Law School and the Obama administration's chief reviewer of agency regulations, looked carefully at the history of the arsenic regulation and concluded, somewhat with his hands in the air, that "EPA could make many reasonable decisions here, and in the range below 50 parts per billion and above 5 parts per billion, there is no obviously correct choice."

Nor is this dilemma limited to arsenic. One could tell a similar story about a wide range of compounds in drinking water. Consider, for example, the case of chlorine, the single largest contributor to safe drinking water in the history of public health. Perhaps surprisingly, the debate over chlorination continues today. A class of compounds known as trihalomethanes can be produced as a by-product of chlorination in the presence of water containing organic materials such as humic acids. Trihalomethanes, most notably chloroform, are carcinogens. While there is uncertainty over the data, they suggest a connection between chlorinated water and bladder, colon, and rectal cancer. Such controversies over chlorination pose risk-risk dilemmas. Earnest efforts to make our water safer may expose us to a new class of harms. And it is not just protection from microbial disease versus heightened risk of cancer. Other trade-offs pose disease versus mortality, younger versus older victims, and well-understood threats versus significant uncertainty. Experts feel that the benefits from chlorination outweigh the harms from increased risk of cancer. They are probably right, but there are significant unknowns in this assessment.

DANGEROUS CHEMICALS IN OUR WATER ARE NOT MERELY CONFINED to poisons such as arsenic and cyanide. Recently, evidence has mounted that some chemical contaminants may disrupt the development of humans and animals by fooling our endocrine system. The endocrine system controls the production and release of hormones, the chemical signals that regulate critical aspects of our development and behavior. Crucial to the development of the fetus and the young child, hormones are, in certain respects, as important as genes in determining physical and psychological characteristics. Endocrine disruptors, a class of synthetic compounds, are able to mimic hormones and potentially interfere with the endocrine system and sexual development.

About fifty chemicals have thus far been shown to have the capacity to act as endocrine disruptors. Research has linked endocrine-disrupting chemicals to adverse effects on sexual behavior, structural deformities in the reproductive tract, lowered sperm counts, and atypical sex ratios in populations of wildlife. These studies suggest such chemicals can also harm the immune systems and perhaps even change the behavior of certain wildlife species. Chemically stable and difficult to remove with conventional drinking water treatment methods, endocrine disruptors' presence in our drinking water and likely impact on human populations are highly disputed.

What makes endocrine disruptors particularly worrisome is that they behave contrary to basic assumptions about toxicology. The working premise of toxicology is that "the dose determines the poison." A drop of chlorine in a tank of water can make it safe to drink by killing microbes. Drinking a cup of chlorine will kill you. The more exposure to a pollutant, the greater the impact. The very mechanism of hormones, however, relies on minute exposure at particularly sensitive times—tiny amounts at precise periods can lead to gross developmental changes. In contrast to traditional assumptions, this is a nonlinear relationship—a small amount may be enough to cause major developmental change—and it suggests that we should be concerned about trace amounts of endocrine disruptors, particularly when ingested by pregnant women (because of the fetuses they carry) and growing children. The development of both a fetus and a young child is critically regulated by hormonal levels. The concern is that synthetic hormones will disrupt this process.

In the Great Lakes, for example, certain species of fish as well as eagles, gulls, and cormorants are all showing increased birth defects and other harm that some scientists have linked with the high level of PCBs (polychlorinated biphenyls, used for electrical transformers and coolants), dioxins, and other persistent organic pollutants in the ecosystem. Researchers have suggested the decline in beluga whales in the St. Lawrence Seaway is likely related to the high levels of such compounds found in their bloodstream. One beluga whale had levels of PCBs in its body ten times higher than the level necessary to qualify as a hazardous waste under Canadian law. Albatross living on remote Midway Island in the center of the North Pacific also carry heavy loads of persistent organic pollutants and display symptoms consistent with exposure, including eggshell thinning, deformed embryos, and a drop in nest productivity. These birds are believed to be contaminated by DDT coming from the coast of Southeast Asia, where it is still widely used for controlling mosquitoes and crop pests.

Troubling data have demonstrated the presence of so-called intersex fish—fish that show both male and female characteristics —in rivers and bays in many parts of the country. Alligators exposed to a pesticide (dicofol) in Florida's Lake Apopka—a freshwater lake about 125 square kilometers in size—have suffered severe damage to both male and female reproductive organs. In many cases the linkage to specific endocrine disruptors is still debated, but the body of circumstantial evidence is growing. Trace amounts of endocrine disruptors have been detected in drinking water sources, but does that make the water unsafe to drink?

Others are concerned about levels of pharmaceuticals and personal care products in our drinking water. Millions and millions of people ingest pharmaceutical products every day of the year, drugs treating a dizzying range of conditions from cancer, arthritis, bacterial infections, and hair loss to blood pressure, depression, and high cholesterol. These drugs are specifically designed to change our bodies' chemistry, so their presence in the water we drink has caused alarm in some quarters. And these drugs are surely present in our water. A 1999 study by the U.S. Geological Survey identified eighty-two contaminants, many of them pharmaceuticals and personal care products, in 80 percent of the streams they sampled in thirty states. A 2006 Geological Survey study of private wells was similarly eye-opening. In a widely publicized study, the Associated Press documented the presence of fifty-six pharmaceuticals or their by-products in treated drinking water, including in the water of metropolitan areas supplying more than forty million people across the nation. But how do the drugs get in the water?

The dominant contributor seems to be us. Despite warnings against the practice, many people flush unused drugs down the toilet. We contribute unintentionally, as well. When we take a pill, our bodies metabolize some of the active ingredients but not all.

The remainder are excreted and flushed down our toilets, making their way through sewers and treatment plants into the environment and, eventually, drinking water sources. Most treatment plants are not designed to remove drug residues, and few actually test for their presence. Nor is this only a concern in highly populated areas. Drugs given to cattle make their way into water tables in agricultural areas, as well. Studies have shown high levels of steroids and antibiotics near cattle feedlots.

There are no regulations requiring testing for the presence of pharmaceuticals in drinking water or limiting their concentration. The Associated Press study contacted sixty-two major drinking water providers. Twenty-eight of those, just under half, tested for drugs in water. Those not testing included facilities serving some of our nation's largest cities—New York, Houston, Chicago, and Phoenix.

Should we be concerned? Dr. David Carpenter, director of the Institute for Health and the Environment of the State University of New York at Albany, states the fear factor in plain terms: "We know we are being exposed to other people's drugs through our drinking water, and that can't be good." A review of the literature in a peer-review scientific journal hedged its bets: "Water scarcity, climate change, aging and increasing population density, increasing use of pharmaceutical products, and rising dependence on water reuse may lead to an increase in the presence of pharmaceuticals in groundwater, surface water, and drinking water in the near future that might pose a risk to water safety or an exacerbation of perceived risk."

As with arsenic, however, the question is whether the levels present are high enough to cause harm or simply perceptions of harm. Scientists tell us that the concentrations are extremely low—sometimes in parts per billion or even parts per trillion. This is far, far below the level of a prescribed medical dose. Nor are there any documented cases of pharmaceutical traces in drinking water leading to harm in people drinking that water.

The EPA refers to these chemicals and others as "emergent contaminants." The risk may be real, but it is largely unknown. Christian Daughton, one of the EPA's leading authorities on the topic, explains the safety dilemma well: "Scientists have only recently become able to detect contaminants at the extremely low levels at which drugs appear in water supplies—typically, around one part per trillion. You're at the outer envelope of toxicology. Historically we've worried about substances like pesticides that are present in much higher concentrations. It's also very hard to study effects at that level because the doses are so small, and the effects are subtle and delayed."

Our scientific progress has created two sorts of problems. The first, seen with endocrine disruptors and pharmaceuticals, is that we are introducing compounds into our environment and drinking water sources that quite literally did not exist decades ago. We are creating risks that have never existed before. So how can we assess the unknown? The second problem, ironically, is that our detection capability has dramatically improved. We can now identify traces of pollutants at excruciatingly tiny levels, at parts per billion and some even at parts per quadrillion. It's worth pausing to consider this awesome power of detection. One part per trillion is the equivalent to one drop of water diluted into twenty Olympic-size swimming pools. It seems hard to believe that such trace amounts could harm us.

But we can't say for sure. Our progress in detection of harmful compounds has not been matched by equal progress in our ability to link the presence of these compounds at very low levels with the actual risks they pose to us. Toxicology and epidemiology studies often rely on data from animals that have been exposed to or ingested massive amounts of the compound being studied. Making these results meaningful in the everyday human context requires three significant extrapolations: (1) from mice or other test animals to humans, (2) from mega-doses the control animals were exposed to the trace levels that we ingest, and (3) accounting for differences among humans exposed to the compound (e.g., adults versus children). These all require significant assumptions and modeling. If you read somewhere that a level of fifty parts per billion of some compound in our drinking water will lead to ten, twenty, or any specific number of cancers or deaths, then you are not getting the whole story. Any responsible risk assessment will result in a range of impacts depending on the specific assumptions within the model. Moreover, it may well be that some of the contaminants we are detecting at smaller and smaller levels are not new problems. They may have been in our water for decades.

But people are concerned, and they may have good cause. The number of synthetic compounds in the environment is steadily increasing. If public demand and scientific data grow strong enough, then government action may follow and some of the compounds will be regulated, but this is by no means a given. Keep in mind, as well, that removing truly trace amounts of compounds from drinking water will not come cheap. The combination of treatments used in the high-tech treatment works of Orange County, California—ultraviolet light, reverse osmosis, and peroxide—appear to effectively remove emerging contaminants. But this is a cutting-edge and costly approach. Traditional treatment methods will not be nearly as effective, so more than a general unease may be needed to justify such expenditures to a public unwilling to spend much on water treatment in the first place.

Nor is there reason to think that our laws will address this situation any time soon. The Safe Drinking Water Act is the primary law safeguarding the water we drink. The law works in three steps. The first is to decide "what's in and what's out," which contaminants the law will regulate and which will remain outside legal control. The EPA is supposed to assess the risk posed by contaminants and their likelihood to occur in public drinking water systems. For those posing the greatest risks, the agency sets maximum contaminant level goals (MCLGs)—the highest concentration of the contaminant in water that allows an adequate margin of safety. For many contaminants, such as microbes and carcinogens, this number is zero. It may not be practical to eliminate these contaminants, though, so in the second step, the EPA then sets a maximum contaminant level (MCL). This is the practical standard, and it is as close to the MCLG as feasible, given technology and cost limitations. In the third step, the agency carries out a risk assessment and considers the costs to achieve the mandated reduction. The final level can then be modified to a level that "maximizes health risk reduction benefits at a cost that is justified by the benefits."

Put simply, if the presence of a regulated contaminant in a drinking water sample does not exceed the MCLs, then drinking water from our tap is legally determined to be safe. The EPA is supposed to periodically reevaluate the stringency of the standards, revising them in light of new data and considering new contaminant candidates to add. The EPA's obligations do not extend to private well water, which supplies more than forty-five million Americans.

Since its passage in 1974, the Safe Drinking Water Act has regulated ninety-one contaminants. That sounds impressive until one realizes that more than sixty thousand chemicals are used within the United States, and the number is growing. Moreover, since the year 2000, *not a single chemical* has been added to the list. Indeed many of the standards for chemicals that are listed have not been revised since the 1980s or 1970s, when the law was first passed. As a result, the director of water quality for the city of Los Angeles, Dr. Pankaj Parekh, has explained, "People don't understand that just because water is technically legal, it can still present health risks." Given this track record, it seems unlikely that the new generation of water pollutants—endocrine disruptors and pharmaceuticals—will be addressed by the law anytime soon.

And even if these compounds are regulated, the law still needs to be enforced and this is by no means a given. A major investigative study by the *New York Times* in 2009 reported that more than 20 percent of the water treatment systems across the country had violated key provisions of the Safe Drinking Water Act over the past few years. Yet only a handful of these systems, a mere 6 percent, had been fined or punished by state or federal officials. Part of this meager enforcement record is due to inadequate funding, but part of it is institutional. Most water treatment systems are operated by local government, and the lion's share of violations occur in the smaller systems, those serving fewer than twenty thousand residents. This should not be surprising, since it is at these smallest systems where resources for testing and maintenance are smallest, as well. As Professor David Uhlmann, former chief of the Environmental Crimes Section at the Department of Justice, explained, it is difficult for one arm of government to sue the other: "There is significant reluctance within the EPA and Justice Department to bring actions against municipalities, because there's a view that they are often cash-strapped, and fines would ultimately be paid by local taxpayers."

This is mainly a problem of enforcing laws against public or publicly regulated bodies. But enforcement against private parties has also been problematic. Most of the enforcement of our nation's water laws takes place at the state level, and not all states take a strong approach to violations. The *New York Times* investigation found that from 2005 to 2009, factories and other regulated sites had violated water pollution laws more than half a million times, yet state officials sanctioned less than 3 percent of Clean Water Act violations with fines or other punishments. The administrator of the EPA in the Obama administration, Lisa Jackson, acknowledged these failings in an internal memo where she stated that "in many parts of the country, the level of significant noncompliance with permitting requirements is unacceptably high and the level of enforcement activity is unacceptably low."

For their part, officials plead insufficient resources. While the number of regulatory targets has increased more than twofold over the past decade, most state enforcement budgets have not increased and remain under tight control in the face of state funding crises. Politics has also taken its toll. An EPA official speaking anonymously complained that, under the administration of President George W. Bush, "We were told to take our clean water and clean air cases, put them in a box, and lock it shut. Everyone knew polluters were getting away with murder. But these polluters are some of the biggest campaign contributors in town, so no one really cared if they were dumping poisons into streams." Enforcement picked up in the Obama administration, with more inspections and prosecutions, but uneven and inadequate enforcement in some states continues.

And note that this assessment does not even take into account so-called nonpoint source pollution, pollutants swept into waterways and seeping into groundwater from pesticides and fertilizer spread on farm fields. In most cases, these are completely exempted from the Clean Water Act and Safe Drinking Water Act. Their largely exempt status has caused nonpoint sources to now become one of the most significant sources of water pollution, contaminating wells and aquifers with bacteria, nitrates, and phosphates.

THE EXEMPTED SOURCE CAUSING THE MOST CONTROVERSY AT THE moment is hydraulic fracturing, known as fracking. Fracking is a method for extracting natural gas from deep within shale formations. Traditionally, natural gas drillers have sunk pipes straight down into gas deposits. In fracking, special technology developed by Halliburton Corporation allows the drill to change directions from vertical to horizontal, running along shale formations. Holes are blasted through horizontal well pipes and into the rock. To fracture the shale even more, a special mixture of water, sand, and chemicals is injected at very high pressure miles deep into these geologic layers. The combined impact of blasts and forced fluids creates fissures releasing natural gas (also known as shale gas or methane) that has been trapped in the shale formations for millions of years. The fracking fluids flow back up the well through steel pipes encased in concrete to the surface, opening a passage for the natural gas to follow.

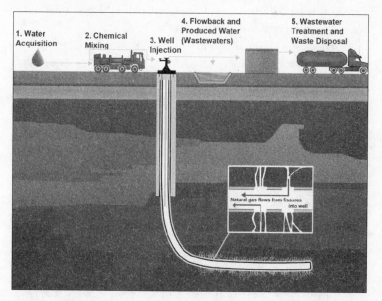

The potential of fracking is enormous, turning assumptions about America's energy security upside down. As recently as 2003, Alan Greenspan, chairman of the Federal Reserve, reported to Congress that the country would soon need to import significant amounts of natural gas from overseas. Reports of massive stores underneath parts of the East Coast have led some to predict that fracking could satisfy the nation's need for natural gas for fifty or one hundred years. Natural gas is familiar to us as the blue flame used on gas stove tops and water heaters. It can generate electricity and even power cars, buses, and trucks, dramatically reducing America's dependency on foreign oil while creating domestic jobs. Natural gas produces fewer greenhouse gases than other fossil fuels, so there could be climate change benefits, as well. As a result, in a modern-day miners' rush, investment is pouring into the field, and we can expect thousands upon thousands of new wells across the country in the next few decades.

There are shale deposits across the United States, but most of the action has centered on a geologic formation known as the Marcellus Shale, a formation extending from West Virginia and Ohio through Pennsylvania and New York. The northeastern Pennsylvanian town of Dimock lies in the heart of the Marcellus and has become ground zero for fracking controversy.

Dimock is a poor community—one in seven are out of work—so when representatives of the Cabot Oil & Gas Corporation knocked on doors, offering $25 an acre to drill for five years, plus a share of royalties when they started pumping gas, it seemed pretty attractive. Pat Farnelli's husband was working two jobs—farmer by day and diner chef on the interstate at night—to make ends meet. When the Cabot Oil offer was made, she recalls, "It seemed like God's provenance. We really were having a tough time then—that day. We thought it was salvation. Any ray of hope here is a big deal."

Cabot Oil had chosen wisely, for its wells in Dimock did well, producing almost $60 million of natural gas every year. But it came at a cost. Starting in 2009, a number of drinking water wells exploded. Other residents complained of polluted wells. While the idea of explosive drinking water may seem hard to believe, if you search YouTube with the words "methane faucet fire," you will find a series of videos showing home owners turning on the faucet, lighting a match, and watching flames shoot out of their kitchen sinks. Cabot Oil replied that the methane in the water occurred naturally and had been there before the fracking began. The concrete casing lining the well safely trapped the methane within the pipe.

A careful study by Pennsylvania's Department of Environmental Protection sided with the home owners, concluding that Cabot's operation had caused methane seepage in water wells. The company was ordered to install methane gas detectors for some residents as well as alternate sources of drinking water. Cabot has since placed a protective covering of cement along the entire well casing.

Nor is Dimock alone. In the suburban Cleveland house of Richard and Thelma Payne, methane built up in the basement, "shattering windows, blowing doors two feet from their hinges and igniting a small fire in a violent flash. The Paynes were jolted out of bed, and lifted clear off the ground." The Ohio Department of Natural Resources laid the blame for the explosion on a nearby fracking site's inadequate concrete casing that had allowed methane to escape near the surface.

Similar controversies are raging across the country. The documentary *Gasland* won a Special Jury Prize at the Sundance Film Festival and was nominated for an Academy Award. Its view on fracking is clear: "The largest domestic natural gas drilling boom in history has swept across the United States. The Halliburton-developed drilling technology of 'fracking' or hydraulic fracturing has unlocked a 'Saudi Arabia of natural gas' just beneath us. But is fracking safe? When filmmaker Josh Fox is asked to lease his land for drilling, he embarks on a cross-country odyssey uncovering a trail of secrets, lies and contamination."

Amid the charges flying back and forth, there are three basic concerns about fracking and drinking water. The first is that the fracking fluids blasted thousands of feet below the surface are finding their way into shallow aquifers that provide drinking water. The second is that methane is escaping from well casings as it is brought back to the surface. And the last is that the recovered fracking fluid is polluting local water sources.

As with other emerging contaminants, there are currently more questions than answers. The best science on the subject to date may be found in a recent peer-reviewed study by researchers at Duke University and published in the prestigious *Proceedings of the National Academy of Sciences*. Researchers compared the chemistry of water found near fracking sites with more distant water. The data showed that water samples near fracking sites contained higher levels of methane than distant drinking water sources. This, in itself, was not surprising. Industry has generally not denied this, arguing that methane was naturally present in water sources before the fracking even began but no one was looking for it.

The Duke study ruled this out by using a detection technique called isotopic analysis. The samples closest to the fracking sites contained a special form of methane known as thermogenic methane. Thermogenic methane only occurs deep within the earth and has a different structure than naturally occurring surface-level methane. The most plausible way this could have been brought to the surface was through poor concrete casing of the drilling rigs, allowing some thermogenic methane to leak as it rises.

Importantly, the Duke study did not find any fracking fluids in the waters they tested. This supports the industry position that the liquids are injected well over a mile beneath shallow aquifers, making contamination virtually impossible. It should be noted that most states do not require disclosure of what exactly is in the fracking fluid. Industry has argued it should remain a trade secret. At a recent conference speech, the CEO of Halliburton, an industry leader in the field, held up a glass of the company's new fracking fluid and asked an executive to come on stage and drink it. Observers were impressed, but said they would have been more impressed had the CEO himself drunk the fluid.

The U.S. EPA has started to get involved, testing drinking water for some of Dimock's residents and drafting regulations for air pollution from fracking operations. Why has it not been more active in such an important area? Perhaps surprisingly, it has been prevented from doing so. In the 2005 energy bill, at the behest of Vice President Dick Cheney, text was adopted that specifically exempted fracking from coverage under the Clean Water Act and the Safe Drinking Water Act. The efforts of Cheney, a former chief executive of Halliburton, led some to dub the exemption as the "Halliburton Loophole." Regulation and enforcement occur at the state level but are very uneven, with stretched resources. The nonprofit ProPublica reports that West Virginia has one inspector for every 3,300 wells. Nor is methane regulated in drinking water. It is not thought to be harmful to health, but there is very little research on the topic.

The fracking debate continues to rage, but two things are certain. Fracking will become an increasingly important industry in the coming years, raising greater concerns about its impacts on drinking water supplies. And the term "fire water" is likely to take on a new meaning.

THE PREVIOUS CHAPTER BEGAN WITH THE OBSERVATION THAT, although we do not give a second thought when filling a glass from a nearby faucet, for most of human history, safe drinking water has been the exception, not the norm. And this seems obvious. The high levels of cholera, typhoid, dysentery, and other waterborne diseases that were commonplace in times past have thankfully become rare, if not nonexistent, in developed countries today. Consider that in 1900, an American had a 1 in 20 chance of dying from a gastrointestinal infection before the age of seventy. In 1940, this had been reduced to a 1 in 3,333 chance; and in 1990 to a 1 in 2,000,000 chance. This is a staggering achievement—a 100,000-fold public health improvement in less than a century.

No surprise, then, that from the vantage of twenty-first-century America, we view the quality of drinking water in the past and in much of the developing world as unsafe, and for good reason. It goes without saying that if we got into a time machine and exited in 1854 at the pump on Broad Street, we would be wise enough not to drink that water. If the history we have traversed means anything, though, it is that our assumption about safe drinking water generally being the exception rather than the norm is wrong.

While *we* may look with horror on the water drunk in days

gone by, people at the time often did not. People generally regard their water as safe. The widow in Hampstead liked the Broad Street Pump water so much she sent her servant specially down to bottle it for her. It is only later, when we look back through the lens of modern microbiology and public health, that the water seems unsafe and the laws inadequate.

The interesting question, then, becomes how such transitions occur, why formerly safe water becomes regarded as unsafe and norms adapt. Think back to the example of the communal cup at Tian Tan Buddha. Why did attitudes toward shared drinking water cups change so rapidly in America in the early 1900s, indeed forcing a change in laws, despite the fact that this practice persists in parts of Asia today? Why was chlorination welcomed in some communities in the early 1900s yet strongly opposed in others? Why do some Bangladeshis continue to draw water from red-painted tubewells and others do not? And of direct relevance today, should we regulate pharmaceuticals and personal care products in drinking water? In these cases and others, common understandings of safe drinking water are in flux; norms are contested.

What explains these transitional periods and their influence on what we regard as safe water? The answer is multifaceted. A large part of the explanation clearly turns on changing conceptions of disease. Imagine there was no time machine and you really were a Londoner living in Soho a hundred fifty years years ago. If you, an educated person, *knew* that diseases such as cholera and typhoid were spread through airborne miasma, then getting your water from a covered well would be prudent. Through this perspective, the cesspit located next to the well would, in fact, be very convenient. You can dump your garbage and collect your day's water at the same place. How thoughtful of the municipality.

Put another way, the demand for safe drinking water is not what has changed over time. That has been a constant in every society. What has shifted is our *relationship* to water, driven by our changing conceptions of threats to health and what makes drinking water unsafe. Our views about safe drinking water are shaped by a continuous co-evolution of norms and knowledge. Over time, as we learn more about the nature of waterborne diseases and the trade-offs of choosing particular water sources over others, our norms for identifying, protecting, and treating drinking water change as well. But this takes time and can lead us down false paths.

The miasmatic theory of disease taught us to avoid water that smelled but gave no reason to be concerned about pollution near the water source. John Snow's insights into the transmission of cholera and the subsequent rise of the germ theory alerted us to the dangers posed by unseen killers and the need for filtration and chlorination to ensure safe water.

There are particular historical junctures when the very identity of safe water becomes contested. It is at these moments that we find John Snow at the Broad Street Pump, chlorination of municipal water, bans on communal cups at drinking fountains, the tragedy over arsenic-contaminated wells in Bangladesh, and the debate over endocrine disruptors today. At these moments, concepts as basic as the causes of disease and the rules over provision of water become unstable and eventually untenable, replaced by new assumptions, laws, and policies. But such change does not come easily or quickly.

Pushing against change is the stickiness of social norms. As we discussed earlier, people in Yorubaland identify their drinking water sources from a set of rules, the most important of which is that the water should come from a clear, flowing stream. While one can understand that this norm could be very practical—for example, reducing the microbial problems associated most with standing water—it posed a riddle for the anthropologist Eva-Marita Rinne.

The villagers in Yorubaland have been told that drinking from flowing water can cause disease. They have been told of the benefits of point-of-use strategies—using chemicals, filtration, and boiling to disinfect their water. Some use these treatment practices, but not many. Their norms have not changed. Why do they continue drinking unsafe water?

Rinne cannot really explain. She suggests that poverty plays a role, since not everyone can afford the treatment options. She suggests passivity, since people do not "regard themselves capable of solving environmental health problems, but rather they rely on the local governments." She finally suggests a catch-all explanation of tradition, concluding that rules for drinking water sources result from "common experience of past generations, the visual evidence of how safe water looks, and of everyday life practices of ensuring safe water." The basic explanation of why they drink unsafe water is, quite simply, that on balance, they have always thought the water was safe enough. Occasional illness or worse is just part of life.

And part of the answer turns on the relative nature of safety. It is understandable that a miserable lost explorer, parched and wandering in the desert, might happily drink out of a fetid pool of water to slake his thirst. In that case, to paraphrase the famed economist Adam Smith, water clearly would be far more valuable than diamonds, even unclean water. For the desperately parched soul, such water would have been safe enough, even though you or I would probably not even use it to wash our car. Drinking water, even if teeming with microbes, is always a safer option than death from dehydration.

In Yorubaland, Bangladesh, and many other parts of the world today, the determination of whether the water is "safe enough" is not as straightforward as it is for a dying explorer. Determining safety turns on a complicated balance of threats to health, opportunity costs of collecting cleaner water (time spent gathering water versus time spent for other important needs such as earning money or collecting firewood), and social pressures. What should a villager in Bangladesh do with a red-painted well nearby and a green well more than an hour's walk away? How can one decide the best option—drinking from surface water with the known risk of waterborne disease, drinking from the green well but losing several hours each day to gather the water, or drinking from the nearby red well and accepting the possibility of arsenic poisoning sometime in the future?

This fundamental challenge is equally true in the developed world as well. We assume we know what safe water is. Part of our view is technocratic. As expressed in the Safe Drinking Water Act or standards set by the World Health Organization, our focus is on biophysical assays of water, maximum contaminant levels, and economic and technical feasibility of treatment. The norms of water safety are determined for us by scientists in lab coats somewhere.

Yet this veneer of knowledge can mask significant uncertainty. As the cases of arsenic, pharmaceuticals, and fracking make clear, exactly what we should regulate and how stringently are no easy matters, especially when money for our water systems is so hard to come by. And we can expect the number of poorly understood challenges to increase.

TAKING THESE CONSIDERATIONS TOGETHER, WE NEED TO FIND A WAY to discuss more honestly and openly what we mean by safe drinking water. There are three fundamental points that should underpin this discussion.

The first is that safety is a relative concept. We would all be safer if we drove in semiamphibious tanks, yet some people—indeed many—choose to drive motorcycles or tiny cars that will crumple in a crash. They prefer to spend their money for benefits other than car safety, and these are perfectly rational decisions. Just as with the Bangladeshis, people living in Yorubaland, and us, safety ultimately is a judgment about choices. We can reduce the level of arsenic in drinking water to five parts per billion or even lower, but choosing this comes at a price, particularly high for many small water systems in the West. It is hard to disagree with someone who says they want safe water from their tap and, to an impressive degree, the water from our taps today justifiably is regarded as safe by most people. Is it totally safe, in the sense of risk-free? No. But it is not at all clear that this would be a desirable goal.

The second point is that we water drinkers must ultimately rely on the judgment of experts and accept that they don't have all the answers. Few consumers, indeed, have the technological savvy to test their water for arsenic, *Cryptosporidium*, endocrine disruptors, and the myriad other potential threats to our water, much less at concentrations of parts per million. One can use household water filters, and these will remove some pollutants but surely not all. Do emerging contaminants pose serious threats to our drinking water, to our safety? Our current understanding does not provide cause for alarm; hence they are largely unregulated. But our current understanding is also admittedly incomplete. Because we thought our water was safe before, does this mean we have no need to worry, or have we uncovered an unseen harm that must now be addressed for our safety and that of our children?

The key point to keep in mind is that just because a poison or carcinogen is in our drinking water does *not* mean it poses a significant hazard. The August 2011 cover of *Reader's Digest*, for example, certainly captured readers' attention with the bright red warning that our water "MAY CONTAIN: ROCKET FUEL, BIRTH CONTROL PILLS, ARSENIC, AND MORE SHOCKING INGREDIENTS." While this may be both accurate and alarming it is, at the same time, misleading. There is reason to believe that traces of many compounds are harmless below certain levels. Arsenic's mere presence in a glass of water does not mean you're poisoning yourself by drinking it. The equally key rejoinder, though, is that low levels do not necessarily mean *no* harm. Some compounds are harmful at any level.

We ultimately have no choice but to trust the decision by our government's regulators that the water coming out of our tap and the bottled water we buy at the store are, in fact, safe to drink. But many of us are unsure whether to trust government authorities when it comes to drinking water. A 2009 survey of environmental problems found that the top concern was water—59 percent of those polled worried "a great deal" about pollution of drinking water. An additional 25 percent worried "a fair amount." This explains in part the popularity of bottled water and its branding strategy. Effective ads for bottled water are all about the natural, pure essence of the clear liquid. Aquafina, Pepsi's successful bottled water brand, could not make this clearer. The product's slogan, spelled out in big letters on the label, reads, "Pure Water." But, as we shall see in Chapter 6, this is by no means a given because the regulatory standards for bottled water are less demanding than those for tap water.

There is no question that our ability to understand the risks posed by drinking water has dramatically improved over the centuries. Measuring traces of contaminants in parts per trillion is now possible. We also have a far deeper understanding of the toxicology of drinking water contaminants. But in some cases—indeed, many cases—our sophisticated tools of risk assessment, toxicology, and cost-benefit analysis of drinking water contaminants are indeterminate. They provide numbers, but with significant error bars or extrapolation from trace levels. The experts unavoidably, necessarily, operate with significant uncertainty. In the face of such uncertainty, should the EPA rely on public perceptions of safety when these, too, can seem fallible or irrational? We know far more than John Snow ever did about what makes water unsafe but must still grapple with imprecision more than we like when forced to make decisions. And this ignorance is both humbling and unsettling.

The last point is that certain things are not in doubt. We, as a society, need to realize that providing safe water requires funding to pay for it. This means rebuilding our aging water infrastructure. It means increasing funding for enforcement of the Safe Drinking Water Act and making the tough political calls to sue local authorities that are violating the law. And it means holding accountable agency officials who are not protecting the public's health. All easier said than done, but until we act as "citizen drinkers," using our political process to demand a sustained focus by government officials on provision of safe drinking water, the problems of lax regulation and enforcement will continue.

CAN DRINKING TOO MUCH WATER KILL YOU?

As part of its *Morning Rave* program, the disc jockeys on the Sacramento radio station KDND were talking up the latest racy on-air contest, "Hold Your Wee for a Wii." The idea was simple enough. The person who drank the most water without urinating would win a Nintendo Wii video game console. Twenty-eight-year-old Jennifer Lea Strange was ready to go. She told the woman beside her that she really wanted to win the game for her two kids. After the first few rounds of drinking eight-ounce bottles of Crystal Geyser water, Jennifer was going strong, watching as one bloated contestant after another dropped out. After downing close to two gallons of water in three hours, though, Jennifer just could not take another sip. She finished a frustrating second. Once in the car, she felt more than frustration. She called her boss, saying she had a terrible headache and was heading home. She was found there several hours later. The cause of death was determined to be "water intoxication."

Hilary Bellamy trained for months to run the Marine Corps Marathon in Washington, D.C., steadily working up the endurance through daily runs to make it through 26.2 miles on the day of the race. Her goal was 5:45, a steady pace of 13 minutes a mile. At the halfway point she was on pace, slowing a little by the 18 mile mark. Every two miles there were water stops where cups of water or a sports drink were handed to runners. Hilary made sure to stay hydrated and drank steadily. By mile 19 she was having trouble, complaining of a headache and blurry vision. At mile 20 she collapsed in the arms of her husband, there to cheer her on with her three-year-old daughter and nine-month-old son. Rushed to the hospital, Hilary died two days later.

Jennifer and Hilary both died from a condition known as hyponatremia. Drinking too much water causes salts in the blood to become too diluted, and water floods into cells. This is a particular problem with neurons in the brain, which do not have the space to expand. The result is swelling of the brain, which can lead to coma, seizures, brain damage, and even death. As Paracelsus famously expounded, the dose determines the poison. Water is the vital ingredient for life, but extremes on either side are dangerous. If you don't drink enough water you will die of thirst. If you drink too much, you can die of hyponatremia.

5

Blue Terror

LACKSTONE, MASSACHUSETTS, IS A SMALL TOWN OF NINE thousand people on the border with Rhode Island. It's named after William Blaxton, an Englishman who sailed to the New World in 1623, just two years after the Pilgrims arrived on the *Mayflower*. Blaxton made his mark in history as a famous first settler—the first European settler in Rhode Island, the first settler in what would become known as the city of Boston. The Blackstone River meanders through the south part of town. Its place in history is assured by powering the first textile mill in the United States in 1790, a date marked by many as the start of the Industrial Revolution. The town of Blackstone made history for quite a different reason the evening of March 28, 2006.

That night, there was a break-in at the town's water tower. Climbing over a twelve-foot-high security fence topped with barbed wire, the group of intruders methodically pried open a two-inch steel door, smashed an electrical panel, scaled the water tower, and kicked in the fiberglass cover on top, exposing the town's water supply. The next morning, officials discovered the damage and found a bucket with an unknown substance nearby. They naturally assumed the worst—that terrorists had poisoned the town's drinking water supply—and responded immediately. The water system was shut down while the 1.3 million gallon water tower was flushed. The town's schools, restaurants, and laundromats were closed. Fire trucks with loudspeakers drove down streets telling people not to use the water. Notices were put in mailboxes with the stark warning

"Important!!!!!!! Do not use the drinking water for any purpose." Residents threw out anything that might contain the tainted water —ice cubes, baby formula, even cooked pasta.

By the time lab results came back a few days later showing no contamination in the water, the mystery had been solved. Two fifteen-year-old high school kids, looking for excitement, had apparently caused all the mayhem so they could pee into the water tower. The *Boston Herald* newspaper humorously called them the "Whiz Kids." But it was no laughing matter. Their teenage stunt had cost the town $40,000 in response costs and, most important, starkly revealed what municipal water managers have long known. Our drinking water supplies are vulnerable.

As Ralph Mullinix, water manager for Loveland, Colorado, put it, "It's not that difficult to get up on top of a water tower. Every high school kid in the country has done that during his senior year, usually to write his girlfriend's name on it. You can harden your perimeter around your key facilities, but the fact is that water systems are very vulnerable." Elizabeth Hunt, Vermont's drinking water chief of planning, adds more darkly, "After 9/11, we can't just assume that it's only some kids goofing off."

The previous two chapters explored whether it is safe to drink the water, focusing on natural and emerging threats such as sewage and synthetic hormones. But *intentional* threats to drinking water can pose just as great a danger. The Blackstone incident showed just how easy it is to contaminate water supplies on purpose. Fortunately, no one was harmed by the high school prank, but what if the Blackstone intruders had been terrorists intent on causing real injury, not just thrill-seeking juvenile delinquents? Standing on top of the water tower, the fiberglass cover pried off, could they really have poisoned the whole town? Just how vulnerable are our drinking water sources? And what should we be doing in the face of these potential threats?

While the attacks of 9/11 focused immediate attention on the safety of our drinking water, these are hardly new concerns. Poisoning the enemy's water is a longstanding military strategy. When Solon of Athens laid siege to Cirrha in 600 BC, he ordered that the poisonous hellebore roots be placed in the local water supply, making the Cirrhaeans violently sick. During the Civil War, both Union and Confederate forces were accused of dumping diseased animal carcasses in drinking wells and ponds. Japan allegedly introduced cholera strains into drinking water during its conquest of China. Poisoning has served its political purposes as well. The Roman emperor Nero routinely dispatched his enemies by pouring cherry laurel water, which naturally contains cyanide, into their wells.

In 1941, concerned over domestic attacks from Nazi or Japanese agents, J. Edgar Hoover, the famed director of the Federal Bureau of Investigation, wrote, "It has long been recognized that among public utilities, water supply facilities offer a particularly vulnerable point of attack to the foreign agent, due to the strategic position they occupy in keeping the wheels of industry turning and in preserving the health and morale of the American populace." And he was right. Since his warning, there has been a series of attempted attacks on American drinking water supplies.

In the early 1970s, the domestic revolutionary group the Weather Underground sought to blackmail a homosexual officer working at the bacteriological warfare facility in Fort Detrick, Maryland, in the hopes of obtaining microorganisms to contaminate water supplies. A decade later, the FBI foiled a plot by the white supremacist group "The Covenant, the Sword, and the Arm of the Lord" to poison urban water supplies with potassium cyanide. In 2002, four Moroccans were caught planning a tunnel under the U.S. embassy in Rome so they could contaminate the water with ten pounds of potassium ferrocyanide. In his State of the Union address that same year, President Bush stated that soldiers in Afghanistan had found diagrams and information on U.S. water facilities.

These are just a few of the most publicized incidents, but there are countless more. An editorial in the *Journal of Water Resources Planning and Management* put this in broader context, claiming that "threats to attack, or, more commonly, contaminate, water systems are not unusual. There are hundreds of threats against municipal water systems each year." A classified 2012 U.S. intelligence assessment leaked to the *Washington Post* concluded that water infrastructure could become a high-visibility structure for terrorists to attack, particularly as water problems become more acute across the globe.

Even popular culture has picked up on the threat. The 2002 action movie *The Tuxedo* features Jackie Chan chopping and kicking his way to thwart the evil designs of a bottled water manufacturer trying to poison municipal water supplies (all the better to grow his market share). The plot of the 2005 movie *Batman Begins* turns on a secretive and ancient group attacking Gotham City by injecting fear-inducing compounds into the water system. The 2006 film *V for Vendetta* features corrupt government leaders contaminating London's water supply to kill, spread fear, and consolidate power.

To date, large-scale attacks have fortunately been limited to the big screen in movie theaters. There have not been any successful, major attacks on American water supplies, but the threat and fear remain. And for good reason. The simple fact is that our water supplies cannot be fully protected. We can erect more fences, higher fences, locks, and security cameras, and hire more guards—and we have—but these will never make us completely safe. To understand why, you need to appreciate the sheer size of a municipal water system.

Most water systems are linear designs, from source to faucet. They start at a supply source, typically some combination of a reservoir, dam, river, or groundwater aquifer. The water is then moved to a treatment facility. Depending on the quality of the water, the treatment plant may use mechanical and chemical processes for purification. These can range from settling pools and fine filters to adding chlorine, bubbling ozone gas, or passing the water through ultraviolet light. The drinking-quality water is then passed through distribution systems to a faucet and the point of consumption. Depending on the setting, distribution systems can include water towers, pipes, and pumping stations.

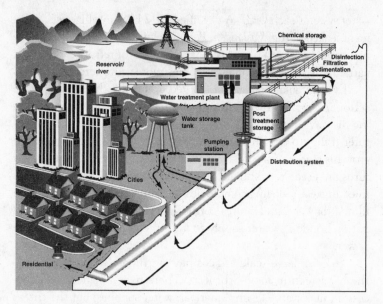

The architecture of a modern water system

So why is protection so difficult? Consider that, nationwide, water is drawn from more than 75,000 dams and reservoirs. This water courses through two million miles of pipe, with millions more access points. There are more than 160,000 drinking water facilities, mostly owned and operated by local government and private parties. Some of these utilities are huge, delivering water to major cities. Others are tiny, serving communities of just twenty-five people. When you add up all the reservoirs, dams, wells, pumping stations, water towers, water tanks, and water treatment facilities, not to mention the miles of pipes connecting them all, it becomes evident pretty quickly that the different parts of our water systems present a big—an impossibly big—target to protect.

Moreover, most of the water sources and distribution system are easily accessible to the public, or at least accessible without much trouble. The Blackstone teenage vandals were hardly master criminals, and they did just fine. There have been similar reports of teen damage in Florida, Washington, and Vermont, just to name a few. In facing the challenge from determined terrorists, it seems clear that we have to further "harden" our water infrastructure against threats but, in a world of limited budgets, which parts of the system should be hardened? To answer this intelligently, we need to better understand the nature of the threats.

BATMAN BEGINS AND OTHER POPULAR VERSIONS OF WATER ATTACKS often portray the evildoers skulking in shadows of a huge, churning treatment plant, pulling out a test tube or flask, and pouring the nefarious contents into the water. But what would an attack look like in real life? Leaving aside the super-fear-inducing toxin of the movies, there are basically four types of threats water managers are genuinely concerned about.

The most obvious is chemical. We all know arsenic in a glass of water can kill, and there are plenty of historical examples to persuade those who remain in doubt. Nor is arsenic alone as a dangerous powder that can be slipped into the drink of an unsuspecting victim. So-called "date rape" drugs rely on spiking a drink with sedatives that impair motor control and can cause amnesia. Other threats may be posed by a whole slew of water-soluble chemicals, including cyanide or even a "designer chemical" specially designed for the task.

The second class of threat is biological. In some respects, this is an ever-present concern because every year we find unanticipated contamination of drinking water by microbes. The 103 deaths in Milwaukee described earlier were caused by the presence of the cryptosporidium bacteria in the drinking water. The small town of Gideon, in southwest Missouri, was hit by an epidemic that afflicted almost half of the population. Fifteen people were admitted to hospital, and seven residents in a nursing home died. The cause was eventually attributed to salmonella spread by bird droppings in the town's water tank. Either the treatment plant's chlorination of the water was inadequate, or these were bacterial strains resistant to chlorine.

These examples were unintended biological contaminants. The government is also concerned about the intentional introduction of these organisms. The U.S. Army Combined Arms Support Command carried out a study of potential biological weapons. In all, twenty-seven biological agents were examined. Seven of these were identified as "weaponized"—able to be used as a weapon in a drinking water system—and a further fourteen were assessed as possible or probable weapons. This does not include, of course, bio-engineered agents.

Increasing attention has recently been focused on the third threat, cyber attacks. Computers play a critical role in operating water systems. Known generally as SCADA systems (for Supervisory Control and Data Acquisition), these computer programs monitor, control, and, when necessary, intervene to ensure proper operation of a water system. A hacker with evil intent could potentially take over the system and release toxic levels of water treatment chemicals prior to distribution or, alternatively, not release the required water treatment chemicals.

A related scenario might involve, for example, a terrorist hacking into the water system's computers and manipulating valves and gates to drain a reservoir or manipulate flow pressures to burst pipes (a so-called water hammer). This would mimic the urban myth surrounding water pipes and popular television shows. Every year, around the time of the Super Bowl, there are occasional newspaper warnings that TV viewers running to the toilet at halftime and collectively flushing at the same time will cause a surge and burst pipes. Years ago, in fact, Harvey Schultz, the commissioner of New York City's Department of Environmental Protection, actually issued a "bowl warning" encouraging football viewers to alternate their trips to the bathroom. His warning presumably was tongue-in-cheek, but there have been legends of surges as a result of collective flushes— after the final episode of the series M*A*S*H, in 1983, for example. Apparently people stayed riveted to the show for the full two and a half hours and then all sprinted to relieve themselves in a giant synchronized water ballet.

Apart from poisoning and the unlikely possibility of massively simultaneous toilet flushing, the fourth and most obvious threat to water systems comes from conventional explosives. As described above, most water systems are linear. Blowing up one part of the chain, whether treatment plant, pumps, or pipes, can effectively disable the entire system, making the water undrinkable for perhaps a very long period of time. We have often seen the natural equivalent of this after natural disasters such as Hurricane Katrina in New Orleans. Many treatment plants store large quantities of chlorine, which is a dangerous poison when inhaled, so attacks on treatment plants would also pose a chemical threat to neighbors. And, of course, water systems use a lot of energy, so blowing up the electric grid can wreak havoc.

This chapter is not intended to provide an instructional guide for would-be terrorists on how to poison water supplies. All of the threats outlined above have been described in great detail in the public literature. The key question is whether these potential threats warrant serious attention. *Batman Begins* is just a movie, after all. In real life, which of these threats really are serious?

For starters, it would be a mistake to assume that our water systems present completely soft targets for poisoning. Quite the contrary. Water systems are designed specifically to *prevent* contamination. That's why we have them in the first place. Water managers deal every day with real attacks to our water quality by bacteria, protozoa, algae, and biofilms. We have become very good at eliminating biological pathogens. Chlorination, ozonation, ultraviolet radiation, and filtration are standard lines of defense, and redundancy is built into the system. If one type of treatment does not destroy the threat, the next one should. Reservoirs are often fenced to keep out wildlife and their excrement. Wachusett Reservoir, one of Boston's primary water sources, has even spread netting over the surface, floated "scare eye" balloons, and used remote-controlled loud noises to prevent birds from settling in the pond and defecating. The question is how well our safeguards work when the evildoers are human and bent on a harmful purpose rather than birds and deer just doing their business.

Poisoning a water system is qualitatively different than poisoning someone's glass of water. The material first and foremost needs to be suitable as a weapon. It must be effective when dissolved in water and remain potent while it courses through the water mains. It needs to elude easy detection by system monitoring. It has to be procured or produced in large enough volume to contaminate a water system. It has to remain dangerous in the face of standard water treatments such as chlorination and filters. And, of course, it needs to inflict harm when drunk. Luckily for us, this is hard to do.

The threat posed by chemical contaminants is limited. While it may be theoretically possible to poison an entire community's water supply system, the effect of dilution makes it practically impossible. Putting a few drops of cyanide in someone's glass will lead to a gruesome death (and likely ten to twenty years for murder if you're caught). Putting a few drops, or even a few barrels, in a reservoir is pointless. Reservoirs generally hold anywhere from three million to thirty million gallons of water. One expert has estimated that poisoning a moderate-sized reservoir with cyanide would require "millions of pounds" of the poison. Even assuming you could back several trucks up to the reservoir and dump their loads without being detected, and assuming further that the enormous number of fish floating on their sides in the likely fish kill that followed was not noticed by anyone, you would still need to get huge quantities of the poison in the first place. The Department of Homeland Security keeps track of biological and chemical agents that might be used by terrorists, and these substances are not easy to come by in large quantities. Nor are they easy to produce at home.

What about the threat from biological agents? This is probably the least likely source of harm. Chlorination is effective against many infectious agents. The alleged Japanese use of cholera to poison Chinese water supplies in World War II, for example, would not work today. The bacteria are too susceptible to chlorine. Filtration excludes parasites and most bacteria. Use of even finer filters—so-called microfiltration or ultrafiltration—screens out even more, including viruses. Biological agents cannot simply be ignored, however. Most of the research on biological and chemical threats has focused on airborne contaminants, and there are large gaps in our knowledge of their behavior in treated drinking water, so some agents may be more dangerous than we think. Some biological agents are resistant to chlorine treatment, and not all water systems use sophisticated (and expensive) filters.

The weakest point lies in the distribution system. In an independent experts' review of water system security carried out by the Government Accountability Office in 2003, distribution was singled out as the most vulnerable point in the system. Poisoning water in the pipes after it has passed through the reservoir avoids the problem of massive dilution and leapfrogs some of the treatment processes, such as filters, upstream. It also makes detection quite difficult, since the water is directly on its way to the consumers. There have been plenty of examples of accidental contamination through this route, so it could happen again.

In 1969, for example, most of the Holy Cross college football team mysteriously contracted hepatitis. This is not an easy disease to get, and even less likely for an entire football team. So how did they get sick? After a great deal of detective work, the answer, surprisingly, came from a golf course and a burning house. The day before the outbreak, kids playing at a nearby golf course had opened a hose on the course and made a big puddle to splash around in. One of these kids had the hepatitis virus and somehow discharged it into the pool of water. Meanwhile, elsewhere in town, a house was on fire. The fire department attached its truck to the nearby hydrant and hosed down the blaze. What links these two events? The sudden drop in water pressure in the water system from turning on the fire hose literally sucked the water from the golf course puddle, through the hose, and *back into* the pipe—the same pipe that now carried this slug of infected water to the nearby athletic building's faucet and the football team's water jug.

Reversing the flow of contaminants into water mains is known in the water industry as "backflow" and happens from time to time. In Woodsboro, Maryland, the failure of a water pump caused a precipitous drop of water pressure in the town mains. A hose that had been extended from a faucet into an herbicide holding tank started sucking the herbicide back into the town's water supply. Once the pressure was restored, water started flowing back into the holding tank but the herbicide was already in the mains. It now flowed out of faucets around the town. The Charlotte Fire Department in North Carolina accidentally back-pumped gallons of fire-retardant foam into the city's water mains. The Sikorsky helicopter plant in Bridgeport, Connecticut, similarly pumped corrosion-proof chemicals into the town's water system. In all these instances and many more, residents were warned not to drink the water, bathe, or wash until the contaminants had flushed through the system.

Sudden losses of pressure that actually suck contaminants into the system (known as back-siphonage) are unusual and hard to predict. A more likely scenario would involve back-pressure, akin to blowing up a balloon. Imagine someone hands you a balloon that is still being blown up with air and nearly full. If you let go of the balloon, it would go whizzing around the room like an out-of-control jet. The air pressure in the balloon is greater than the air pressure in the room, so air flows out from the high-pressure area to the low. This is what happens when a water pipe bursts. If you clamp the balloon in your mouth and start to blow, though, the balloon fills up even more. The air pressure created by contracting your lungs is greater than the air pressure pushing *back* from inside the balloon. Back-pressure is the same thing, but in this case the pressure forcing contaminants into the pipe needs to be greater than the water pressure in the pipe.

Backflows are dangerous because there are many places in the distribution system where contaminants can be introduced, so-called cross connections. Water faucets are an obvious example. As a result, water managers have long been concerned about backflows. As John Sullivan, chief engineer of the Boston Water and Sewer Commission, has bluntly stated, "There's no question that the distribution system is the most vulnerable spot we have. Our reservoirs are really well protected. Our water treatment plants can be surrounded by cops and guards. But if there's an intentional attempt to create a backflow, there's no way to totally prevent it." In 1984, well before 9/11 made water infrastructure a national concern, a group known as the American Backflow Prevention Association (ABPA) was created. Dedicated to education and technical

assistance, ABPA has more than forty chapters around the country and brings together elected officials, water officials, and engineers. Seeking to popularize the issue, it has even published a comic book with the catchy character Buster Backflow. The first issue was called "A Visit from Buster Backflow."

Traci and David are trying to give their dog a bath in an outside bucket. When the dog runs away, they leave the hose running in the soapy water. When they return, standing over the tub is Buster, wearing a skintight red costume and a lock of blond hair looping over his forehead. After explaining the fluid mechanics of backflow, Buster warns the kids, "If you don't want to *drink it*, don't connect your water system to it!!"

In a message aimed at an older audience, Gay Porter DeNileon, a member of the national Critical Infrastructure Protection Advisory Group, has been blunter. Writing in the journal of the American Water Works Association (AWWA), she said, "One sociopath who understands hydraulics and has access to a drum of toxic chemicals could inflict serious damage pretty quickly."

Fortunately, introducing a large backflow is hard to do. Water mains are under very high pressure. When a main bursts, it can create a geyser that blasts up from six feet underneath a road, splintering the asphalt. Blowing up a balloon is one thing; taking a sip out of a fire hose is quite another. If you're not careful, you can get your lips blown off. Moreover, backflow contamination will be localized, limited to the area where contaminants were introduced.

While no water system can be completely protected from attack, there obviously are steps that can be taken to minimize the threat. Since the mid-1990s, the national government has taken a serious interest in protecting water infrastructure. In 1996, President Clinton issued Executive Order 13010, creating the Commission on Critical Infrastructure Protection. The commission was charged to produce a strategy for protecting critical national infrastructure from serious threat that could incapacitate the nation's physical or economic security. They ended up choosing eight sectors, including telecommunications, gas and oil storage, banking and finance, and water supply systems, among others.

Congress became involved following the attacks of 9/11 with passage of the Public Health Security and Bioterrorism Preparedness and Response Act of 2002. Known as the Bioterrorism Act, this law has forced water suppliers to confront explicitly the many types of threats they might face. Most important, it requires water systems serving more than 3,300 people to perform a Vulnerability Assessment and submit the assessment to the U.S. Environmental Protection Agency. These 8,600 communities' water providers must consider the potential weaknesses in their systems, their specific vulnerabilities to terrorist attacks, and efforts they can undertake to prevent them. In practice, this means determining which components of the system are most at risk (whether pipes, treatment facilities, or chemical storage), assessing the likelihood of attacks from terrorists or vandals, identifying current countermeasures, and creating a prioritized plan for future actions to harden the system. Some parts of the country already have useful experience through developing emergency response plans to earthquakes and hurricanes.

Yet water managers are hydraulic engineers. They are not trained to assess terrorist threats or conduct strategic assessments of the most likely means of attack. They need help, and are assisted in these efforts by other agencies. The EPA, for example, periodically issues the Baseline Threat Report. This collates current thinking on the most likely types of terrorist attack as well as useful countermeasures. For obvious reasons, this is not publicly available information.

The EPA has also created the Water Information Sharing and Analysis Center (WaterISAC). This is a secure, web-based portal that shares sensitive information among utilities, law enforcement, and intelligence agencies. It currently has as members more than three hundred utilities that collectively provide water to more than 60 percent of the country. Its products and services include alerts on potential terrorist activity; information on water security from law enforcement and public health agencies; a database on chemical, biological, and radiological threats; and resources on security solutions.

Beyond developing plans and sharing information, the primary defenses to terrorist threats are hardened infrastructure and improved system monitoring. Since 9/11, most water systems have restricted access to treatment facilities and reservoirs. But, of course, they could always do more. Perimeter security would surely benefit from higher fences, motion sensors, more patrol guards, greater use of remote cameras, etc. And, to a certain extent, this is being done.

The Coast Guard, for example, has increased its patrols of Chicago's intake sites in Lake Michigan. New York City has spent upward of $100 million on fencing, security cameras, and other measures, while tripling the dedicated police force to guard its upstate reservoirs and lakes. Across the country, California has closed off many of the roads and access points to its reservoirs. The Los Angeles Department of Water and Power has almost doubled its security personnel, increased its testing of water by 50 percent, acquired two helicopters for patrolling infrastructure, and started fingerprinting and background checks of its employees. Water managers have also focused on reducing threats within the system. Many utilities, for example, have replaced highly poisonous chlorine with sodium hypochlorite or even switched to nonchemical treatment like ultraviolet light.

The more innovative developments have focused on monitoring. As described above, our overall water system, from headwaters to tap, is simply too large to completely prevent contaminations, so a critical factor comes down to how quickly a contamination event can be detected, located, and the nature of the contaminant identified. Early detection and warning are key to minimizing harm by shutting down supplies and letting people know not to drink the water. That's why the town of Blackstone acted so quickly once it learned of the break-in at the water tower.

All water systems are required by the Safe Drinking Water Act to test their water periodically for a range of contaminants. This is not often enough, however, to detect a specific attack soon after it has occurred. Some systems routinely track drug stores' sales of antacids and diarrhea medications. These can serve as a public health proxy for wide-scale gastrointestinal upsets from drinking water. One clever approach used by both large and small systems relies on biological sensors. The town of Loveland, Colorado, for example, keeps a tank of drinking water (chlorine removed) full of trout. When the trout start to die, water manager Ralph Mullinix knows something is wrong with the water and investigates. Sure enough, after one such event a few years ago, he found that copper sulfate, added by upstream farmers to kill algae in irrigation canals, had contaminated the town's drinking water. The trout, he said, were "like the canary in the mine." Rather than just looking for dead fish, wealthier systems actively monitor the common bluegill fish's respiratory behavior using electrodes linked to software programs. If six out of eight fish show signs of stress, an alert is sounded.

The sensitivity is remarkable; the fish have detected sediments disturbed by divers in a reservoir forty miles away.

The most effective monitoring would be real-time, sensitive monitors throughout the system that can detect a whole range of contaminants. Many water managers, for example, regularly monitor pressure in the pipes. Generally, a sharp and unexpected drop in pressure indicates a burst pipe. But it may also indicate a backflow incident that can then be explored.

Bigger systems can take multiple measurements at different points in the system every day. Following 9/11, New York City increased the number of daily water samples. These samples still have to be taken to the lab and analyzed, which can take a day or longer. Of great interest are new, sensitive monitors that can detect a whole range of contaminants in real time. These have cool-sounding names such as DNA microchip arrays, immunological techniques, microrobots, flow cytometry, molecular probes, etc. None of these is commercially available yet, but the hope is that they and other emerging monitoring technologies will be placed throughout the water system, providing real-time warning of contaminants early enough to allow quick responses by water authorities.

New York City mayor Michael Bloomberg has stated the challenge clearly: "Our drinking water really is the lifeblood of this city, and that, unfortunately, might make it a target for sabotage. We need to be vigilant in protecting our water systems." What is left unsaid, though, is the vexing question: Just how much should we spend and where should we spend it?

The Bioterrorism Act requires preparation of Vulnerability Assessments, but it does not mandate that they be implemented. The key to all these hardening and monitoring strategies, not surprisingly, is money. Not only are these emerging technologies expensive, but they and others like them are also unlikely to be developed commercially if the market payoff appears small. As with so many public policy issues, knowing what to do is only half the battle. You also have to pay for it.

Given limited resources, the initial choice concerns whether the focus should be on protecting large- or small-scale systems. Larger systems, of course, serve more people. As the Congressional Research Service suggests, "A fairly small number of large drinking water and wastewater utilities located primarily in urban areas (about 15% of the systems) provide water services to more than 75% of the U.S. population. Arguably, these systems represent the greatest targets of opportunity for terrorist attacks, while the large number of small systems that each serve fewer than 10,000 persons are less likely to be perceived as key targets by terrorists who might seek to disrupt water infrastructure systems." To date, most grants have gone to big cities, but it's not clear that's the best choice. Smaller systems may, in fact be more vulnerable because they do not already have significant protections in place. In general, smaller systems have fewer resources, less well-trained staff, and weaker capabilities. As a result, the same dollar amount invested in small systems may provide greater benefit than the equal investment in a large city's system.

Congress and the Bush administration provided funds to help water systems get started. The Bioterrorism Act authorized $160 million for preparation of Vulnerability Assessments. Seventy percent of this amount, $113 million, was eventually provided. That seems like a lot of money, but the American Water Works Association, the professional trade organization of water providers, has estimated the total cost for assessments at $500 million. One water system servicing 1.2 million people, the size of Dallas, estimated it needs $90 million to strengthen the security of its operations. AWWA's overall estimate for basic system hardening measures—improved lighting, locks, fences, etc.—was as much as $1.6 billion.

One, of course, needs to take the million- and billion-dollar cost estimates with a grain of salt, or chlorine. There are many reasons why a water manager and an organization of water managers would argue for greater resource needs. But potential costs go well beyond simply adding fences or more guards to basic capital costs. A utility may decide to build two treatment plants instead of one, intentionally creating system redundancy in case a plant goes down.

Distribution pipes may be extended to soften the linearity of the system and increase the capacity to draw water from different sources during an emergency. Pipes may be buried instead of elevated. Virtually every construction choice, in fact, might look different if security became an explicit design priority.

THE FUNDAMENTAL QUESTION OF HOW MUCH TO SPEND GETS BACK to how worried we should be about terrorist threats to our drinking water. How much is improved defense against a terrorist attack worth? To answer that, we might also want to consider how much improved defense against an asteroid is worth. After all, an asteroid could collide with Earth next year. Last time it happened, dinosaurs went extinct. Perhaps we should dedicate immense funds to developing an anti-asteroid laser cannon (some people think we should). Why don't we?

It turns out that asking whether our drinking water is vulnerable to terrorist attack is an unhelpful question. *Of course* it is vulnerable. The question is *how* vulnerable, and how great the risk of harm is compared to other potential threats. There are always trade-offs over how best to spend taxpayers' money. The key points are the likelihood of such an attack, the harm that might result, and the costs necessary to prevent such an attack.

There surely are plausible threats to America's drinking water security. At the same time, though, we need to keep them in perspective. Our water systems are already designed to prevent contaminants from getting into the pipes and coming out of the tap. Getting large quantities of chemical or biological contaminants remains difficult. And dilution makes the challenge of a large-scale attack even more challenging. Thus the likelihood of a successful, far-reaching attack on our drinking water supplies is quite small. Just because a compound or biological agent can be described as a weapon of mass destruction doesn't make it so in practice. It is very difficult to poison an entire city's water supply and, given advances in monitoring technology, it will likely become more difficult in the future. Small-scale attacks, though, remain quite possible. Backflow contamination cannot be fully prevented and this gives some cause for concern.

The good news is that small-scale attacks do not threaten large populations. Simply because an attack is not a "worst-case scenario" and does not inflict massive harm, however, does not make it any less horrible. After all, the root of the word "terrorist" includes "terror" for a reason. The fear of being a victim, even if small in number, can impose real psychological harm on the greater population. The loss of confidence in the water coming out of the tap from even a small-scale attack could well impose large-scale fear and loss of confidence in the security of our overall water supplies. As a result, the serious attention devoted to the security of our drinking water supplies remains warranted.

WAS FLUORIDATION A COMMUNIST PLOT?

Scientists have been studying the effects of fluorine on teeth for close to a century. Early research focused on the discoloration and weakening of teeth (known as "Colorado brown stain") by naturally high concentrations of fluorine in the water. Studies in the 1940s in Grand Rapids, Michigan, established that adding low levels of fluorine to drinking water supplies (fluoridation) did not weaken teeth but, quite the contrary, was effective in strengthening tooth enamel. This, in turn, prevented cavities and painful tooth decay.

Creating fluoridated water, indistinguishable from untreated water in both appearance and taste, became a goal of the U.S. Public Health Service in the 1950s. By 2006, almost 70 percent of Americans were served by water systems that fluoridated their water. Britain, Canada, Australia, and a number of other countries fluoridate their water as well.

A series of studies have demonstrated the effectiveness of this public health intervention, reducing the incidence of children's cavities by up to 40 percent. The World Health Organization, U.S. Surgeon General, American Dental Association, and a range of other public health organizations have similarly endorsed fluoridation. Indeed, the U.S. Centers for Disease Control included fluoridation of drinking water on their list of the Ten Great Public Health Achievements of the twentieth century. Other achievements on the list included vaccination and control of infectious diseases. Impressive company.

Despite this glowing success, fluoridation of public water supplies has been extraordinarily contentious, with conspiracy theorists asserting nefarious plots. To be sure, fluoridation does pose a clear conflict between individual choice and government coercion. If you want to avoid fluorine in your water, you may need to go to great lengths. Much bottled water contains fluorine, since it starts as tap water, and standard filters

At the Sign of THE UNHOLY THREE

won't remove fluorine. The objections to fluoridation, though, go deeper to an anxiety over mass medication decisions by government officials.

During the height of the Cold War, some groups asserted that fluoridation was a Communist plot to attack the public's health. The fact that some fluorine compounds were used as rat poison made this at least sound plausible. Stanley Kubrick's classic film *Dr. Strangelove* wove this conspiracy into the movie's plot when General Jack D. Ripper launches a preemptive strike against the Soviet Union to thwart their strategy to contaminate the "precious bodily fluids" of Americans.

In a sensationalist brochure put out by the anti-Communist Keep America Committee in 1955, water fluoridation stood accused with vaccination and mental health services as the "Unholy Three," part of a nefarious plot against America by world communist powers. If one is deeply distrustful of spies subverting society-wide government programs, vaccines and fluoridation likely would raise genuine cause for concern.

In any case, with the fall of the Soviet Union in the 1990s, it seems clear that even if fluoridation was a Communist plot, it did not achieve its intended purpose.

6

Bigger Than Soft Drinks

SATURDAY, SEPTEMBER 15, 2007, WAS A BANNER DAY FOR THE University of Central Florida and its football team, the Knights. They were playing the University of Texas' powerhouse squad, ranked fourth in the nation. The Knights had gone to their first bowl game just two years earlier, and a win against Texas would put them on the national stage. The game was the very first in the university's new $54 million stadium. Excitement couldn't have been higher. The stadium was packed with fans, hoping for an upset. It was hot and humid, of course, since average temperatures in Orlando can be more than ninety degrees in September.

Security guards at the entrance had prevented people from bringing water into the stadium. When fans went to get a drink of water to cool off, though, they found no drinking fountains. Not one. Anywhere. The only water to be found was in $3 bottles at the concession stands or in cupped hands at bathroom sinks. The concession stands soon sold out, and matters turned serious. The heat and humidity took a heavy toll, sending eighteen people to the hospital for heat-related illnesses. To make matters worse, the Knights lost, 35–32.

The Monday after this debacle, a university spokesman acknowledged they had not had enough bottles of water. Trying to put a positive spin, he played up the fact that the stadium project had been completed on time and within budget. "That is a pretty remarkable thing in this day and age," he said. "Granted, it did not have water fountains and some people will say you took a short cut. I don't choose to view it that way. . . . Part of the stadium, of course, is the concession, and frankly, water is a big chunk of it. . . . So my sense is that we will not be offering free water."

This tale is remarkable not merely because of the university's tone-deaf efforts to spin the story. More troublesome, the stadium designers saw nothing wrong with failing to provide drinking fountains in a place where high temperatures and humidity are commonplace. Indeed, they saw it as a clever way to increase concession revenues. Nor is this unusual. When is the last time you saw a drinking fountain, much less one that worked? They are becoming more rare than pay phones. The common understanding seems to be that if you need water, you buy it in a bottle.

Yet not too long ago, the opposite was true. If you had asked for water at a gas station in the 1970s, you would have been pointed outside to the hose used to fill radiators. Even thirty years ago, bottled water occupied a niche, elite market—a chic symbol for the healthy and wealthy. In a mere matter of decades, though, bottled water has become the drink of choice in the classroom, workplace, conferences, restaurants, health clubs, and, of course, at sporting events. Celebrities ranging from Madonna, Tiger Woods, and the Jonas Brothers to Weird Al Yankovic and Sarah Palin demand the stuff.

As a society, we clearly have deeply conflicting feelings about bottled water. As the story of McCloud in the introduction made clear, there are deep divisions within society over whether our relationship with drinking water should be based on the market or considered a human right. Nowhere is this starker than with bottled water. What explains its remarkable ascent not only to market dominance but to cultural dominance, as well, where bottled water is now taken for granted as the *primary* way to drink water? Is it really better for us than tap water?

These are current questions, but the answers lie many years back, for the story of bottled water is older than the introduction of Perrier a few decades ago—far older, and much more surprising.

THE NEED FOR BOTTLED WATER GOES BACK TO THE VERY FIRST SOCIETIES. Whether in goatskins, gourds, or clay pots, hunters and groups on the move needed containers to transport water with them, particularly if they were unsure where the next source of safe water might lie. There is no evidence, however, of a true market for bottled water in ancient times, in the sense of containers of water sold for consumption somewhere else. Instead, local water needs were satisfied by water sellers who provided a drink or filled containers brought by customers.

The famous seventeenth-century painting by Velázquez of a water seller in Seville suggests the human precursor of the modern vending machine.

The origins of bottled water markets lie not with water sellers, however, but with an entirely different and unexpected source: the veneration of spring waters thousands of years ago. After all, what could be more mysterious to premodern people than a natural spring? How the water came to the surface, literally flowing out of rock, could not be easily explained, much less the mysterious minerals, carbonation, heat, and smells of the strange waters. How else to explain these but by mystic origins? No surprise that springs and wells were often explained by a divine presence, by local gods who looked after the waters, sometimes for good and sometimes for ill.

From earliest times, natural water sources have been linked with mystical healing and divine powers. The Bible is filled with references to particular wells. Other regions, such as the Scottish Isles, have long boasted their own special waters. As recounted earlier, in Scotland in the Middle Ages, those suffering from insanity were cured by drinking at St. Maelrubha's Well, while those suffering from toothaches could seek relief by drinking from the healing well on the isle of North Uist.

Similar stories from around the world speak of waters with miraculous healing powers. According to local legend, different wells could cure the sick or restore movement to the lame, eyesight to the blind, and fertility to the barren, not to mention provide relief from rickets, lameness, whooping cough, leprosy, paralysis, etc. These cures may sound ridiculous to modern ears. Spring waters, though, really can have curative powers. Like Coke, some of these waters are the Real Thing.

There is no such thing as pure water in nature. Lots of substances, both organic and inorganic, like to dissolve in water. All spring water starts originally as rain or snow falling to the ground. Water's particular nature comes from both the downward path it takes as it seeps through the earth and its upward path as it slowly ascends through geologic layers, emerging at a different point. As with all journeys in life, the nature of the passage makes all the difference. Water passing through limestone will be higher in dissolved calcium and magnesium. Water filtering through igneous rocks will pick up dissolved sodium in its slow years-long migration returning to the surface.

While it may sound pretentious to compare water to wine, it's a fair analogy. Just as wine grapes are flavored by their vines' soil, so, too, does mineral water gain its chemical composition through the rock strata it has passed. The precise composition of the water—its *terroir*, if you will—depends on the local geology, and, it turns out, so does the water's therapeutic value.

Modern medicine has demonstrated that natural salts can soothe the pains of arthritis. Sulfates and bicarbonates found in some spring waters are routinely used to treat gastrointestinal ailments. Calcium strengthens bones and teeth. And water containing naturally dissolved lithium, a drug long used to treat depression, may even be useful for those with mental health problems. Thanks to their dissolved minerals, some healing waters really *do* heal beyond the power of positive suggestion.

In the era before modern medicine, and even today in some regions, these mineral-bearing waters were particularly important to health. Because of their unique natural composition of salts and minerals, many spring waters became widely known for their curative powers. Specific waters were recommended for specific ailments. Julius Caesar favored the hot waters at Vichy in France, known in Roman times as the Hot Town (Vicus Calidus). The great Renaissance artist Michelangelo suffered from kidney stones. His doctor ordered him to take the waters from a nearby town, and Michelangelo reported, "I am much better than I have been. Morning and evening I have been drinking the water from a spring about forty miles from Rome, which breaks up the stone. . . . I have had to lay in a supply at home and cannot drink or cook with anything else." The German Romantic author Goethe swore by Fachingen waters near Wiesbaden with their high bicarbonate content. He wrote his daughter-in-law that the "the next four weeks are supposed to work wonders. For this purpose, I hope to be favored with Fachingen water and white wine, the one to liberate the genius, the other to inspire it."

While we now understand the chemistry behind the curative powers of sacred springs, people at the time obviously looked to different explanations. In a society with no understanding of geology or modern disease, there was a need to attribute some cause to these waters' origins and medicinal benefits. Attributing divine creation and curative powers to springs made sense from both a physical and metaphysical view. Thus did waters become sacred and imbued with special powers because of their mystic origins. These holy waters married the myth to the real, and their reputations endured over time.

Despite particular springs gaining notoriety for their curative powers, visits to distant springs for health were quite uncommon. Prior to the eighteenth century, traveling in Europe purely for health reasons was simply too expensive and often too dangerous. Yet people still traveled great distances to visit wells and springs, indeed large numbers of people. They traveled not for physical but for spiritual health. Particularly during the Middle Ages, pilgrimage routes were popular throughout Europe. Some, as Chaucer recounted, led to great cathedrals such as Canterbury; others led as far as Jerusalem. Near or far, however, many led to holy waters.

Most springs' creation myths involved a miracle of some sort. To entrepreneurial Church officials, this created an intriguing business opportunity. Indeed, a number of holy wells began to compete with one another for the burgeoning commerce of pilgrims and holy objects. In a precursor to modern travel websites extolling white beaches, bronzed bodies, and pulsing nightlife, boosters of holy wells entered into an arms race of hyperbole. A comprehensive history of ancient wells relates, for example, how a monk of Winchecombe Abbey in Gloucestershire:

> invented a story that Prince Kenelm of Mercia was murdered by his sister Quendreda's lover, who buried Kenelm's head under a thorn tree. A white dove carried a scroll that described the evil deed to the Pope in Rome, who ordered the body be found. Local

clerics used a white cow to locate it on the slopes of Sudely Hill, where a spring burst forth. Quendreda tried to curse the ensuing funeral procession by reading Psalm 108 backwards, but her eyes exploded. On the strength of this amazing tale, Winchcombe Abbey became a popular destination for pilgrims and one of the largest abbeys in England.

This incredible—truly incredible—tale invented at Winchcombe Abbey was a likely result of such boosterism, as pilgrimage sites competed with one another to get a cut from the revenue stream. One can just imagine the enterprising pilgrimage marketing materials. "You think going on pilgrimage to St. Maelrubha's Well is holy? Just listen to what happened at Winchcombe Abbey! Exploding eyeballs!"

The intense interest in visiting such holy places and offering contributions created a sizable stream of revenue to Church coffers. In fact, the Church often had well-managed staff in place precisely to gather the pilgrims' offerings. Holy wells had strongboxes strategically located to accept donations, and priests collected the daily inflow. The take could be huge.

The Church was not entirely corrupt, of course, and men of good faith were troubled by this practice. Thus one can find a series of canons and laws from the period that forbade pilgrims to travel to wells and holy water sites or to worship there. King Egbert declared in the ninth century, "If any keep his wake at any wells, or at any other created things except at God's church, let him fast three years, the first on bread and water, and the other two, on Wednesdays and Fridays, on bread and water; and on the other days let him eat his meat, but without flesh." The Bishop of Lincoln actually threatened to excommunicate pilgrims journeying to holy wells in Buckinghamshire. These paternalistic efforts to protect pilgrims and their money seem to have had little effect. The allure of holy wells and their sacred waters was just too strong.

So how do these stories of holy waters and pilgrims explain the rise of bottled water?

A sketch of water bottles with their distinctive seals from
St. Menas's holy well in Egypt

Pilgrims that chose to visit a famous well or spring faced a problem. While drinking or being blessed with the holy waters was all well and good, many wanted to bring some of the waters back with them. There was, after all, a booming trade in holy relics at the time. But how could pilgrims prove that the water they carried was really filled with holy waters? Just as a skeptical neighbor might cast doubt on whether a pilgrim had returned from Jerusalem with a piece of the True Cross, so, too, might he question whether the water the pilgrim carried was from distant Winchcombe Abbey or the nearby stream. "You say that's holy water? Prove it!" The ingenious solution to this challenge provides the first example of bottled water marketing.

To validate pilgrims' claims of authenticity, each holy well produced its own special flask that could only be obtained at that particular site. Every site had its own ceramics works, producing its own distinctive container with a special seal. These represent the earliest known case of water branding through packaging—a full fifteen hundred years before Perrier's distinctively shaped green bottle.

While the market for bottled waters originated in the holy

relics trade, it was concerns over physical rather than spiritual health that transformed the market into what we see today. Starting in the eighteenth century, spas became the vacation spot to go and to be seen, both in America and Europe. As described above, the chemical content of mineral waters often provided real medical benefits. Contrexéville in France was renowned for its water's powers in breaking up kidney stones and curing urinary complaints. Ferrarelle in Italy, described by Pliny the Elder as "miraculous waters" in his *Natural History*, was known to soothe digestive complaints. Évian-les-Bains near Switzerland was effective against skin diseases. Other spas' waters were recommended for sufferers of arthritis, confusion, and an impressive range of ailments.

Clever entrepreneurs transformed the towns around the waters into destination sites themselves. The best-known spa town of all, the aptly named Bath in England, had been a popular site since Roman times. With hot mineral springs supplied by virtue of an underground volcanic fault, the Romans constructed a temple to Minerva and the English crowned King Edgar beside the springs in 973. By the eighteenth century, Bath had become a fixture in the aristocracy's social calendar. During "The Season," the great and the good would venture to Bath and revel in the balls, gambling, and promenades, all the while "taking the waters"—the convenient excuse for being there in the first place. This involved not only drinking the mineral waters but bathing in them, as well. Christopher Anstey described in 1766 the fully clothed men and women in what must have been a peculiar stately promenade in the steaming spa waters:

> And tho' all the while it grew hotter and hotter,
> They swam, just as if they were hunting an Otter;
> T'was a glorious sight to behold the fair sex
> All wading with gentlemen up to their necks.
> And today many persons of rank and condition
> Were boiled by command of an able physician.

Similar stories of spa towns could be told of Contrexéville, Évian-les-Bains, or Vittel in France. The French government passed decrees in 1781 and 1856 declaring these waters of "public interest" for their medicinal benefits. Vichy, in particular, became favored by French returning from overseas colonies and hoping to regain their health after the rigors of serving in tropical Asia or Africa. New York's Saratoga Springs, long famed for its horse racing, first attracted visitors because of the more than one hundred mineral springs in the area. Diamond Jim Brady, the celebrated magnate of the Gilded Age, was a regular luminary in the 1890s. Nearly a century later, James Bond enjoyed the social scene on behalf of Her Majesty's Secret Service in the novel *Diamonds Are Forever*.

Spa towns reached their zenith in the nineteenth century, as railways made travel easier for the wealthy and affordable for the cost-conscious. Ornate hotels, decked with marble, stained glass, and great rooms, became the norm. Promenades, casinos, theaters, and concert halls provided a range of entertainments, all so the well-dressed visitors could see and be seen. Amid this swirl of activity, the central attraction remained the health benefits of "taking the waters."

If the waters were so valuable, a question naturally arose: Could one not only take the waters at the spa but, quite literally, take the waters home with you, as well?

If there is a dollar to be made, clever people will figure it out. The business plan of holy wells one thousand years earlier played out yet again. Just as enterprising priests in the eighth and ninth centuries had transformed local monasteries near popular springs into wealthy abbeys, so, too, did local businessmen in the eighteenth and nineteenth centuries transform spa towns into resort destinations. And, of particular importance for our story, just as the holy sites created specially branded flasks to sell water from holy wells to the pilgrims, so, too, did spas develop a vigorous trade in bottled mineral waters.

Until well into the 1800s, bottled water was uncommon except for the wealthy. Produced by hand and in small quantities, the glass and stoneware bottles were sealed by porcelain or cork. Tradition holds that Benjamin Franklin was responsible for the first imported bottled waters to America: impressed by the spring water during his service as ambassador to France during the American Revolution, he arranged for the shipment of a supply to Philadelphia upon his return, delighting his dining companions with French wine *and* French water.

By the middle of the nineteenth century, however, bottled water was becoming available to the average consumer. In 1845, Poland Spring sold its first bottled water in a three-gallon clay jug. Vittel bottled its waters for sale in 1855, Deer Park followed in 1873, and Arrowhead in 1894. Rapid advances in bottling technology and industrial processes allowed large-scale production of bottled water that remained safe to drink for long periods of time far from its original source. Vichy bottles were popular in French colonies. The German water Appollinaris became a favorite not only in Britain but in the American West, as well, where it was offered on railroad cars. The famed French scientist Louis Pasteur would order cases of his cherished Badoit water ten at a time.

The rapid growth of the bottled water market can be attributed to a number of fortunate events. Bottling technology was one, of course, but the growth of railroads also played a role. Dependable rail lines to spa towns brought more people to spas, which increased the interest in and knowledge of their waters. Freight rail made transport of heavy bottles feasible and affordable. For the first time, large amounts of bottled mineral water could be transported far distances to people who had enjoyed the waters at their origin or, even more important, had never even visited there at all. For these customers, marketing was critical, and nowhere is this more evident than in the rise of the most famous pedigree of bottled water, Perrier.

The carbonated waters from the town of Vergèze, close to Nimes in southern France, have been celebrated since Roman times. The general of elephant fame, Hannibal, is reputed to have enjoyed the spring's waters when marching to Rome in 218 BC.

In 1863, the French emperor, Napoleon III, granted Dr. Alphonse Granier, former mayor of Vergèze, permission to sell waters from the local spring that formerly had been free for the taking. Granier's business venture offered not only bottled water but also showers, mud baths, and "inhalations" of the waters. His first slogan was "The Princess of Table Waters." Granier hired Louis Perrier, a young doctor interested in the use of hydrotherapy to treat arthritis, to help run the spa. Three decades later, Perrier and a group of financial supporters recognized the market potential of its waters and purchased the spring, increasing the bottling operations. Seeking additional capital, Perrier joined forces with a young Englishman, Saint-John Harmsworth, who had been impressed with the waters while traveling in France. Harmsworth's family had made a fortune in the newspaper business, publishing the London *Daily Mail* and *Daily Telegraph*. Seeking to create his own success, Harmsworth sold his interests in the family business and bought the spring outright.

Harmsworth was paralyzed below the waist, the victim of what must have been one of the very first car accidents. He chose to keep the Perrier name but create a new brand image for what he now called "The Champagne of Bottled Waters." His inspiration for the unique Perrier bottles supposedly came from the Indian clubs he used in physical therapy. Under Harmsworth's management, sales by his new Compagnie de la Source Perrier rocketed, reaching eighteen million bottles by the 1930s. Ironically, his French spring water was most popular in the British Empire, where, it was said, there was no substitute for Perrier when mixing whisky.

Perrier was the first of many such success stories to come. One of the most popular Italian bottled waters of the time was Ferrarelle. As with Perrier, Ferrarelle was marketed through two different but complementary strategies. Relying on its origins as therapeutic waters, Ferrarelle publicity emphasized its medicinal properties. An early ad declared, "Ferrarelle battles stomach problems. It is unique, unsurpassable and unmistakable. If you have stomach problems but do not try this water, you deprive yourself of the greatest of fortunes, your health." This strategy targeted the traditional market of medicinal waters for sale in pharmacies.

The other market, new but growing, was intended for the table. As Perrier's "Princess of Table Waters" branding made clear, bottled water was making its way to the dining room. Thus a 1904 ad praised Ferrarelle as "a sole superior quality table water. . . . It is cold, clear, completely colorless and odor free, effervescent, fresh-tasting, pleasant, acidic, bubbly." As bottled waters became commonplace at restaurants and dinner tables across Europe, discriminating diners favored particular waters' sparkling qualities and taste. And it was a growing market. France alone had 188 brands, and Germany more than 300 brands of bottled water.

In much of America, by contrast, the idea of drinking bottled water for pleasure would have seemed as odd as serving hay for the salad course. The primary market was medicinal. What fledgling market there had been for quenching thirst was dealt a severe blow by the introduction of chlorine into municipal water systems in the 1920s. The very idea of chlorination, safe water from a tap, was revolutionary and came to be seen as more stylish than bottled waters—quite an irony, given the trendy image of bottle water compared to boring tap water seventy years later.

Through most of the 1900s, while local brands enjoyed a loyal customer base, there were only two major markets in America for bottled water: the traditional therapeutic trade in pharmacies and five-gallon office water jugs. The idea of hanging out at the office water cooler has fallen out of popular usage recently, but for decades it was the central meeting point for workplace gossip. The consumer market for bottles of water, though, remained tiny.

THE ORIGIN OF THE MODERN MARKET THAT WE KNOW TODAY, where bottled water slugs toe-to-toe with soft drinks as America's favorite beverage, dates to 1976 and the transatlantic marketing launch of Perrier. The challenge was clear. As Kim Jeffery, the

CEO of Nestlé Waters North America, later described, back in the 1970s Perrier was basically unknown: "People didn't know whether to put it in their lawn mower or drink it." Seeking to move from a small number of fancy restaurants to mass market, Perrier used the largest advertising budget ever by a bottled water company to position its product as a healthy and chic drink. The face of the campaign was the famed actor and director Orson Welles. Rotund and deep-voiced, Welles rhapsodized about a special site in the south of France, where "there is a spring and its name is Perrier." Moving beyond its elitist image, Perrier's branding emphasized the healthy aspects of its product. It sponsored the New York City Marathon in 1979, where six thousand runners crossed the line in Perrier T-shirts.

Lucky timing proved crucial to Perrier's success. Its marketing campaign coincided with the unexpected explosion of interest in fitness. Aerobics classes were packed with tight-fitting leotards and pounding music. Jim Fixx's simply titled book *The Complete Book of Running* topped the best-seller list for an improbable eleven weeks. The health craze sweeping the nation fit perfectly Perrier's positioning as a classy alternative to sugar-filled, fattening soda. The brand's growth was rapid—from a mere half a million bottles in 1974 to 157 million in 1989, an increase of more than three-hundred-fold. In short order, Perrier grew synonymous with bottled water, holding prime place in an extremely fragmented market.

Other bottled water companies followed Perrier's example. As San Pellegrino's U.S. manager later described, "That was what everyone else was doing, advertising that [mineral water] is a healthy thing to drink, as opposed to a soft drink. The category had an exercise and fitness orientation." As with Perrier, there was a dual strategy. San Pellegrino sought to use its position on restaurant menus as branding. Waiters were instructed not only to pour water in glasses but also to keep the bottle and its label on the table. San Pellegrino did not have a big advertising budget, so they used the dining experience as a marketing opportunity—"putting our liter bottle package on the table, handling it like a fine wine [would] enhance consumer awareness." By the end of the 1980s, bottled water had become a mass-market beverage seen as both healthy and chic, and the best seemed yet to come.

In February 1990, however, an unexpected test result threatened the very future of Perrier and the bottled water industry. A lab in North Carolina had decided to use Perrier as a control for other samples, assuming its purity would provide a baseline for testing the pollution of other water sources. After all, Perrier's brand identity was its pure spring in that special place in France, virgin and unpolluted. To the lab technicians' surprise, they found traces of the cancer-causing chemical benzene in the Perrier samples. Additional tests by the U.S. Food and Drug Administration confirmed benzene levels in some bottles up to four times the maximum contaminant level allowed in public drinking water supplies.

Perrier's first responses blamed the contamination on U.S. bottling procedures rather than the source. Ultimately, though, to reassure its customers it recalled seventy million bottles and was off market shelves for eleven weeks. The *New York Times* reported that, when told of the recall, André Soltner, owner of the trendy Lutèce restaurant in Manhattan, exclaimed, "Oh, my God," followed soon after by the optimistic observation, "Maybe we'll sell some wine now." Perrier's recall may have saved the brand and the market. The intense media coverage had the unexpected effect of *increasing* interest in the bottled water market. While Perrier's sales took a massive hit, the sector redoubled its dramatic climb. The climb this time, however, was fueled not by clever marketing by a small foreign company but by the brute power of multinational corporate giants.

The success of Perrier was carefully followed in boardrooms, and the opportunity for growth in the U.S. market was too good to pass up. The Swiss food and beverage company Nestlé purchased the Perrier brand in 1992. Two years later, PepsiCo entered the bottled water market. In 1997, within months of each other, Pepsi launched the Aquafina brand and the Coca-Cola Company launched Dasani. Backed by their powerful network of distributors and retailers throughout the country, Dasani and Aquafina quickly gained market share and are currently the two leading brands in the country. Bolstered by Perrier, Nestlé remains the largest global player in bottled water, closely trailed by Danone, which sells brands such as Evian and Badoit, the favored drink of Louis Pasteur a century ago.

The strategy and marketing of bottled water have been stunningly effective. Consider that, across America, people are opening about 1,500 bottles of water *every second*. Here are some illuminating statistics:

- Over the past two decades, the bottled water market has been the fastest-growing drinks segment in the world.
- Three hundred million gallons of bottled water were sold in the 1970s. That figure has grown thirtyfold, to roughly nine billion gallons sold annually.
- More than half of Americans drink bottled water and more than one-third do so more than once a week. The average American drinks thirty gallons of bottled water per year, mostly from single-serve plastic bottles.
- More than 50 percent of students polled at the University of California, Santa Barbara, said they rarely or never drink tap water.

These trends have translated directly into company profits. Whether pumped from a spring or purchased from the municipal water authority, the raw material for producing bottled water is cheap—costing anywhere from 240 to 10,000 times less than the final sales price in a bottle. Put another way, the $1.50 you pay for 16 ounces of Dasani would buy about 1,000 gallons of tap water in many cities. This translates to costing Pepsi about $0.0002 for the basic raw material in each bottle. Can you imagine paying such a markup for any other consumer product? Could I interest you in a $10,000 sandwich?

Of course, the consumer is also paying for the treatment, packaging, shipping, marketing, and other expenses, but there's no hiding the fact that bottled water provides a tidy profit margin. Bottled water often has the highest markup on a restaurant menu. It's no coincidence that the trade publication *Hotel Online Special Report* advised that "as we all know, the profit margin with bottled water is astronomical. As such, every restaurant should be offering it to their guests, all the time." So don't act surprised when the first thing you are asked after sitting down at a restaurant is whether you would like bottled water or tap or, better yet, when the waiter brings bottled water to the table without asking and then makes you feel gauche for requesting tap water instead.

With the cost of bottling equipment around $100,000, this is an easy market to enter if you can find the right marketing angle and distribution network. As the bottled water marketing manager for Nestlé complained, "We have what we call the 'San Pretendos,' the little regional guys that are just nipping at you all the time with their regional programs." And there are plenty of folks trying to enter much smaller niche markets, as well. With choices such as K9 Quencher and Woof Water, what is a concerned dog owner to do? As Bill Fels, the entrepreneur behind Pet Refresh, described, "My thought was that if your water tastes bad to you, how does it taste to your pet? And how healthy is it?" He may have a point, and it sure beats drinking out of the toilet. But he may be laughing all the way to the bank if he can make inroads to the more than $30 billion a year spent by pet owners. And there are countless other niche market opportunities out there. Yale University and other fine schools provide their own branded bottles on campus.

The growth of bottled water, both in mass and niche markets, truly is impressive. In a mere three decades, a product that would have seemed as ludicrous to most people as bottled air now battles the iconic Coke and Pepsi for bragging rights as the dominant commercial beverage in the United States. Surely, though, this was not an ascent without wires. Now, let's take a closer look at this commercial juggernaut and the important questions it implies. First and foremost, why are so many people buying so much bottled water? Is bottled water really better for you than tap water? And should we feel guilty about buying this stuff?

AS THE CHAIRMAN OF THE BOARD OF PERRIER ONCE INCAUTIOUSLY observed, "It struck me . . . . that all you had to do is take the water out of the ground and then sell it for more than the price of wine, milk, or, for that matter, oil." And he wasn't exaggerating. A moment's reflection, though, suggests two big assumptions in his observation. The first is that consumers will want to buy bottled water rather than tap water or another beverage. The second is that they will pay a premium. Neither is self-evident. Indeed, if he had said the same thing about dirt, he would sound like an idiot.

In some respects, selling bottled water is the ultimate marketing challenge because, well, it's water in a bottle. And if water is water, then why should consumers choose one brand over another? In this sense, bottled water is no different than any other generic commodity, and the only real difference among brands should be price or marketing. But low price clearly is not seen as a competitive advantage; indeed, the opposite is true. Hence, it's no surprise to see the emphasis on branding. Names such as Arctic Falls, Arctic Spring, and Glacier all suggest pure snow-fed waters; images of mountain peaks and remote places such as Fiji and Poland Spring reinforce the notion of clean water. These are all culturally recognizable references.

Surprisingly, though, one successful marketing strategy has been to use a *meaningless* name. Unlike Perrier or Badoit, the brands of Dasani and Aquafina are not named for spring waters, much less from a specific location. Instead, Coke and Pepsi take tap water; run it through a series of fine filters to remove minerals and bacteria, ultraviolet and ozonation treatments to kill any remaining organisms, and reverse osmosis to remove any remaining materials; and then add minerals (nicknamed "pixie dust") back in because all the taste has been removed. Just as the taste of Coke is the same regardless of where it is bottled, Aquafina, Dasani, Pure Life, and others have become the water equivalent to the McDonald's french fry—identical in consistency and taste no matter where you buy it.

The irony is stunning. America's leading bottled waters have moved as far as possible from the distinctive aspects of spring waters that made them attractive in the first place. Badoit and Evian became famous precisely because the water *came from* Badoit and Evian, each with its particular taste and therapeutic qualities. The Coke, Pepsi, and other major brand waters, by contrast, bear meaningless names that have evolved through focus group selection and that are intentionally tasteless. Not that they taste bad. The companies simply try to make their waters as indistinctive as possible, at least in terms of taste. Aquafina's label features a panoramic mountain range, presumably to suggest the glacier quality of its water. Yet you'll have to look hard to find the snowcapped peaks closest to Ayer, Massachusetts (about two thousand miles away, in fact), one of the eleven or so major municipal water sources for Aquafina's water. Not, of course, that any ordinary consumer could figure out the water's origin from looking at the label (until a few years ago, when Pepsi changed its labeling to state that it came from public water sources).

This strategy has carried over to the spring water brands, as well. To carry the name "spring water," federal regulations require the water to be drawn from an underground aquifer that flows naturally to the surface. Poland Spring doesn't wait, drawing its bottling water to the surface using a borehole drilled straight into the aquifer. But the success of Perrier and its subsequent owner, Nestlé, in managing Poland Spring's growth to more than $600 million in sales led to a problem. The spring simply couldn't provide enough water to meet the demand. As Peter Gleick describes, to keep the spring water label the company needed to find more spring waters somewhere else. As a result, "Poland Spring is no longer a 'source' but a 'brand.' The water in the bottle might come from Poland Spring, or it might come from Clear Spring, Evergreen Spring, Spruce Spring, Garden Spring, Bradford Spring, or White Cedar Spring—other Maine water sources owned by Nestlé Waters North America. There is no way to know. And Nestlé isn't saying."

So a lot of thought goes into the product names, but why are people buying the product? Some critics of bottled water place great emphasis on the strategy of "manufactured demand." A clever video,

"The Story of Bottled Water," distributed by the consumer group Food & Water Watch puts it this way: "Imagine you're in charge of a bottled water company. Since people aren't lining up to trade their hard-earned money for your unnecessary product, you make them feel scared and insecure if they don't have it. And that's exactly what the bottled water industry did." Without effective marketing campaigns, the argument goes, there would not be a market. It's no coincidence, many have observed, that "Evian" spelled backward is "naive."

Attributing the market's rise solely to effective marketing, though, doesn't hold water, if you'll excuse the pun. Companies would sell Pet Rocks, if they could—and that worked for a while—but there's a limit to what marketing alone can achieve. For the type of multidecade sustained growth we have seen with bottled water, it needs to meet more than just a manufactured need. So what else explains the demand?

A series of polls over the years have asked why people drink bottled water. They all come up with the same basic explanations—convenience, style, taste, fitness and health concerns—all credible though, as we will see below, some more legitimate than others.

Convenience

Pervasive store displays and vending machines clearly make buying a bottle of water convenient for quenching thirst, as does the steady demise of drinking fountains. The main explanation behind the convenient attraction of bottled water, though, lies in the often-overlooked PET bottle. Polyethylene terephthalate plastic is ideally suited for holding beverages. It is cheap, light, and commonplace, and does not leach into the liquid it contains. The bottle was introduced in the soft drink market in 1977 but not in the bottled water market until 1990. As the CEO of Nestlé Waters North America later observed, "It revolutionized our industry because now people could get bottled water in the same format they were getting soft drinks in." Consumers now had an easy choice in the convenience store to buy a bottle of juice, soda, or water, all in the same packaging. Water looked like it belonged on the store shelf.

Style

As *Time* magazine presciently declared back in 1985, "Water snobbery has replaced wine snobbery as the latest noon-hour recreation. People order their eau by brand name, as they once did Scotch. The fastidious will not take it on the rocks, because ice bruises the bubbles." Trendy rock stars and supermodels have long had their favorite brand in hand. Jack Nicholson made waves twenty years ago when he snuck a bottle of Evian into the no-beverages section of the Academy Awards. As bottled water has become increasingly mainstream, the chic factor has diminished some, but only some. There are still plenty of stylish bottles and names selling at a premium. While denouncing the environmental impacts of Fiji Water, the progressive magazine *Mother Jones* could not help but admiringly admit that the company has managed to position its product "squarely at the nexus of pop-culture glamour and progressive politics." Two can play at this game, however, and the ever-stylish government authorities in Paris have enlisted the help of Pierre Cardin to promote the use of tap water by designing a water carafe that neatly fits on a refrigerator door. So far, they've distributed thirty thousand for free.

A number of fancy restaurants have taken advantage of the bottled water cachet with the service of a tableside "water sommelier" who can provide counsel to diners looking for just the right choice of bottled water to match the dish and mood. As the noted connoisseur Arthur von Wiesenberger has counseled, when drinking bottled water, ask yourself whether it has "a slow, medium bead, or random bead, or a profuse, fast bead. Is it crisp? Bubbly? Slippery on the palate? Alkaline or slightly acidic on the tongue? Well-balanced? Refreshing? Can it claim a full, elegant mousse, a sharp spritz, a cheerful entry followed by a clean refreshing finish?" This is all wonderfully pretentious, of course, but also accurate. Because of their mineral content, many bottled waters do offer different tastes and carbonation.

Taste

Indeed, taste is a common explanation for buying bottled water. This surely is a concern in some parts of the country where local geology provides tap water with strong odors and bottled water is clearly preferable. Despite claims of caring about taste, though, there is little evidence this really matters to most consumers. Blind taste tests continue to show not only that most people cannot distinguish among bottled waters, but also that they can't even distinguish between bottled and tap water. This has been the case on popular shows such as ABC's *20/20* and *Good Morning America*. New York City tap water routinely wins blind taste tests against bottled water. Nor should this be surprising. After all, as described above, Dasani, Aquafina, and other mass-market bottled waters are intentionally designed for a bland, flat taste. This could not be further from the view in Europe, where they drink particular brands precisely because of where they come from and how they taste.

Ever wonder why it is so hard to order water with ice in Europe? It's not snobbery. Cold suppresses our tongue's ability to taste minerals in water. This only matters, of course, if you care about taste in the first place. For most people, the sort of taste that really matters is more the taste in choosing a particular brand than the taste on the tongue.

Fitness and Health

Because bottled water has been marketed so successfully in vending machines and display cases alongside sodas and sports drinks, health-conscious consumers concerned about their waistlines can easily compare drinks filled with sugar, caffeine, and sweeteners to water, which has none of these. Perrier's initial success was largely due to its branding as a healthy alternative to soda and juice, and this remains an effective strategy. As an aside, though, it is revealing that some have attributed the rise in tooth cavities to the growing use of nonfluoridated bottled water.

The bigger health concern, and by far the most controversial, comes when comparing bottled water with tap water. While bottled water executives will loudly argue that their competition is soft drinks and juices, there's a good deal more to the story. Consider, for example, some of the slogans of Fiji Water ("The Label Says Fiji

Because It's Not Bottled in *Cleveland*") or Poland Spring ("Sip smarter. Live Longer."). Susan Wellington, head of Quaker Oats' beverage division, could not have been clearer when she vowed, "When we're done, tap water will be relegated to showers and washing dishes." Fighting words, indeed. In fact, she seems to be winning. Personal drinking habits clearly are changing. Compared to 1980, the average American drinks twenty-five gallons more bottled water, seventeen gallons more soft drinks, and thirty-six gallons *less* tap water.

And what about reasons to avoid bottled water? While it may seem obvious that bottled water is safer than tap water—that Fiji Water, of course, is cleaner than Cleveland tap water—the simple fact is that we don't know. And there are reasons to think that in some cases bottled water is less safe. One thing is certain: Bottled water is less stringently regulated than tap water.

While tap and bottled water are subject to the standards set by the Safe Drinking Water Act, the U.S. Environmental Protection Agency (EPA) regulates tap water but bottled water is regulated as a food product by the Food and Drug Administration (FDA). As a result, the monitoring and inspection requirements for bottled water are, in practice, a good deal weaker than those for tap water. If contaminants are found in tap water, which is tested daily, the water utility must quickly inform the public. If contaminants are found in bottled water, which is tested weekly, manufacturers must remove or reduce the contamination but there is no similar requirement to notify the public. Perhaps most important, FDA regulations only apply to goods in interstate commerce, i.e., traded across state lines. Yet anywhere from 60 to 70 percent of bottled water never enters into interstate commerce. As a result, two-thirds or more of bottled water passes is effectively exempt from federal regulation.

This means it is subject to state regulation, which wouldn't be a problem if states had strict regulations and well-funded inspection and enforcement teams. But they don't. Ten states do not regulate bottled water at all. Massachusetts has some of the strongest regulatory requirements in place, yet it dedicates only one-quarter of one person per year to supervise bottled water in the state. A study by Co-op America found that forty-three states fund one or fewer officials to supervise bottled water. Contrast the frequency and thoroughness of the inspections these people could possibly conduct with the fact that New York City tests its tap water more than 330,000 times every year. Moreover, the potential fines for violating the bottled water rules are small—just $100 for a first offense and $500 for subsequent offenses in Massachusetts, if fines are ever levied in the first place. How do states justify this scant dedication of resources to ensure the safety of bottled water? Quite simply, they have other important food safety concerns and only so much money in their budget.

The nutritional label on a bottle of water suggests the complete lack of anything unhealthy—no fat, no cholesterol, no carbohydrates. What we don't see, however, is what we ought to care about and information that, in fact, is mandated for public water sources—the levels of chlorine, coliform bacteria, trihalomethanes, nitrates, turbidity, etc. Requiring the use of a standard nutrition label for bottled water amounts to a sin of omission. All of the "0 percent" daily values tell us precisely 0 percent about the water's specific source, mineral composition, and quality.

Bottled water manufacturers have sought to fill this regulatory gap through private certification. The industry's trade association, the International Bottled Water Association, has created a set of inspection standards that all members must satisfy. These include submission of daily samples for independent laboratory testing and surprise inspections by a third party. The trade association covers 85 percent of the bottled water sold in the United States, so this might well be sufficient to ensure product safety. Studies of what is actually on the market, though, give one pause.

A study in the *Archives of Family Medicine* compared fifty-seven samples of bottled water in Cleveland with the local tap water. While thirty-nine of the samples were cleaner than the tap water, fifteen bottles (almost 25 percent) contained higher bacteria levels. So much for Fiji's boast that it wasn't bottled in Cleveland.

The study concluded that the "use of bottled water on the assumption of purity can be misguided." A four-year study by the environmental group NRDC of more than a thousand bottles of water from more than a hundred different brands concluded that while most of the bottled water was fine, overall quality was "spotty." About one-third of the bottles contained arsenic and other carcinogenic compounds that, in some cases, exceeded state or industry standards. A report by the California state assembly similarly found cases of bottled water that contained excessive arsenic, benzene, chloroform, nitrates, and other nasty compounds. Analysis of eighty bottled water samples gathered by the Kansas Department of Health and Environment found levels of chlorine, fluoride, sodium, nitrites, chloroform, arsenic, and lead, among other compounds. The FDA does not require disclosure on the label for any of these materials.

To be fair, similar analysis of tap water might also reveal instances of nasty compounds in excess of regulated standards. Indeed, as described previously, there are very real problems with our drinking water infrastructure—from treatment plants badly in need of upgrades to spotty enforcement to leaking or contaminated pipes. The key difference, however, is that we require extensive testing and recordkeeping for tap water on a regular basis precisely because we want to ensure the safety of our tap water. We can't know it's unsafe if we don't look.

Yet the same is not true for bottled water. Much of it may in fact be cleaner than tap water and perhaps safer to drink, but we have no way of really knowing. Compared to tap water, bottled water is subject to weaker regulations, much less frequent monitoring, largely meaningless labeling, and broad exemptions. And the few large studies that have been conducted suggest there are plenty of examples where bottled water is more contaminated than tap water, sometimes significantly so. Assuming bottled water is safer than tap water may make us feel better, but there is little reason to think this is necessarily so.

STILL, IT IS NOT CONCERNS OVER WATER PURITY THAT HAVE STARTED to turn the tide against bottled water but rather the environmental impacts. While PET bottles are well suited for storing water and cheap to make, they come at a cost. Resource consumption is one concern. It takes three to four liters of water to make a liter PET bottle. While hard to imagine, PET bottles are generally made out of petroleum, roughly one ounce for every liter bottle. What bothers most consumers, though, are the waste issues. The Container Recycling Institute estimates that thirty million bottles are discarded daily in trash cans (later taking up landfill space or burning in incinerators) or simply dropped and forgotten as unsightly litter. California receives about one billion water bottles in its trash every year.

Seeking to counter these concerns, Pepsi's Aquafina launched in 2009 the Eco-Fina bottle, which it claimed was the lightest bottle on the market, using 50 percent less plastic than the liter bottle sold in 2002. As Robert Le Bras-Brown, Pepsi's vice president of packing innovation and development, boasted at the time, "Consumer research confirms that we achieved our desired objective, which was a 'sustainable design trifecta'—a bottle that looks better, functions better, and is better for the environment."

It is true that PET bottles are recyclable (hence the number 1 on many bottles to show the recycling code). Plastic recyclate enjoys a second life in mattresses, fleece jackets, and other popular products. But few bottles actually are recycled. The overall recycling rate for plastic is 25 percent, and water bottles fall well below that. The California Department of Conservation estimates that only 16 percent of PET water bottles are recycled. This is not surprising when one realizes that water bottles are exempted from most bottle legislation. After a long battle, New York state extended its deposit requirement to water in 2009, making it just the sixth state to do so.

Yet energy concerns go beyond the packaging. It takes energy to filter and purify the water, package and transport it from source to store, and chill it at the point of sale, not to mention the energy required for transporting and recycling the bottles that are collected. It goes without saying that drinking a bottle of Fiji Water, shipped from halfway around the world, results in a lot more greenhouse gas emissions than filling a glass from the tap in the other room. The NRDC has calculated that bottled water imports from France, Italy, and Fiji to California account for 9,700 tons of carbon dioxide, the equivalent of 1,700 cars on the road for a year.

To counter this charge, Fiji Water launched a major campaign to burnish its environmental credentials. Its website lists a series of initiatives, including dedicating 1 percent of its profits to environmental causes, partnering with Conservation International for forest restoration projects, and claiming "carbon negative" status by purchasing greenhouse gas emission offsets for 120 percent of its emissions. The public radio program *Marketplace*, however, gave Fiji Water top billing in its 2008 "Greenwashes of the Year" list. In the reporters' view, a pig is still a pig whether it wears lipstick or not.

Finally, as we saw in the story of McCloud, there are battles underway around the world over water withdrawals from local aquifers. Until recently, concern over the environmental impacts of bottled water was limited to communities directly affected by the bottling operations and a handful of environmental and consumer groups. A broader-based coalition, though, is starting to take shape. At the vanguard have been religious groups. Given the historic origins of bottled water in the holy relics market, perhaps this is fitting.

In 2006, the General Council of the United Church of Canada declared that congregations should avoid purchasing bottled water where possible. Soon after, the National Coalition of American Nuns similarly voiced disapproval of the bottled water culture promoted by multinational corporations and urged its members to avoid buying bottled water "unless absolute necessity requires such a purchase." As we'll see later, much of this opposition goes beyond selling bottled water to the more fundamental idea of privatizing the delivery and sale of water at all.

An increasing number of "locavore" restaurants have taken stands against bottled water, as well. The high priestess of the local food movement, Alice Waters, has barred the sale of commercial bottled water from Chez Panisse, her restaurant in Berkeley, California. A few other leading restaurants, such as Del Posto in New York and Poggio in San Francisco, have taken similar actions. Given the markup on bottled water, though, it's not clear whether this will be widely adopted. As Geoffrey Zakarian, the chef and owner of the restaurant Country in New York City, bluntly put it, "Alice is very commendable and extraordinary, and we look to her, but I think she gets carried away sometimes. . . . You have to make a profit."

Money talks, and the more significant threat is coming not from restaurants but from institutional purchasers, particularly government purchasers. In a time of tight and shrinking budgets, a number of mayors and city councils have looked at their bottled water bills and identified a cost-cutting opportunity they can feel good about. Thus St. Louis, Vancouver, Toronto, San Francisco, and other cities have reduced or outright banned the use of public funds to purchase bottled water. The mayor of Salt Lake City, Rocky Anderson, went so far as to call bottled water "the greatest marketing scam of all time." It makes a nice sound bite, and the potential savings can be significant. At least twenty universities, such as Penn State and Washington University, have similarly restricted purchases of bottled water as part of a "Take Back the Tap" campaign. Taken together, these initiatives and changing attitudes may be having an impact. Following years of double-digit market growth, since 2009 sales of bottled water have flattened while the water filter and reusable container markets are taking off.

IN THE FINAL ANALYSIS, BOTTLED WATER ACTS AS A PROVOCATIVE mirror reflecting back on us. Attitudes run the spectrum. Strong opponents to the sale of water would go thirsty before buying the offensive product. Others simply regard bottled water as a commercial product no different than Coke or Pepsi. But there are many consumers, indeed a growing number, that feel conflicted. There is no simple response to put them at ease.

We seem to have a particular blind spot when it comes to bottled water. The environmental impacts surely give cause for concern, but that can't be the whole story. Soft drinks pose almost identical concerns—packaging in PET bottles, energy impacts from transportation and cooling, huge appetites for extracted groundwater—yet the only major backlash or worry in this segment is over obesity.

Nor, on the flip side, can the strong demand for bottled water simply be concern over the quality of our tap water. The very same people who swear by the safety of bottled water don't give a second thought to the ice cubes they drop in their glasses or the water they use to boil pasta or make soup. Yet this water that comes straight out of the faucet seems so harmful when poured in a glass.

For many, bottled water strikes a dissonant chord, yet identifying the particular wrong note is hard to do. Is it that bottled water stands as an embarrassing symbol of our throwaway culture, that we are just too lazy to fill a reusable water bottle or drink from the tap? Does it lay bare our increasing distrust of institutions and their ability to protect our health? Does it encapsulate our fear that the public goods we have taken for granted are being sold out to the highest bidders?

Some can take solace that the University of Central Florida did eventually decide to install fifty water fountains in its football stadium. And somehow this seems reasonable. Yet it seems unreasonable to demand that a convenience store provide a water fountain beside its stock of bottled water. Why do we have such different intuitions for what, on their face, seem similar situations of public water provision in private spaces?

In the end, perhaps bottled water remains troublesome precisely because it symbolizes so starkly the privatization, the creation of a marketable product, of something that just feels should be ours by right.

SHOULD RESTAURANTS SERVE BOTTLED WATER DURING A DROUGHT?

The Piedmont region of North Carolina experienced a serious drought from 2007 to 2008. During this time, a number of higher-end restaurants in the region stopped serving tap water. As a waiter patiently explained to a patron one night, "We are doing our part by serving you bottled water at cost." He was not amused when the diner suggested the restaurant would serve its part even better if it put stones in the holding tank of its toilet. Nor was this restaurant alone. A number of New York City's trendiest restaurants, such as Lure, Park Avalon, and Blue Fin, served bottled water instead of tap water during the city's 2002 drought, and often not at cost. Many Atlanta restaurants did the same in its drought of 2007. So who was right, the waiter or the customer?

The more cynical, perhaps, might suggest that altruism is less important here than greed, since bottled water represents one of the highest-margin items on a restaurant menu. But let's assume the best in our restaurateurs and their well-intentioned efforts to play their part in reducing water usage in times of drought. If their goal is to minimize water use, is serving bottled water instead of tap water worthwhile?

In terms of pure numbers, banning tap water is more symbolic than effective. Assuming a restaurant with twenty-five tables that turn over twice in an evening, an average of three diners per table, and six glasses of water per group (i.e., each diner's glass is refilled once in addition to beer, wine, and soda), then the restaurant saves about fifty-six gallons of water. Not bad—about the water used to fill a large bathtub. But they would be better served by taking pasta off the menu (thereby saving the gallons needed to boil noodles); using disposable plates, cups, and cutlery (saving even more gallons needed for the dishwasher); or, as was brazenly suggested, putting stones in the toilet holding tank (saving gallons from flushing). A low-flush toilet would be even better, since that can save up to four gallons per flush compared to older, traditional bowls. While glasses of drinking water do add up and every little bit helps, there are other measures, both more and less obvious, that would achieve even greater savings.

This is not to say that the restaurant's gesture is meaningless. Far from it. Beyond the diners' feel-good glow from easy self-denial for a worthwhile cause, refusing to serve tap water can be an effective means to highlight the seriousness of the drought. This uses conspicuous consumption as a teachable moment. Their consciousness raised, diners may think twice about how they use water at home. Perhaps this will lead to taking shorter showers instead of baths, not hosing down the driveway, and modifying other personal behaviors that consume large amounts of water during times of drought. It appears the waiter and diner are both right.

7

Need Versus Greed

HIGH IN THE ANDES, THE BOLIVIAN CITY OF COCHABAMBA rests in a fertile valley astride the banks of the Rocha River. Bolivia is the poorest country in South America. Two-thirds of its population lives below the poverty line. The simplest things can be difficult and, as in many developing countries, more than 40 percent of Cochabamba's residents lack access to a water faucet. And even those who do get piped water cannot depend on reliable service. The poor often live in squatter settlements on the outskirts of town, relying for their drinking and domestic water supplies on private vendors. In a cruel irony, the poorest end up paying more for their water than wealthier citizens connected to the city's water mains. Sometimes up to ten times more.

As part of a nationwide project to improve city services, the government of Bolivia launched a major privatization reform effort in the late 1990s. Guided by financial institutions such as the International Monetary Fund and the World Bank, the government actively sought out private investors to manage Cochabamba's water and sewage services. Bringing in companies to run the systems, it was widely argued, would bring multiple benefits. Private capital would improve the water supply system infrastructure and delivery. Private management would ensure greater efficiencies. And the market would ensure increased attention to customer needs.

In the end, a forty-year concession for water and wastewater services in Cochabamba was granted to a private consortium.

Headed by the giant international construction company Bechtel, the group was known as Aguas del Tunari. In the national law passed to facilitate this transaction, water was declared the property of the state, available for licensing to private companies for distribution.

Aguas del Tunari immediately set about laying new pipe, as well as digging the new reservoir and hydroelectric dam required by local politicians as part of the deal. To cover its costs, the company raised the price of water and waste services charged to consumers. Just how much the prices went up remains disputed. Some residents claimed they had to spend more than 20 percent of their household income on water alone.

What is not in dispute is that the public's reaction was swift. Just four months after the privatization scheme commenced in 2000, protests began. These soon mushroomed into street demonstrations and violence. In the face of property damage approaching twenty million dollars, dozens of injuries, and mass unrest, the government terminated the privatization concession. The city has since taken back control over the water supply system in Cochabamba. The poorest still buy their water from vendors.

During the heady days of protest, grassroots organizations met and issued a common statement to the press. They called it the Cochabamba Declaration, and their view of the conflict was clear. Drinking water should not be a market commodity. They were fighting for a basic, inalienable entitlement. As the Declaration pronounced:

> Water is a fundamental human right and a public trust to be guarded by all levels of government, therefore, it should not be commodified, privatized or traded for commercial purposes.

In their eyes, selling the concession to Aguas del Tunari had been a fundamental breach of the government's responsibility to safeguard the public trust.

The ringing prose from Cochabamba was a response not only to the politicians of Bolivia but to the international community, as well. It could not have contrasted more starkly with the recommendations of water experts at the International Conference on Water and the Environment held a few years earlier in Dublin, Ireland. Known as the Dublin Statement on Water and Sustainable Development, the consensus statement had declared in 1992 that "water has an economic value in all its competing uses and should be recognized as an economic good."

As the saga of McCloud suggested, Cochabamba's conflict over who should control water was not a unique event. Similar protests have played out in Paraguay, South Africa, the Philippines, and elsewhere. Cochabamba, however, remains the best-known example and has become the rallying point for opponents of water supply privatization in developing countries. It serves as a perfect morality play. Rights versus markets. Human need versus corporate greed.

The popular recounting of Cochabamba and its fiery Declaration fit neatly into the rhetoric of the globalization debates, as does the Dublin Statement. Rights-based and market-based access to drinking water are depicted as antithetical, while arguments revolve over whether access to water should be publicly or privately managed. Indeed, much of the popular discourse over drinking water has revolved around morality tales. Venal transnational companies will commodify our water, warn antiglobalization bards, while free marketeers calmly reassure us that savior transnational companies bring cleaner water and local investment.

Each version clearly features good guys and bad guys. At their core, they raise questions over the very nature of drinking water—whether it should be treated as a basic human right or tradable commodity. And these stories have shown a striking persistence despite the fact that they're neither particularly accurate nor helpful.

IF THE FACILE DICHOTOMY OF RIGHTS VERSUS MARKETS AND PUBLIC versus private obscures more than clarifies, then how should we think about this conflict? As a first step, we need to better understand the problem that everyone acknowledges they are trying to solve.

To appreciate the breadth of the drinking water problem at the global scale, we must consciously step outside our daily experience. In developed countries, we do not think much about drinking water on a daily basis. It is plentiful, safe, and easily available. Nor do we often consider the quality or quantity of drinking water. We simply turn the tap or open a bottle of water. Most of us do not know the source of our water, and do not particularly care to know. Water supply is seen as a government or corporate responsibility, not an individual concern.

In much of the world, by contrast, neither water quality nor quantity can be assumed. Over one billion people, almost exclusively in the global South, do not have access to even a basic water supply. Well over two billion people lack adequate sanitation. In sub-Saharan Africa, 62 percent of people do not even have access to a basic toilet. As a result, approximately half of the developing world's inhabitants suffer from illnesses caused by contaminated water supplies. It is not hard to imagine the implications for lost productivity.

Though it is an inexact figure, researchers estimate that diarrheal diseases are responsible for the death of one child every eighteen seconds, 200 children an hour, 4,800 children a day. To place this in a different context, imagine the outcry to the equivalent of a classroom of children in America dying from waterborne diseases every six minutes, and an entire elementary school dying every hour. The numbers of those incapacitated by nonlethal disease are, of course, much greater. One study estimated that every dollar spent to improve sanitation creates nine dollars of economic benefit.

Because water supply infrastructure is not provided in the poorest urban areas or in many rural areas, obtaining water is regarded as an individual or domestic responsibility. In contrast to the ease of turning on a faucet, lack of infrastructure means a high labor input as someone from the household (in most cultures, a woman or a girl) must collect each day's water, whether from a communal pond or well, a tanker, or a kiosk. Less than half of the population in Africa lives within a fifteen-minute walk of a safe drinking water source. The daily average for water gathering in 1997 across East Africa was an hour and a half, triple the time spent three decades earlier. In India, roughly 170 million people have to walk to gather their water.

Where communal or free water sources are too far away or clearly contaminated, the poor purchase their water from street vendors or tanker trucks. These prices are always higher than the price of water from municipal supply systems, often twelve to twenty times as much, with the tragic irony of the poorest in society paying the most for their water. The resulting social and economic impacts are immense.

The time women and girls spend walking for water not only exposes them to a greater risk of assault. Carrying such heavy loads day in and out also takes a continuous toll on the body, condemning many women to lower back pain. It keeps them from attending school, from working, from helping take care of their families.

While the statistics alone are shocking, they do not tell the whole story, nor can they. Sterile numbers and photos cannot capture the hardships, the grinding necessity of devoting so much time day after day to collecting water that often makes you sick. To put a human face on the situation, consider the tale of twenty-five-year-old Aylito Binayo.

Aylito lives in the mountain village of Foro, in the southwest of Ethiopia. The height of the town has long kept it safe from malaria in the valley below and cool in the hot summers, but it makes collecting water an arduous chore. Working beside her mother, Aylito stopped going to school when she was eight years old and started carrying water. Every morning, well before the sun rises, she walks down the foot-worn path over rocks, beside cactus and thornbushes, to the Toiro River below. A fifty-minute descent. The drought has lowered the river level, and the water sits in muddy pools. When she gets there, other women are already at the river—providing water is not fit work for a man—so she must wait her turn, losing more time that she needs to spend on her other chores—growing cassava and beans with her husband, grinding grain to make flour, cooking, and taking care of her three young sons. Of all these chores, water carrying takes the most time and is the most physically demanding.

A group of Indian girls stopping to pose while carrying water

Finally taking her place in the river, she works with a plastic scoop, trying to drain water that is not muddy into her six-gallon jerry can. This is difficult because other women stirred up mud as they filled their cans. Donkeys wander in the riverbed, as well, drinking their fill and muddying the waters. Once it is finally filled, she straps the fifty-pound plastic jerry can to her back and turns back up the steep climb to the village. By the time she gets there, between the time for the trips, waiting her turn, and filling the container, she has spent at least two hours, usually more. She will repeat this three times a day, every day of the year.

On top of all this, the water she carries back is teeming with parasites and bacteria. Seventy percent of the patients seen at the village clinic suffer from diarrhea they contracted from drinking Toiro River water and following poor hygienic practices. The villagers in Foro are too poor to buy soap for washing their hands after using latrines, if they even have a latrine to use.

With a significant proportion of women's time and family income dedicated to gathering domestic water—walking to the river, waiting for the tanker trucks to arrive—opportunities for economically productive activities such as education or other employment are squeezed out. It is no exaggeration to say that the introduction of piped water can transform the social and economic fabric of a community. While climate change has taken hold of the media as the greatest threat facing humanity, many environment ministers would disagree. To them, unsafe drinking water is clearly the single greatest threat facing their citizens, particularly children.

Yet the trend is worsening. From 1950 to 1985, the percentage of the world's urban population doubled. The United Nations estimates that more than half of all people on earth now live in urban, rather than rural, settings. As a result of growing urbanization, the number of clean communal water sources is decreasing as water and sanitation provisions come under increasing pressure. Indeed, social scientists have introduced the term "water deprivation"—"the inability reliably to obtain water of adequate quantity and quality to sustain health and livelihood"—as a basic index of poverty.

The journalist Charles Fishman describes the consequences well: "Water poverty doesn't just mean your hands are dirty, or you can't wash your clothes, or you are often thirsty. Water poverty may mean you never learn how to read, it means you get sick more often than you should, it means you and your children are hungry. Water poverty traps you in a primitive day-to-day struggle. Water poverty is, quite literally, de-civilizing."

It is not hard to imagine just how different the lives of Aylito and her children would be if they had ready access to clean water. No time lost gathering water. No time lost due to sickness from drinking dirty water. No need to drop out of school. Newfound opportunities to pursue jobs, take care of their families, and build their communities.

In recognition of these pressing issues, the governments of the world committed one of the eight Millennium Development Goals to drinking water. By 2015, the UN has pledged to "reduce by half the proportion of people without sustainable access to safe drinking water." Given the poor state of water provision in much of the world and the limits on debt-burdened governments to fund significant infrastructure, this remains a challenging goal.

The problems from water deprivation are clear and have been for years. Everyone can agree that increased access to safe water and improved sanitation are both desperately needed in developing countries and absolutely necessary to improving quality of life. There is little agreement, however, over how actually to achieve this.

COCHABAMBA SERVED AS THE FLASHPOINT OVER SEVERAL CRITICAL areas of disagreement. What is the proper role of the market in water allocation? Should access to drinking water be regarded as a basic human right? Regardless of how one answers these questions, practical question remains. What are the appropriate roles of companies and government in providing water whether by right or by price?

The water sector is often described as a natural monopoly. The high costs of infrastructure create significant barriers to entry, thereby making competition difficult because it is hard for new businesses to enter the market. This has often justified state intervention and public provision of drinking water. Almost 95 percent of water systems in the United States are under public control. But that is not inevitable. Nor is it necessarily desirable.

Public water utilities, particularly in developing countries, face a number of potential challenges. Funds to pay for laying new pipes, upgrading old ones, or building new treatment plants can be hard to come by, not to mention the basic costs of maintaining the current aging system. Civil service protections may make the employees insensitive to concerns over customer service. If politicians control jobs, there may be abuses of patronage or corruption, undermining morale. This is not to say, of course, that all water utilities suffer from these shortcomings or even that most do. The basic problem is that current water provision in many developing countries is woefully inadequate, and this has occurred under a tradition of public service provision.

In light of these concerns, many have argued that the answer to safe drinking water in the developing world lies in privatization. Growing demand and shrinking supply make the perfect ingredients for a market solution. The arguments for contracting the operation of water utilities to corporations are similar to those for privatizing other traditionally public services, whether prisons, registries of motor vehicles, or trash collection. Only the private sector, they contend, can mobilize the necessary capital for investments to improve service and ensure efficient management.

At the heart of all these arguments lies the assumption of state failure. It is indeed ironic that international financial institutions funded by governments often made privatization a core condition for lending funds to nations such as Argentina and Bolivia.

Spurred by the consensus of the Dublin Statement, there has been an unprecedented expansion of private sector participation in water supply over the past two decades. The global water service market has been estimated at over $250 billion and growing at an annual 6 percent rate. Water supply services have been privatized across the globe, from the United Kingdom, Poland, and Morocco to Argentina, Indonesia, and the Philippines. "Privatization," of course, can mean many things. Such arrangements have ranged from outright privatization of water supply infrastructure to public/private partnerships, management contracts, leases, etc.

In theory, private provision should provide benefits over public provision, particularly in developing countries. The first advantage is access to private capital. A common and understandable excuse offered by many local and regional governments in developing countries for poor water service is the simple fact that building and maintaining water treatment plants and water mains is enormously expensive. Cities across the United States are barely doing enough to maintain their own infrastructure. How realistic is it to expect Cochabamba to do the same? Companies have access to private investment capital and can bring much greater funds to bear toward water supply infrastructure and delivery in a shorter amount of time than can local governments. Moreover, the profit motive ensures that companies will focus on efficiency. A public utility, shielded

from competition and guaranteed a fixed rate of return, has no similar incentive.

Private provision of services should also be less vulnerable to
patronage and corruption than local governments where politicians
influence hiring decisions. The problem, of course, is that deals can
be cut when the initial terms are negotiated. Bechtel had no interest in building the hydroelectric dam above Cochabamba, for
example, but local politicians demanded that as a concession for
the contract. In a telling statistic, fully 70 percent of the water concession contracts in Latin America have been renegotiated, at least
opening the possibility for additional side payments and concessions
to the authorities rewarding contracts.

The privatization arguments go beyond private management,
however, to the nature of drinking water itself. The failure to treat
water as a scarce commodity, advocates argue, only ensures its
inefficient distribution and use. A basic axiom of resource economics is that we overconsume goods that are underpriced. Since the
market is more efficient than governments at allocating scarce
goods, it follows, market prices should be charged for water. This
would promote conservation and more efficient use of scarce water
resources by making waste expensive.

Perhaps surprisingly, the plight of the poor actually reinforces
this argument. The fact that the very poor do pay for water, and
pay quite a bit in relative terms, suggests both that they could and
would pay for piped water. Thus the principle of "full cost recovery"
—charging a price to cover all the costs of investment as well as
profit—has seemed both possible and desirable, but also risky.

Private operation of a water system may provide the capital necessary for maintenance and upgrades, yet it requires amortization
periods that can run several decades for the investments to pay back.
A long-term return on investment also requires general economic,
political, and social stability over that period. In many developing
countries this is far from a given. Hence the difficult challenge: privatization may hold the greatest social potential in developing countries because it can inject needed capital, yet it is in precisely such
settings where investment environments are least certain.

The immediate concern that can arise with full cost recovery is one of inequity. If water access is based on ability to pay rather than willingness to pay, then what are the implications for poor and marginalized communities if water prices rise? Does changing the management regime effectively deny them access to adequate clean drinking water? More fundamentally, will private water providers only choose to service wealthier areas and not bother to invest in poorer areas, making privatization a losing proposition for the poor? These are primary concerns of opponents to privatization.

The answer is not as obvious as may first appear. Consider, for example, the privatization of water services in Argentina. Much like Bolivia, spurred by the International Monetary Fund and World Bank in the 1990s, Argentina engaged in a large-scale privatization campaign. Over a decade, roughly one-third of Argentina's municipalities privatized their water systems. Case studies carried out by researchers from the University of California, Berkeley, and the Universidad de San Andrés in Buenos Aires, Argentina, found that privatization resulted in measurable benefits. Service quality improved (in the form of cleaner water, faster repairs, improved water pressure, fewer stoppages), and the network of both water provision and sewer lines expanded into poorer areas not previously connected at all. The authors surmised that networks expanded into poorer areas because the wealthy parts of the city were already connected.

Using statistical analysis, they also found that privatization of the water system reduced child mortality by 5 to 10 percent. This impact was greatest in poor municipalities, where the marginal improvement in water supply and cleanliness was much greater. As one of the authors concluded:

> In spite of the concerns about inducing negative health effects or worsening health inequality, our evidence suggests that the deterioration of water systems in Argentina under public management was so large that it allowed for a privatization that generated profits, expanded service, and reduced child mortality. While the regulated private sector might have been providing sub-optimal services, it seems it was doing a better job than the public sector.

As with the question of whether drinking water is safe, the key question in assessing the public versus private debate is "Compared to what?" Privatization of water systems surely poses its own set of concerns, but these may still be preferable compared to the miserable state of public provision. It's not as if Cochabamba had a great situation before Aguas del Tunari came in. Robert Glennon recounts an illuminating exchange in this regard between "an Argentinean opponent of privatization, who argued that water 'is a gift from God,' and the president of Veolia Environnement (which supplies water to 100 million people throughout Europe, Asia, Africa and the Americas), who responded, 'Yes . . . but he forgot to lay the pipes.'"

Interestingly, despite the benefits researchers attributed to privatization in Argentina, they found that public disapproval increased from 49 percent in 1998 to 85 percent in 2002. It's important to keep in mind the broader context, since many services beyond water and sanitation were privatized, and low-income households were more supportive of privatization than others polled. There is no doubt, though, that antiprivatization positions were politically popular.

The Argentine research is described in detail because, in such a highly charged area, facts are hard to come by. The terrain of the water privatization debate features a contested landscape, dominated by mammoth multinational corporations and savvy non-governmental organizations (NGOs). With polarized advocates on both sides, it can be difficult to know where the truth lies.

The academic researchers painted a generally positive view of Argentine water privatization. Contrast that, however, with the description by the advocacy group Food & Water Watch of the privatization of the water utility in Buenos Aires: "Before privatization, nonpayment of tariffs had been somewhat of a problem. Aguas Argentinas [the private provider] effectively dealt with this problem by cutting off poor Argentines after three unpaid bills. Consequently, the company 'persuaded' 90 percent of its customers to pay." As two prominent figures opposed to water privatization put it, "The major water privateers are facing mounting and fierce public opposition to their operations in many parts of Latin America. As in the rest of the world, the damaging effects of water privatization are well-documented: rate hikes, cut-offs to customers who can't pay, reduced water quality, huge profits for corporate investors, secret contracts, bribery and corruption." It's hard to imagine two more contrasting assessments of the same situation.

AS PART OF THE LARGER ANTIGLOBALIZATION WAVE, A VOCAL RIGHTS-based movement has arisen to challenge the growing pressure for water privatization. For this group, the status quo is equally unacceptable. Rather than reliance on the market, though, their strategy calls for a bold change in how we conceive of the broader issue, arguing for the recognition of a human right to water. We saw such a demand expressed in the grassroots Cochabamba Declaration and its statement that "water is a fundamental human right and a public trust." Similar calls for a human right to water may be found in more than a dozen international documents. What, though, does this mean in practice?

As a statement of formal international governmental policy, the right to water has been presented most strongly in General Comment 15, adopted in 2002 by the United Nations Committee on Economic, Social and Cultural Rights. General Comment 15 recognized the right to water as an independent human right, defining it as "sufficient, safe, acceptable, physically accessible and affordable water for personal and domestic uses." These terms were carefully negotiated, and it is worth considering them in detail.

A "sufficient" amount implies the government's responsibility to provide a minimal quantity of water for basic needs to prevent dehydration and disease, often seen as seven to fourteen gallons a day per person. "Safe" implies not only a responsibility for treatment but also a corollary responsibility to prevent pollution from contaminating drinking water sources. "Acceptable" and "accessible" suggest that the sources must be reasonably close to where the water is consumed.

The term "affordable" is less obvious. It could mean that states must provide access to water even to those who cannot pay for it. After all, the General Comment goes on to say that "water, and water facilities and services, must be affordable for all." This would not be possible if the availability of water were solely determined by market forces in a full cost recovery approach. At the same time, the text never says water must be provided for free. And while its critics rarely note the concession, even the promarket Dublin Statement made clear that there is a "basic right of all human beings to have access to clean water . . . at an affordable price."

Many advocates for a right to water reject this possibility, demanding that water be provided for free to those too poor to afford the fees. Others go further, arguing that water belongs to the people and therefore cannot be subject to commerce. As the Council of Canadians, one of the most influential groups in the debate, proclaims on its website, "Water is a public trust; it belongs to everyone. No one should have the right to appropriate it or profit from it at someone else's expense. Yet that's what corporations and investors want to do."

General Comment 15 was adopted in 2002. The UN General Assembly adopted a resolution in 2010 declaring "the right to safe and clean drinking water and sanitation as a human right that is essential for the full enjoyment of life and all human rights." Forty-one countries abstained in the final vote, including the United States, the United Kingdom, Canada, and Japan.

It may seem strange that there has been so much controversy over recognizing a right to water. It is not as if General Comment 15 or other UN pronouncements will lead to an immediate change in behavior, so what are the implications in recognizing a right to water? On a fundamental level, human rights change the nature of the discourse. If we start to think of water more as a right and less as a commodity, supporters hope, then we will also think more naturally of state obligations to respect and fulfill these rights. Just as a state should not deny an individual his or her right to personal liberty, so, too, should no one be denied access to safe drinking water because of their inability to pay. It certainly puts a dent in the principle of full cost recovery.

As lawyers know well, rights talk trumps markets talk. As one scholar put it, "Utilizing human rights protections changes the terms of discourse from one of charity or commodity to one of entitlement with corresponding state obligations." And, it follows, if states have such an obligation, then they should be legally and politically accountable when they fail to meet this obligation. No one speaks in favor of slavery because there is a profit to be made. The right of liberty is nonnegotiable. The same should be true for the right to water.

This is all fine talk, but what would such a right look like in practice? The General Assembly resolution and General Comment 15 are equally unhelpful in detailing what states need to do to comply. Yet it is at the state level—where the rubber meets the road— where obligations are respected and enforced. It is here we must look to see how a right to water would operate. While most countries do not recognize a right to water, there are at least fifteen national constitutions that recognize basic water rights. Among these, India and South Africa provide the most interesting examples to consider.

While no statute or constitutional provision speaks directly to a right to water, the Indian Supreme Court has developed an expansive reading of Article 21 of the Indian Constitution. Article 21 provides that "no person shall be deprived of his life or personal liberty except according to procedure established by law." This short text has served as the justification for a flowering of Court decisions establishing rights-based protections, including the right to go abroad, the right to shelter, and the right to water, among others. As the Court wrote in a 1998 case, the "right to life guaranteed in any civilised society implies the right to food, water, decent environment, education, medical care and shelter."

Like the right to water in General Comment 15, though, the question still remains how to apply this in practice. We can find an instructive and wonderfully creative example in a 1998 case from the northern part of the country, in the city of Allahabad in Utter Pradesh. A lawsuit filed by Shri S. K. Garg, the vice president of the Allahabad bar association, asked the presiding judge,

Markandey Katju, to ensure a regular supply of water to the people of Allahabad. The pleadings cited example after example of broken or inadequate water supplies. Three out of the four water tanks at Khusroobagh were not working, and the functioning tank was full of filth and mud. The tubewells and hand pumps installed by the Jal Sansthan were out of order. The water pumps at Ashok Hagar and Rajapur had been broken for the past week. The list went on and on.

Faced with this litany of public failure, most judges in other countries might throw up their hands. Suing public authorities for inadequate water service provision and forcing action is difficult to do, even in the United States. Indian courts, however, have developed a strong tradition of public interest litigation over the past thirty years. In a small number of cases, courts have stepped in to demand specific improvements in local governance by authorities. This happened most notably in the case of M. C. *Mehta v. Union of India* where, in response to the pleading of a public interest litigator, the court ordered the local government of Kanpur to take specific actions to protect the water quality of the Ganges for drinking and bathing, including construction of sewage works, moving dairies away from the river, and stopping the burial of bodies in the river. And that type of bold intervention is precisely what happened in the courtroom of Judge Katju. Part of his opinion bears quoting:

> The English poet Coleridge in his poem The Ancient Mariner wrote "Water, water everywhere but not a drop to drink."
>
> This is precisely the plight of the people of Allahabad which has been highlighted in this writ petition. Despite two mighty rivers, the Ganga [Ganges] and Yamuna, at whose confluence the city is situated, a large number of colonies and the people living there have been hardly getting even a drop of water for days on end, and even in the places where water comes, it very often trickles for hardly 15 minutes or so in a day, and people have to rush with their buckets to get some. . . .
>
> In our opinion the right to get water is part of the right to life guaranteed by Article 21 of the Constitution but a large section of

citizens of Allahabad are being deprived of this right. Without water the citizens of Allahabad are going through terrible agony and distress particularly in this hot season when the temperature goes up to 46 or 47 degree Celsius [115 degrees Fahrenheit]. Without water the people are bound to die in large numbers due to dehydration and heat stroke and in fact many have died already.

Judge Katju ordered the creation of an Allahabad Water Committee, naming its chair and eleven members. The committee was charged to meet within a week and at least every two weeks after that to decide immediate and long-term remedial steps. The local authorities were also directed to repair the broken wells and pumps within a week, as well as test the water for pollution. Both the committee and general manager of Allahabad were ordered to appear before the court two months later to report on progress.

This kind of judicial intervention in municipal governance is virtually unheard of in other systems. It seems as strong an exercise of the right to water as might be possible. And yet, despite this powerful exercise of judicial authority, the fact remains that roughly 17 percent of Indians do not have access to clean water. Even a motivated judiciary has its limits in poor countries.

South Africa has taken a different approach. Confronting the legacy of apartheid, much of South Africa's black population suffers from the same lack of access to clean water as in other parts of Africa. This was addressed in 1996 when the new constitution created a right to water. Section 27 mandates that "everyone has the right to have access to . . . sufficient . . . water. . . . The state must take reasonable legislative and other measures, within its available resources, to achieve the progressive realization of each of these rights."

To make concrete this broad and abstract right, government legislation established a Free Basic Water entitlement of twenty-five liters per person per day (6.6 gallons) or six kiloliters per household per month, available within two hundred meters of a household. Under what is known as the Free Basic Water policy, this ration of six kiloliters is to be provided free to all citizens, supplied from the local government's portion of the national allocation. Municipalities are required to adopt a block tariff system, where the cost of water increases for consumption in excess of the free six-kiloliter allocation. The result is a cross-subsidized system, where large users of water subsidize the initial basic supply for the poor. In addition, the Water Services Act stated that government actions cannot "result in a person being deprived access to basic water services for nonpayment."

While it seems sensible on its face, the policy has had limited success. Collection of revenue, in particular, has proved challenging, especially in areas where there are not enough high-volume users to subsidize free water. Up to 75 percent of water pumped to some areas goes unaccounted for because of leaks and unpaid bills. In response, some municipalities have installed prepaid water meters. These meters shut off a household's water supply once the free basic supply has been provided. Any additional water must be paid for.

This practice was challenged by residents of the Soweto area of Johannesburg in 2008. The lower court said the practice was unconstitutional because it unlawfully and unreasonably discontinued the supply of water. The court also found that the twenty-five-liter free basic supply allotment was insufficient and should be raised to fifty liters per day. On appeal, the Constitutional Court overruled this decision. The Court made clear that the constitutional right to water provided in Section 27 "does not require the state upon demand to provide every person with sufficient water without more; rather it requires the state to take reasonable legislative and other measures progressively to realise the achievement of the right of access to sufficient water, within available resources." The decision was deeply pragmatic, recognizing that inadequate resources pose a legitimate barrier to realization of the right. Indeed, in 2006, more than 8 million South Africans did not have adequate access to water, and 3.3 million had no access to a basic, safe water supply at all.

India's active judiciary and South Africa's legislative guarantee of a basic supply offer promising approaches to realize the people's right to water. Even the strongest proponents of a rights-based approach, however, recognize that simply declaring a human right to water will not, by its mere pronouncement, solve problems on the ground. But it can help change how people think about the problem and, importantly, the basic responsibilities of government.

The rights-versus-markets debate remains highly contentious, with strident advocates on both sides of the issue. As with most complicated issues, both sides have a point yet neither owns the debate. Indeed if our survey of drinking water management in different societies in Chapter 2 showed anything, it was that the popular discourse is both simplistic and distinctly ahistorical. While making for powerful rhetoric, framing access to drinking water as a binary conflict of rights versus markets, of public versus private management, forces a false choice.

Consider that more than 150 years ago, the New York Committee on Fire and Water addressed the very same issue of private versus public provision that we continue to fight over today. Its 1835 report recommended a hybrid approach.

> The control of the water of the City should be in the hands of this Corporation, or in other words, in the hands of the people. From the wealthy and those who would require the luxury of having it delivered into their houses; and from the men of business, who would employ it in their workshops and factories, the revenue should be derived. But to the poor, and those who would be content to receive it from the hydrants at the corners and on the sidewalks, it should be as free as air, as a means of cleanliness, nourishment and health.

Markets and rights both have coexisted and can coexist, one reinforcing the other.

The centuries-long stability of the Roman drinking water system provides an even more nuanced perspective. When viewed from the broader vantage of natural resource management, drinking water was consciously managed as a physical resource (the aqueduct and distribution system within Rome), a social resource (free water in the communal gathering places of the *lacus*), an economic resource (charging the *vectigal* to underwrite maintenance costs), and a political resource (as a justification of imperial rule). Asking whether access to Roman drinking water was by market or by right is not nearly as instructive as considering how the different natures of drinking water were deliberately managed.

Recognizing the various facets of drinking water also frames the Cochabamba story in a different light. There were many issues underpinning the unrest in Cochabamba, but the fundamental problem surely did not lie in treating access to water as a market transaction instead of by right. Water was not free before the uprising in Cochabamba, and it is not free now. By granting an exclusive water concession to Aguas del Tunari and requiring that water withdrawals be licensed by the state, the government was perceived as effectively enclosing the "water commons." Contemporary accounts suggested that people feared the government was outlawing the traditional collection of water from rain barrels, streams, and wells. This likely played a far greater role in people taking to the streets than rising water bills. Such failure to consider the popular conceptions of resource access proved fatal. By treating drinking water as a purely economic resource and focusing on pricing, Aguas del Tunari ignored water's significant nature as a social resource. The mass demonstrations did call for a return to previous water rates but, more fundamentally, a return to previous entitlements.

When a water system seeks to pay for itself, whether government-run or private, it must decide how to value the provision of water in a culturally acceptable manner. As the Cochabamba case illustrates, where cultures view the right to water as an inherent right, full cost recovery is likely to fail. There still is room for market mechanisms, but they may need to be more creative, mindful of the experiences in India and South Africa.

WHILE THE PRIVATIZATION DEBATE HAS DOMINATED MUCH OF THE discussion over drinking water provisions in developing countries, it is by no means the only concern. In fact, it is largely irrelevant for many rural areas. In these places, once one moves outside the big cities, large-scale infrastructure is infeasible and privatization by large companies with access to capital makes no sense. So what is to be done? In recent years, promising strategies have been developed to reinvent how to ensure safe water in the home and how to pay for it. Neither of these is a silver bullet. The problem is far too large and complicated for that, but they do offer some hope to what can seem an insoluble challenge.

The major pathway of waterborne diseases through drinking water in rural areas follows a well-worn route: inadequate sanitation leads to contaminated water sources. The traditional approach to address this problem has involved infrastructure projects such as digging wells, putting in piped water, and building latrines. The focus, in other words, has been on improving water sources and sanitation. And these are obviously important. They can also be relatively expensive for very poor areas. There's a reason beyond ignorance that they are not already in place. And even where wells and latrines are in place, there still may be a high incidence of waterborne diseases.

In recent years, researchers have realized that their model of providing clean drinking water to poor households is incomplete in an important respect. Digging a deep well and building latrines away from the water source are all well and good. But if the water is carried home and stored in a dirty container—if it becomes contaminated during transport or storage—then all the previous protections were wasted efforts. Providing clean water to a village is not enough. It must be kept clean until it is drunk by individuals. As a result, there has been a great deal of work studying behavior at the water's point of use (known as POU).

"POU interventions" is the fancy name for behaviors and technologies in the household to ensure safe drinking water just before consumption. They fall into three broad categories. The first is physically removing pathogens, usually through sedimentation (letting the water settle) or filtration. Filters run the gamut from simply passing water through a cloth rag or sand to more sophisticated membranes, ceramic filters, or even reverse osmosis technologies. The second approach is to disinfect by heat or exposure to ultraviolet radiation. The third approach relies on chemically treating the water with small amounts of iodine or chlorine.

Household chlorination, for example, has proven an effective POU strategy with widespread adoption. It is often dispensed by filling a chlorine container's bottle cap and pouring it into a standard-sized bucket filled with water. Simply stir, wait, and drink. A popular chlorine-based product in Africa, WaterGuard, is available for sale at a reasonable price. Diarrhea can be reduced by 22 to 84 percent and the cost is low, from 0.01 to 0.05 cents per use. The main downside is the chlorine taste in the water and its inability to kill some common parasites.

Solar disinfection is easy to use in sunny climates. Clear water is placed in plastic bottles and left in the sun for six hours, two days if cloudy. The sun's ultraviolet radiation kills common germs such as giardia and cryptosporidia. The technique has been disseminated in more than twenty developing countries and currently has more than one million users. While free (apart from the clear bottle) and easy to use, the range of effectiveness is broad, reducing diarrhea by anywhere from 9 to 86 percent.

Another promising POU approach has been developed by the consumer products giant Procter & Gamble. Called Pur, the powdered product is provided in a small sachet. The instructions are straightforward—add the packet to ten liters of water, stir, let the particles settle, strain, wait, and drink. The cost is one penny per liter of water. Procter & Gamble, in partnership with the Children's Safe Drinking Water program, has distributed over 130 million sachets on a not-for-profit basis since 2004. The main ingredients are ferric sulfate, a compound that binds particles in the water, and the disinfectant calcium hypochlorite. Procter & Gamble claims that studies conducted by the U.S. Centers for Disease Control and Johns Hopkins University found diarrhea incidences reduced by half. The major downsides are the multiple steps required to treat the water and the need for mixing equipment, which can be a challenging obstacle in communities where water collection itself can consume hours each day.

These are only a few of the wide range of POU interventions currently under development, but suffice it to say that this is a vibrant field of activity. These experiences and others suggest that

POU treatments can produce major health benefits at a low cost. Indeed, the research on POU raises a fundamental challenge to drinking water strategies more broadly. As an article in the medical journal *BMJ* concluded:

> Water quality interventions were effective in reducing diarrhea even in the absence of improved water supplies and sanitation. Effectiveness did not seem to be enhanced by combining the intervention with other common strategies for preventing diarrhea (instruction on basic hygiene, improved water storage, or improved water supplies and sanitation facilities). Although the evidence does not rule out additional benefit from combined interventions, it does raise questions about whether the additional cost of such integrated approaches as currently implemented is warranted on the basis of health gains alone.

In plain English, the authors suggest that POU may be more effective and less expensive than the more traditional strategies for assuring drinking water quality. A major review of POU field studies reached the same conclusion. Providing clean water, improving sanitation, and hand-washing with soap may not significantly reduce waterborne disease any more than the POU intervention *on its own.*

The policy implications of these findings are significant. Assume for a moment that you are the head of development for a funding agency. You have been tasked to reduce the incidence of waterborne disease in a desperately poor group of villages in East Africa with contaminated surface water sources and little or no sanitation. Human and animal waste flow into the local ponds and streams. Protecting the water source and improving sanitation are obviously important priorities for poor communities, but what to do if funds are limited? Your budget is tight, and your bosses want quick results. Where should you invest your resources?

In the past, the traditional approach would have focused on digging wells and building latrines, and these definitely can improve quality of life. But they also require construction, labor, and time. The research described above suggests that focusing on POU interventions can provide more immediate benefits, to more people, at lower cost. Over the long term, one can reasonably debate about the relative merits of investing in infrastructure versus short-term POU actions (and experts in the field do indeed debate about this), but the low uptake costs of POU make it very attractive to the donor community, where real results can be seen soon after adoption in poor communities suffering from intestinal diseases caused by dirty drinking water, particularly when the likelihood of funds for large-scale centralized treatment and distribution infrastructure is remote.

Adoption, though, is the key word. Developing effective POU interventions is one thing; ensuring they are used, and used appropriately, is quite another. Changing people's behavior is no easy matter, particularly when trying to persuade them to adopt new ways to handle something as basic and commonplace as water. Are they affordable? Are they easy to use and reliable? Are they scalable? There are too many examples of treatments that work in pilot projects with hands-on education and follow-up. The test is what happens when the support has been withdrawn. Will people return to their traditional practices? Barriers to adoption include timeworn habits, local norms, the smell and taste of treated water, and the lack of disposable income.

One of the more interesting debates concerns this last challenge of poverty. Is it more effective to provide POU treatments for free or to sell at a low price? One might assume that providing chlorine bottles for free, for example, would increase use since poverty will not prevent their purchase. Some research, though, suggests that those who purchase the kits are *more* likely to use them than those to whom the kits were simply given. When we get something for free, we tend to value it at the cost we paid—zero. Paying for the POU kits, by contrast, requires sacrifice and can create a sense of obligation to use them.

We know that the very poor are willing to pay for water, so it would seem reasonable to assume they would be willing to pay for POU treatments, as well, but this is not always the case. Paying for water is not the same as paying for chemicals or materials to treat the water. As one researcher observed, "Some people are willing to pay for water quantity and for convenience, but in low-income countries many households will not pay for quality."

There are some success stories that give reason for optimism, though. To take one example, the nongovernmental group PSI launched a product in Zambia called Clorin, basically a bottle of the disinfectant sodium hypochlorite. PSI developed a brand identity for Clorin, advertised on radio and TV spots, and distributed bottles for sale through traditional retail networks, health centers, and door-to-door vendors. A survey found impressive penetration— 42 percent of households reported using Clorin. Thanks to aid from the U.S. Agency for International Development, the $0.34 cost of the bottle is subsidized and sold to the public for $0.12. In a country that ranks at the bottom of the United Nations Human Development Index, 164 out of 177, this level of use is no small achievement. It bears keeping in mind, however, that the typical adoption rate for chlorination POUs is much lower, closer to 5 to 10 percent. PSI's initiative in Zambia is the greatest success story to date and offers important guidance for program design in other places.

Experts in development can argue about the relative merits of POU versus wells versus piped systems, but regardless of their approach, they all agree there is not enough money available to satisfy the demand for clean water in developing countries. Just as research on POU is challenging how we think about providing clean water, so, too, is the savvy creativity of one man challenging how we think about raising money to pay for clean water.

SCOTT HARRISON STANDS ALONE AT THE BACK OF THE ROOM AS THE students start to enter. With average height, close-cut hair, and a cropped beard, he's well-dressed—a clean white textured shirt, designer blue jeans, leather shoes. The posters at Duke's Nicholas School of the Environment say he'll be talking about something called Charity: Water. Spotting the oldest person in the room, Harrison walks up to me and shakes my hand. "You're a professor? Great. Tell me about the crowd." As I describe the students' back-

*Scott Harrison, the founder of Charity: Water,
speaking at an event in 2010*

grounds, he gives me his full attention and keeps saying, "Cool, cool." A few minutes later, he walks to the front of the classroom, sits cross-legged on a desk, and in even tones starts talking.

The room gets quiet as he shows photo after photo on the screen of Africans with enormous, grotesque tumors on their faces, most sticking out of their mouths. Harrison says he cried the first time he saw someone like this. The photos were taken by him in Liberia, when he was working aboard a hospital ship. He pauses, then starts to tell how he got there.

In 2004, Scott Harrison was one of the top event planners in New York City. He lived the high life, clubbing with the A-list crowd in Manhattan, drinking $350 bottles of vodka, dating a model, taking vacations all over the world. He had grown up in a religious family but he left for New York City and did everything his family had told him not to: "From eighteen to twenty-eight, I partied and did drugs." He was successful by any measure, had a remarkable talent for organization and for engaging with people, but he felt empty.

On a whim he still doesn't completely understand, he walked away from it all and volunteered to work on the Mercy Ship *Anastasis*, heading to Liberia to provide badly needed medical services for free. He bluffed about his experience as a photojournalist to the organizers, reading the Nikon camera manual as the ship steamed east. Arriving in Liberia, he found a capital ravaged by war and literally hundreds of people with facial deformities waiting to be treated by doctors on the *Anastasis*. As Harrison recounted, "I fell in love with Liberia—a country with no public electricity, running water, or sewage. Spending time in a leper colony and many remote villages, I put a face to the world's 1.2 billion living in poverty. Those living on less than $365 a year— money I used to blow on a bottle of Grey Goose vodka at a fancy club. Before tip."

Harrison pauses in the story. He's a powerful speaker and knows it. The slide show is slick. Naked words appear on the screen and fade out, a graphic photo taking its place. The audience is following his every word.

Everywhere Harrison traveled in Africa, unsafe water seemed to be at the root of so many of the hardships he saw. "I saw school after school with no clean water. There were no iPods. Just yellow jerry cans as their accessories." Most communities don't have enough money to boil water before drinking. Charcoal is too expensive. It's illegal to cut down trees, and cow dung, the regular fuel source, doesn't burn hot enough to boil for long enough. Instead, he saw people relying on crude filters, usually just pouring water though a dress or some other fabric. He shows slides of a small water hole, puddles in trampled mud beside cows and children. "This is a common sight at drinking holes. Kids and cows. The cows are bigger, so they go first."

Returning to the States, Harrison was a changed man. He decided to get involved, raise money, and make a difference. The problem was that he didn't think much of organized charity. He had been remarkably effective in getting people to go to club parties and spend money there. Why not do the same raising money for clean water in developing countries? The key, he realized, was clever marketing. And he knew he could do that.

So he founded the group Charity: Water. To raise money, he started selling twenty-dollar bottles of water. All of the money raised went to water projects in Africa. "It was a context-shifting bottle of water. We put on a black label with facts of death and disease. Putting them in hotels was great. They already cost ten or eleven dollars, and business people could expense them to the room." He got others excited and they started selling water bottles, too. Seven-year-old Max Schmidhauser sold seven thousand dollars' worth. Steve Sabba, a small-time accountant in New York working in a cramped office, got in touch. "He said he could sell five thousand of water. We said, 'OK, that's a lot of water.' He set up a credit card terminal in his office." Sabba raised hundreds of thousands of dollars, got his first passport at fifty years old, and went to Liberia to see the wells he had funded

Using his A-list of contacts, Harrison raised fifteen thousand dollars at his thirty-first birthday party. With the money, he fixed three wells and built three more. He took photos and sent emails back to everyone who had contributed—"Some couldn't even remember the party." For the one-year anniversary of Charity: Water and his thirty-second birthday, he decided to invite people *not* to attend a party: "Instead, I gave up my birthday and asked people to give thirty-two dollars instead." Ninety-two people joined him for their September birthdays, giving up their birthdays for gifts. He shows a montage on the screen of ninety-two faces, including a monkey. "I don't know about that one," he deadpans. He eventually raised a hundred fifty thousand dollars, enough for three hospitals and one school.

Harrison is now getting into it. Energetic, hands moving, eyes sparkling, he is fully engaged. You can see why he was so successful on the club scene. You'd love to party with this guy. His birthday giving concept is scalable. He wants to make it ten times bigger, so he created the website borninseptember.org. His goal was to raise $1.2 million. And that's just the beginning. "So you open it up to every month. You can give up your wedding, your anniversary. We already have a hundred fifty schools signed up. Micropayments can really scale, and not just in the U.S." You can see his mind clicking. This is social entrepreneurship in real time.

Harrison went to the management of Saks Fifth Avenue and put his sales skills to the test. As he described, "So I went to them and said, 'Hey, like we're a year old and just got our 501(c)(3), and you should do this with us.' And they got the message." One expects that the discussions were a bit more involved, and Harrison can surely tell a good story. Saks became a strong supporter. The store sold Charity: Water bracelets and dedicated its Fifth Avenue windows for a week to displays of the jerry cans used to collect water. This directly followed their Giorgio Armani display. Quite a contrast. Saks' efforts raised $540,000 in two months.

Using fashion photographers for publicity shots, Harrison re-created photos of gathering water in Africa, but now set in the Upper East Side. Kids dressed for the most expensive schools in the city were carrying forty-pound jerry cans on their backs. "It's not OK for our kids to carry forty pounds of water on their backs to school, so why is it OK in Uganda when the kids don't go to school?" A crew of forty-five filmed a public service announcement. Well-dressed people walk out of their luxury apartment buildings and line up to fill their jerry cans from a dirty pond in Central Park. The entire production was done on a shoestring budget of five thousand dollars, yet it managed to attract big-name talent such as actress Jennifer Connelly. Using Harrison's club connections, the spot was aired for free on the hit show *American Idol*, and seen by twenty-five million people in an ad slot that normally cost one million dollars per minute.

Harrison lists example after example of creative, clever ways to raise money and spread the message. He wanted Charity: Water to be the first charity to use Twitter for fund-raising so he helped come up with the idea for the "Twestival." Through tweeted micropayments, more than two hundred cities around the globe hosted events that more than ten thousand people attended, raising $250,000. The drilling of his first "tweet well" was posted online.

Actor Hugh Jackman tweeted, "I will donate 100K to one individual's favorite nonprofit organization. Of course, you must convince me why by using 140 characters or less." Harrison was in Uganda and immediately went to a local school for his tweet. He also urged Charity: Water's more than 140,000 followers on Twitter to encourage Jackman to give them money. Choosing among thousands of suggestions, Jackman contributed fifty thousand dollars to the group and one other. Harrison says that Charity: Water received three hundred media mentions in its first three years with no marketing budget. In its first two and a half years, the group raised $9.5 million from more than forty thousand donors.

Charity: Water always works with local partners. The community is charged with looking after the well, while the organization contributes to a fund every month so there is money to pay for parts and repairs when the well breaks down. Responsibility stays local.

This is not just a story of clever marketing. Harrison is literally trying to reinvent how charities operate for his generation. From his perspective, it all starts with the brand: "Design is so important to me. Just because you're a nonprofit doesn't mean you have to have bad design." Everything about Charity: Water has a clean, sharp look about it. It has a fashion sense, from the black labels on the bottled water to the organization's website. *People* magazine had a feature on him in its article "Super Heroes," and the teaser headline read, "Think all the Good Ones Are Taken? Meet Three Hot Humanitarians."

But it goes beyond image: "Charities were so bad at proving what they did." Harrison found that his friends wanted to donate but were cynical about their money going to administrative costs or corrupt locals. He decided to show that every penny went to help people: "Every project we funded had to have a GPS coordinate. We partnered with Google Earth so people can see exactly where their well is." He posted videos of the wells actually being built. "Our plan is to go back in five years to audit every water point." Donors can track their donations on another continent. Harrison is committed to full transparency in all aspects of operation. The group's audit reports and tax forms for every year are easily downloadable from the website.

Harrison runs a lean operation and separately solicits donations to cover administrative costs and overhead—that way every dollar Charity: Water raises from the public goes directly to projects. Harrison understands that guilt doesn't sell nearly as well as the satisfaction in making a difference to other people's lives.

"I would have called myself a very noncreative person during the decade of nightlife. I mean, we just did the same thing over and over again, and it was banal and just boring. With water, I mean, oh, my gosh, I have twenty years of ideas. It's such an exciting space. You can tell people stories. If your goal is trying to get people to understand what you're seeing, I mean, I walk between two worlds. I'm in remote villages in Ethiopia and Bangladesh, and then I'm at fancy dinners hanging out with millionaires. And constantly going through my mind is, how do I get the millionaire to understand what the woman just said? I mean, how do I get him to understand about leeches in the water? That's just so foreign."

Surrounded by students after the talk, he is still brainstorming. One student talks about a creative engineer she knows. He picks up a plastic jerry jug and starts showing her how they need a new design so that straps can be put on to carry it more easily. "Maybe it can curve this way," he wonders aloud.

Harrison is a visionary, but he's realistic, as well. Working with local partners, Charity: Water claims to have provided clean water for two million people in its first five years of operation. But, Harrison readily acknowledges, the challenge of providing safe drinking water in much of the developing world remains a daunting challenge. "This only will have solved one-tenth of 1 percent of the problem."

Despite the scale of the challenge, though, there is real progress on the ground. The UN currently estimates that most regions of the world will meet the Millennium Development Goal of halving the population without safe drinking water by 2015. Increased adoption of POU strategies holds out great hope. And if anyone can make a difference in addressing this intractable problem, you get the feeling Scott Harrison will lead the way.

DOES DOWSING WORK?

Where surface sources for water are not available, locating groundwater is as important for a wealthy vineyard in California's Napa Valley as for a poor village in rural Botswana. Digging a well requires a serious commitment of time and labor, so you want to hit water the first time. Today, those seeking to dig a well can rely on sophisticated technologies ranging from low-frequency sensors and ground penetrating radar to geophysical tomographs. Prior to the advent of advanced geological sensing technologies, however, how did people know where to dig when water may (or may not) be ten feet or even lower beneath the ground?

One of the oldest techniques that persists through today is known as dowsing, divining, or water-witching. Depending on the technique, a dowser holds a forked stick (preferably willow or hazel, one fork in each hand), a pendulum, or L- and Y-shaped rods in front, parallel to the ground. He then walks around searching for the presence of water underneath him. When the stick dips sharply, the pendulum shifts position, or the rods cross one another, and the dowser knows he is over water.

Dowsing has also been used to search for mineral deposits at least since 16th century Germany and likely earlier. A founder of the American Society of Dowsing describes the technique as "the exercise of a human faculty, which allows one to obtain information in a manner beyond the scope and power of the standard human physical senses of sight, sound, touch, etc."

Not surprisingly, skeptics have long challenged whether there are any modes of detection "beyond the scope and power of the standard human physical senses of sight, sound, touch, etc." One could imagine, for example, that a dowser is unconsciously aware of subtle physical cues in the landscape suggesting groundwater. Another cause may be what psychologists call the "Ideomotor Effect," unconscious motion that is consistent with the person's expectations.

While many adherents swear to dowsing's effectiveness, scientific studies have yet to confirm this. In a comprehensive and clever experiment in Germany, researchers buried a plastic pipe a foot and a half below the ground. With the flick of a switch they could turn on the flow of water through the pipe. Dowsers were shown the location of the pipes and asked to determine whether water was flowing. Thirty dowsers from Germany, Denmark, Austria and France volunteered to participate. For the first ten tests, they were told the water was flowing and asked to confirm this. The control was important because it provided a baseline and ensured there were no "anomalies" in the landscape that might disrupt the dowsers' detection ability. All the dowsers agreed that water was, in fact, both present and flowing. This was followed by three days of tests when the water flow was turned on and off based on a random pattern. The dowsers' predictions matched what would be expected by pure chance. Other studies have reached similar results.

As the famed skeptic, James Randi, observed, "It is perhaps significant that the German word for the dowsing rod is *Wünschelrute*, which translates as 'wishing stick.'"

8

Finding Water for the Twenty-first Century

A dead Prime Minister.
A country in turmoil.
A battle for Canada's most precious resource—water.
On the eve of testy discussions with the U.S. Secretary of State,
Prime Minister Matthew McLaughlin is killed in an accident. His son,
Tom McLaughlin, returns to Canada to attend his father's funeral
where he delivers a eulogy that stirs the public and propels him into
politics and ultimately the Prime Minister's office. The investigation
into his father's death, however, reveals that it was no accident, raising
the possibility of assassination. The trail of evidence triggers a series
of events that uncovers a shocking plot to sell one of Canada's most
valuable resources—water.

THUS READ THE PUBLICITY MATERIALS HYPING H_2O, one of the top dramas on Canadian television in 2004. It leaves out the most exciting part, where American troops invade Canada to plunder their water supply. The two-part miniseries, produced by the Canadian Broadcasting Corporation, was nominated for a series of awards and won a Golden Nymph for Best Actor. A son succeeding his father as prime minister seems plausible enough, but would anyone really care enough about Canada's water to assassinate its head of state? Would the United States really invade its neighbor to the north for water? From the high ratings, the Canadian public seemed to think so, and with some justification. At the time, the country was embroiled in a contentious national debate over plans to sell and ship off water from the Great Lakes.

The Great Lakes come by the name honestly. They are the largest bodies of freshwater on the planet, comprising about 20 percent of the total accessible water (most freshwater is locked in glaciers and icebergs, but more on that later). Given so much water for the taking, there has been a series of proposals over the past fifty years to transport water from the Great Lakes to Texas, Las Vegas, Phoenix, and other water-scarce regions. None of these previous proposals have gone very far, though, either because of the sheer costs involved or political opposition. None have gotten very much public attention, either.

That all changed in 1998 with a permit application by a company called the Nova Group to the Ontario Ministry of the Environment. Nova requested a five-year permit to fill up to six hundred million liters of water from Lake Superior in tankers. These ships would then transport the water to Asian markets where freshwater is scarce. The business concept seemed a clever way to satisfy the increasing global demand for clean drinking water. In concept, it was little different than shipping grain from Alberta, timber from British Columbia, or oil from the tar sands of Athabasca—moving a scarce commodity from its point of origin in Canada to a foreign market.

While six hundred million liters sounds like a lot of water, keep in mind that Lake Superior, the world's largest freshwater lake, holds roughly twelve thousand cubic kilometers of water. Nova's permit allowed the company to withdraw one five-hundred-millionth of the lake's volume. That's pretty small by any measure. The ministry granted the permit with little fanfare or concern. When the deal became public, officials were in for a surprise.

The public reaction was swift and harsh on both sides of the border. Opposition arose primarily over the treatment of water as a commodity. Maude Barlow, the Canadian campaigner for a human right to water and chair of the Council of Canadians, warned that Canada would lose control of its resources: "Once the tap is turned on, we can't turn it off." While there are no cases on point, she cautioned that international trade agreements such as the North American Free Trade Agreement (NAFTA) and the General

Agreements on Tariffs and Trade (GATT) would leave Canada powerless to restrict bulk water exports if water were viewed as a commodity under trade law.

Part of the opposition to bulk transfers of Great Lakes water has been proprietary on both sides of the border—it's ours and you're not going to get any. Having seen too many of their jobs, population, and prosperity move South and West, America's Rust Belt states were not feeling generous, either. As the governor of Illinois, Jim Thompson, declared, "There has been no effort by Sun Belters to give up their climate or by California to give up its redwoods. That's all right. We don't want that. But fair is fair, and Great Lakes water is not available for export." Highway billboards put up by Citizens for Michigan's Future, a nonprofit group formed to oppose diversions, put it simply. Showing caricatures of a Texas cowboy, a California surfer, and a Utah skier drinking with straws from a trough in the shape of the Great Lakes, the billboard's message read, "Back off Suckers. Water Diversion . . . The Last Straw." North of the border, some of the opposition, and certainly the driving force behind the television series H_2O, was latent anti-Americanism.

Concerns were also raised over the environmental impacts by continuous withdrawal from lakes that had been formed by glacier and slowly replenished. Lake Superior's level has fallen to the lowest levels since measurements were first taken in 1918. Other opponents claimed that the use of Great Lakes water was unworthy. As one critic wrote, "California suburbs also use taxpayer-subsidized water to create gardens that would be the envy of gardeners in rain-soaked England—while living in an area that receives forty centimeters of rain a year. . . . Canada has no interest in feeding this wasteful and inappropriate consumption of water." Another argued that "water shipped halfway around the world will only be affordable to the privileged and will deepen inequities between rich and poor. International trade in bulk water will allow elites to assure the quality of their own drinking water supplies, while permitting them to ignore the pollution of their local waters and the waste of their water management systems."

While overwhelming, opposition to bulk transfers was not unanimous. Supporters pointed out that freshwater was a valuable commodity and Canada should take advantage of its natural good luck just as it had with timber, oil, and other resources. And echoing the plot of the H_2O television series, the cover story in the popular magazine *Maclean's* argued Canada should "sell them our water before they take it."

There was also a good deal of hypocrisy about the sanctity of Great Lakes water at play, though few wanted to hear about it. The Nova Group received a permit to withdraw six hundred million liters over five years. Consider, however, that Toronto withdraws 1.7 billion liters *every day* from Lake Ontario for its use. Chicago withdraws even more from Lake Michigan, more than two billion gallons of water a day, and transfers it into a shipping channel that flows into the Mississippi River. Allegedly this would fill a tanker every two hours. Nor does this include the billions of liters that are diverted from the lake for agricultural use. In the public drama playing out in the media, the Nova Group was the bad guy, threatening the future of the lakes. Local use—orders of magnitude greater and happening right now by cities and farmers bordering the Great Lakes—was scarcely mentioned. As *Maclean's* columnist Steve Maich wrote, "If it's okay to use water to irrigate crops that are then shipped across national borders; if it's okay to bottle millions of litres a year for sale in corner stores around the world; if it's okay to divert water to make steel or refine oil that is then shipped across national borders, then why not the water itself?"

The Nova Group was as surprised as anyone. This was no sophisticated multinational. The company shared an office with an accounting firm above a hairdresser. Trying to respond to the media and political onslaught, the company issued an apologetic PR statement explaining that "what started to be a simple idea to help Third World Asian countries in need of freshwater and in turn possibly help the economic climate in northern Ontario has turned into an international incident. That was not our intention." Not surprisingly, the Nova Group never shipped any water.

Just as we saw with the battle over Nestlé's bottling plans in

McCloud, commercialization of drinking water provokes strong reactions. The furor over the very idea of shipping a negligible amount of water from the Great Lakes laid bare a tender and angry range of concerns—from fear of privatization of water and environmental harm to resentment over other regions squandering their treasured local water. It catalyzed a broad public debate on both sides of the border over whether Great Lakes water should be exported to thirsty markets at all.

Responding to the public's opposition, governors of the eight Great Lakes states, from New York across to Minnesota, joined with the premiers of Ontario and Quebec to announce a ban on large-scale water transfers. Legislation passed by Congress now permits the governor of any Great Lake state to veto a water diversion for use outside of the basin. Canadian law similarly prohibits water diversions outside of the boundary water basins. Amendments to the international Great Lakes–St. Lawrence River Basin Water Resources Compact reinforced these national laws. The net result makes it virtually impossible for a business to ship large amounts of Great Lakes water outside of the watershed. The legal obstacles created to block transfers, however, include an interesting loophole. There is no restriction on the transport of water in containers of twenty liters (5.7 gallons) or less for human consumption. Either politicians or lobbyists, or likely both, were unwilling to shut down the potential bottled water market for Great Lakes water. The danger of depleting the Great Lakes one bottle at a time seems not to have been a concern.

Patricia Mulroy, the general manager for the Las Vegas Valley Water District and the Southern Nevada Water Authority, has earned an international reputation for the innovative and tough water conservation measures she has put in place for one of the fastest-growing and most arid cities in the United States. She has little patience for the Great Lakes saga. "We take gold, we take oil, we take uranium, we take natural gas from Texas to the rest of the country. We move oil from Alaska to Mexico. But they say, 'I will not give you one drop of water!' . . . They've got 14 percent of the population of the United States, and 20 percent of the freshwater in the world—and no one can use it but them? 'I might not need it. But I'm not sharing it!' When did it become *their* water anyway? It's nuts!" Or maybe not. Mulroy, who has seen more than her share of political grandstanding, describes the core problem bluntly: "Nothing makes better cheap politics than water."

As THE PREVIOUS CHAPTERS HAVE MADE CLEAR, MANY PARTS OF THE world are getting thirsty. Access to reliable, clean drinking water is no longer a given in some places and has never been an easy option in others, where assuring water to drink remains a daily challenge. Even for those with currently adequate supplies, access to safe drinking water will only become more difficult as climate change increases the incidence of droughts, pollution despoils existing supplies, and population growth increases demand. These regions, encompassing most of the global population, will need to increase their supplies of safe drinking water. To call this a critical challenge to humanity's future is no exaggeration.

In some respects, the challenge is quite straightforward. There is no "new water" to create. Our planet's atmosphere traps our moisture, so the water we can draw from is fixed. It's the same water that the dinosaurs drank, the same as the primordial soup that served as the incubator for the emergence of life on earth. Given that, there are two basic strategies to provide more drinking water. The first is to move it from water-rich to water-scarce regions. Think tankers full of Great Lakes water plowing the seas toward the Middle East or icebergs towed from the poles. The second strategy relies on generating new supplies of water locally. Think desalination plants or so-called "toilet-to-tap" efforts—capturing, treating, and distributing sewage water.

The rest of this chapter reviews the impressive range of technologies and approaches in use and under development around the globe to increase supplies of drinking water. Some are dizzyingly high-tech, some brilliantly low-tech. As you read about these, imagine yourself as a venture capitalist. Which business opportunities would you invest in? No less a business authority than the *Wall*

Street Journal has proclaimed water as the twenty-first century's equivalent of oil. There is a lot of money to be made, as well as lost, and some very clever people are in on the game.

DESPITE THE ACRIMONY AND SHUTTING DOWN OF WATER SALES FROM the Great Lakes, bulk water transfers are already happening in many parts of the world. Take Barcelona, for example. In 2008, while suffering its worst drought in sixty years, the city began shipping water from the nearby Spanish city of Tarragona and the French port of Marseille in tankers. Six ships per month delivered more than four hundred million gallons of freshwater. The cost per gallon was more than three times higher than that of regular water. The city paid, but is now building a major desalination plant. Israel has entered into an agreement with Turkey for the shipment of fifty billion liters annually from the Manavgat River. Greece and Cyprus routinely import freshwater, as well. Most of the water is shipped in tankers, just like any other liquid commodity. Aquarius Water Transportation, a company supplying far-flung Greek isles, however, tows massive bladders—gigantic rubber bags as long as a football field—behind a ship. Because freshwater is less dense than salt water, the bags float just beneath the surface.

The bulk water market is still relatively small, but many observers think it will increase significantly in the coming decades. Paul Muldoon, executive director of the Canadian Environmental Law Association, uses an intriguing analogy. While it may not make financial sense to move water around the world today, "it's a little like buying a McDonald's restaurant in 1963. Who would have ever thought you'd want to get a drive-through hamburger, but look at the way things are now." Climate models predict that much of the American South and Southwest will continue to suffer periodic droughts, even in states we normally think of as water-rich such as Alabama and Florida. The billionaire T. Boone Pickens needs no convincing. He bought more than $100 million in water rights in Texas and plans to build a two-hundred-fifty-mile pipeline to Dallas, where he will supply the expanding municipality. Dallas says the price is too high at the moment, but Pickens believes time is on his side.

An idea that has no doubt occurred to any entrepreneur clinking ice in a glass on a hot day is towing icebergs. Icebergs float free for the taking near the poles, filled with nothing but clean water. The only trick is getting them from their cold waters of origin to distant ports where they can be used. There have been serious proposals to tow icebergs since at least the 1950s.

The idea is far from crazy, except that pushing makes more sense than towing. Tugboats push massive ships every day in harbors around the world. Indeed, in the North Sea they already push icebergs away from oil platforms. Strong currents flow from both the North and South poles toward the Equator, so most of the navigational force could be supplied by the oceans themselves. Just look at the icebergs from the Arctic that are sometimes carried deep into the Atlantic Ocean, as the passengers on the doomed *Titanic* learned to their dismay.

We don't see an iceberg moving industry, though, so there are obviously some problems in the way. One concerns melting. Ocean water temperatures increase significantly between the poles and the equatorial regions, as much as 20 to 30 degrees Celsius. Moreover, the iceberg must traverse the high waves and occasional storms of the open ocean, either of which could put pressure on fissures within the iceberg, causing it to break into smaller pieces. A tug can only push one piece at a time, so everything calving off would be left to melt in the open water. Since, as we all have been told, only the tip of the iceberg rides above the water, running aground is also a significant challenge. Moving the iceberg into a shallow port where it could be broken apart and placed in tanks to melt could prove difficult.

Nonetheless, entrepreneurs continue to push the idea. As Georges Mougin, an enthusiastic iceberg proponent, explains, "An iceberg is a floating reservoir. And water from icebergs is the purest water. It was formed some 10,000 years ago." A sophisticated computer analysis Mougin developed with the aeronautics firm Dassault calculated that a tugboat pushing an iceberg at one knot per hour could, with favorable currents, move a seven-million-ton iceberg from Greenland to the Canary Islands in 141 days, losing just 38 percent of the bulk en route. This would still leave close to four million tons of frozen water for local use.

Otto Spork sought to avoid the challenges of ocean transport by investing in glaciers, instead. Chief executive of the hedge fund Sextant Capital Management, Spork was confident in his business plan. "Two years ago," he explained, "we were looking for the next big commodity and settled on water. It was underappreciated, mispriced, and growing scarce." Spork purchased water rights to three glaciers in northern Europe. Located near ports for transportation ease, he planned to use the melt from one glacier for bottled water and the other two for bulk transport by tankers and water bladders. We will never know if his plan would have worked, however, since Spork and Sextant were found guilty of fraud by the Ontario Securities Commission in 2011.

While attractive in concept, moving water large distances in tankers or frozen in icebergs remains a niche market. The more important strategy to increase sources of freshwater is creating drinking water where we already are. Entrepreneurs and engineers are combining forces to create some exciting technologies. Few of these are likely to become commercially viable, but they give a glimpse of future directions.

While a high-cost and high-tech approach, desalination holds great promise in converting plentiful ocean and brackish water into freshwater. There are a range of desalination processes currently in use. Reverse osmosis forces salt water at high pressure through a series of membranes that filter the salts out. Passing the water through a second set of finer membranes provides an even fresher water. In a sense, this is learning from nature, for the process of natural selection perfected a process for removing salts from ocean water in the evolution of species as varied as albatross and mangroves.

In distillation, salt water is heated and water vapor rises until it meets a cold surface, condensing into drops of freshwater. You may recognize this as the basis of the natural water cycle. Rather than the sun, clouds, and rain, however, distillation plants rely on industrial boiling and cooling equipment.

The benefits of desalination are indisputable. A secure source of clean water is assured from a virtually limitless supply. There are more than twelve thousand desalination plants in more than one hundred twenty countries. The Middle East accounts for almost three-quarters of global production, most notably in the oil-rich nations of Saudi Arabia, the United Arab Emirates, Qatar, and Bahrain. Israel, Malta, and the Maldives also rely heavily on desalinated water. The United States has more than two thousand desalination plants. The cities of El Paso, which relies on desalination for one-quarter of its water, and Tampa are the major adopters. Barcelona, Sydney, Algiers, and even London are constructing or have recently opened major plants.

Despite such widespread adoption, however, desalination remains a small player at the global level, accounting for less than one percent of total water consumption. Much of this is due to the lower cost of alternative surface and groundwater sources in most places. Desalination is expensive no matter how you do it. Energy and construction costs are high, making the water as much as ten times more expensive than many surface or groundwater supplies. The Saudi Arabian plant at Shoaiba produces a massive 450 million liters a day but cost more than $1 billion to construct.

Desalination also imposes high operating costs. Heating the water or forcing it through filters takes a lot of energy. Most desalination plants rely on coal- or oil-fired power plants, and the greenhouse gases emitted, unfortunately, contribute to climate change. As a result, there is increasing interest in renewable energy. The desalination plant in Perth, Australia, is partly powered by the Emu Downs Wind Farm. The plant in Sydney offsets its energy use with renewable power from an inland wind farm. Delft University in the Netherlands has a project underway that couples a small desalination plant with an on-site windmill. With the catchy title "Drinking with the Wind," the combined operation can provide enough water for five hundred families. While wind holds promise as a means to reduce desalination plants' contribution to climate change, the more common non–fossil fuel energy source is nuclear. India, Japan, Russia, and other countries rely on nuclear power both on the land and at sea to power their desalination plants. A U.S. Navy aircraft carrier uses its nuclear reactor to provide desalinated drinking water to the small city aboard—up to four hundred thousand gallons per day.

Even if the energy source does not generate greenhouse gases, desalination creates a serious waste stream. Ocean water obviously contains a much higher concentration of salt than freshwater. The waste product resulting from desalination, called brine, is even more saline and is produced in large quantities. For every hundred gallons of water treated in a reverse osmosis plant, as much as fifty to eighty-five gallons will be discharged as brine. The Environmental Protection Agency treats brine as a waste regulated under the Clean Water Act. Simply discharging brine into the ocean can cause significant harm to the local marine environment. Because brine is denser than seawater, it tends to sink to the ocean bed, killing filter-feeding animals such as coral and the nonmobile eggs and juveniles of other species at the sea bottom. This is an even greater problem in semi-enclosed areas such as bays and estuaries, where water does not easily mix. As a result, some desalination plants have long pipes that discharge the brine far offshore, often using multiple branches to diffuse the discharge over a larger area.

Despite the high start-up costs, entrepreneurs are entering the desalination market. The strategy of the start-up Water Standard is to rely on desalination plants in retrofitted tankers. These ships, part of the company's H2Ocean product line, will be moored far enough offshore to avoid the environmental problems from discharging brine but close enough that transporting the freshwater to the shore via pipe or ship is practical. The company envisions producing up to seventy-five million gallons of freshwater a day. Venture capitalists clearly think there is money to be made, and have provided $250 million in funding to get the business going.

Despite its financial and environmental costs, whether powered by fossil fuels, wind, or nuclear power, desalination seems certain to become a more significant source of drinking water in the coming decades. Given the likelihood of prolonged droughts from climate change, the prospect of turning salt water into clean freshwater cannot help but be an obvious option as cities seek new sources to satisfy their growing populations. Over time, technology will continue to develop and the problems of high energy use and brine discharge may well become less significant. Desalination is not, however, a silver bullet. Because water is expensive to move across land in large quantities, particularly uphill, cities far from the coast or at high elevations will not find the technology helpful because of its high costs. Nor, of course, will poor communities unable to afford the high capital and energy costs. Peter Gleick, the noted water authority, projects that desalinated water will supply no more than 0.3 percent of the United States' water supply.

As with any market, the future for projects providing large amounts of water, whether tankers or desalination plants, depends, of course, on supply and demand. But there are other factors to consider. How expensive is it to obtain the clean water? How much does it cost to move the water from its origin to the site of consumption? And, critically, what is the city's marginal cost of supply? This last point is subtle but important. The challenge facing local government is not simply how to get water in times of drought but the most efficient way to do so. Every city has a drinking water supply system in place that provides the bulk of the water consumed. The question is how much an additional gallon of water will cost *on top* of what the system already produces. If the system generally provides enough water and extra supplies are only needed sporadically, then an expensive, temporary strategy such as tankers may be appropriate. While costly on its face, transporting water by tankers or giant bladders is considerably less expensive than installing large pipelines. If, by contrast, a steady shortfall in water supply is likely, then more capital-intensive approaches such as pipelines or even a desalination plant with much higher up-front costs that will take decades to pay off may prove a wiser long-term financial investment.

There is a trade-off between water volume and infrastructure cost. Water from a tanker may feel expensive compared to the normal cost of water but prove far less expensive for three months' supply than paying for a permanent desalination plant or miles and miles of pipes to a distant source, not to mention buying rights-of-way through private land. For an additional supply extending two or three decades, though, tankers may prove much more expensive. It all depends on how often the current system will prove inadequate and how much additional water is needed.

The other basic problem faced by water entrepreneurs is that they are not playing on a level field. They know how much it costs per gallon of freshwater to tow an iceberg or sail a tanker but, in the absence of a drought or dire situation where a city will pay almost regardless of the price, they have to match or beat the current cost of water. Unfortunately for them, urban water is not generally subject to market forces. In most cases, both the water and infrastructure are owned by the government. Even when private providers are allowed, the rates are often regulated. The net result is, more times than not, a subsidized good. There are arguments why governments may want to ensure that water is inexpensive, but make no mistake. It provides a strong disincentive for the development of additional sources by entrepreneurs who simply cannot compete on price. Because of this, much of the entrepreneurial energy has focused on emerging technologies for smaller scale supply.

The military is a good place to start. Since the time of the Roman legions and well before, every army on the move has sought to improve its logistical efficiency. Safe drinking water is critical to battle success. Generals from Vegetius to Rommel have emphasized that dangers to troops from dysentery and diarrhea can be as harmful as battlefield casualties. If safe water can be provided locally, all the better, since it avoids the costs of transport. A current initiative under development with the U.S. Department of Defense is capillary condensation. This technology captures the water vapor from burning diesel fuel. Basic chemistry suggests that one could capture one gallon of water from one gallon of diesel fuel burned.

On a smaller scale, the LifeStraw is a simple device intended for individual use to purify drinking water. About a foot long and easily hung from the neck, the plastic casing encloses filter membranes. The only energy needed is from a person who literally sucks through the straw, drawing water through the pores and filtering out bacteria and parasites. Designed to treat a thousand liters, roughly the amount a person drinks in a year, the LifeStraw costs only two to three dollars. There are reports on the web that U.S. troops use LifeStraws to drink from puddles.

Another new technology known as WaterMill produces drinking water from humidity in the air. The machine uses the dew point to create condensation, which then drips into a holding container. The manufacturer claims that the technology can turn outdoor air into approximately thirteen quarts of drinking water every day. To prevent contamination, the machine uses ultraviolet light to sterilize the water collected. Larger atmospheric water generators, such as the Air Water machine, can produce much greater volumes of water. Following the 2004 tsunami in Thailand and Sri Lanka, thirteen 3.5-ton water generators, each the size of a small trailer, were deployed. These large machines have also been used by the U.S. Marines, Indian border police, and South African military.

The PlayPump technology offers a seemingly clever approach to providing drinking water in poor rural areas. Created by a billboard executive from South Africa in the 1990s, the basic idea was to connect a spinning merry-go-round to a borehole. Playing children would provide the power to pump clean groundwater to a 2,500-liter holding tank seven meters above the playground. To create a revenue stream, the tank was enclosed within four billboards that could be leased for advertising space.

The simplicity of pumping clean water through kids having fun on the playground rather than working hard at a hand pump seemed a brilliant inspiration and generated great enthusiasm. It was awarded the World Bank's Development Marketplace Award in 2000. A few years later, First Lady Laura Bush announced funding of $16 million from the U.S. Agency for International Development and other donors, with the goal of raising $45 million more to build four thousand pumps in Africa by 2010. The rapper Jay-Z promoted the initiative in concerts and an MTV documentary.

What looks great on the drawing board, though, often faces unanticipated challenges when tested in the field. Following the installation of several PlayPumps, the initial enthusiasm was doused with the cold water of reality. The well-known development group WaterAid chose not to adopt the PlayPump technology in its projects. Concerns ranged from high installation costs (roughly four times the costs of the alternative hand pump system) and difficulty in finding spare parts locally to a complex design that made local maintenance impractical. A more emotional charge claimed that the amount of pumping necessary to provide sufficient water for a community would require a great deal more power than could be provided by occasional playing, not to mention the fact that children might not want to play when water was most needed, such as during a hot drought. The implication was that "child labor" might be a more appropriate description than "child's play." Moreover, it is hard to imagine much of a revenue stream for billboards in poor, rural areas. As one blogger with development experience observed, "Each time I've visited a PlayPump, I've always found the same scene: a group of women and children struggling to spin it by hand so they can draw water."

REUSING WASTEWATER HOLDS TREMENDOUS POTENTIAL TO FORESTALL expensive alternative supplies of water both on Earth and in space. In May 2009, astronauts aboard the International Space Station first drank water recycled from their own urine. Seeking to celebrate the moment, the astronauts toasted to their own pee, "clinking" the water bags. The American astronaut Michael Barratt claimed "the taste is great. . . . We're going to be drinking yesterday's coffee frequently up here, and happy to do it." Not quite as catchy as Neil Armstrong's "One small step for man, one giant step for mankind," but a nice try. The processor is housed in a space toilet purchased from Russia, which passes urine into an American-made filter. Solid waste in the urine is separated out and stored to be sent back to Earth. This process can recycle 93 percent of the water it receives and reduces the fuel needed to transport the heavy liquid from Earth to space. This source of additional water also increases the number of astronauts the space station can support.

While the space station relies on a distinctly high-tech approach, recycling our sewage is not difficult to do. With enough filters, ultraviolet radiation, and other standard treatment technologies, we can take virtually any polluted water source and produce clean drinking water. Indeed, we already do. While not something most people dwell on, it's a fact that our water treatment plants deal every day with excrement from animals that live beside the rivers and reservoirs where we store our water, not to mention oil leaked on driveways, lawn fertilizer, and other gunk that washes off our streets and drains into water bodies. Where water is scarce, why not capture, treat, and reuse what we flush down our drains? Is it really much dirtier than water we already treat before piping it to our water mains and faucets? If it's good enough for astronauts, it should be good enough for us.

While it might make perfect sense to an engineer, chemist, or economist, selling the idea of "toilet-to-tap" to the general public has proven far more challenging. The basic problem is that it just feels gross. Experts in the field describe this as "the yuck factor." As Charles Fishman has memorably described, "The condoms flushed away, the stagnant water from the vase of roses that stayed too long, the washing machine water from the dog's bath towels, the sour milk poured down the kitchen drain, the deceased goldfish given a toilet-bowl funeral—you can clean all that out of the water, no problem. But no matter how crystalline the water itself, you can't filter away the images of where it comes from."

There are a few places where recycling wastewater has become an accepted, standard practice, including Windhoek, Namibia, and affluent Fairfax, Virginia, near Washington, D.C., where treated sewage makes up about 5 percent of the drinking water. Orange County, California, started reusing sewage water in the 1970s and now relies on this source for 20 percent of its water needs. To address the yuck factor, treated water is pumped into an underground aquifer where it is later extracted as groundwater. As the water percolates through the soil, it is further cleansed by microorganisms and the water's "origin" is scrubbed from the public's consciousness, as well.

The most ambitious use of toilet-to-tap is occurring in Singapore. Branded "NEWater," the reuse strategy is justified in terms of national security. A tiny country at the tip of Malaysia, Singapore has few natural resources and has traditionally relied on Malaysia for most of its drinking water. As twenty-year-old student Khaiting Tan explains, "In the past, we had to get water from another country, but what happens if the ties between the two countries are jeopardized? It's better to be self-reliant." The treated water currently meets about one-third of Singapore's daily water needs and the goal is to meet 50 percent over time. A public education initiative explains where the water comes from, why the strategy is necessary, and that the water is, in fact, cleaner than most piped water. Two remarkable statistics show just how accepted this initiative has become—more than eight hundred thousand people have visited the wastewater purification visitor's center and nineteen million bottles of NEWater have been distributed to athletic groups and at community events.

Singapore's experience proves that toilet-to-tap is clearly a viable strategy, but proof of concept has not assured acceptance in other parts of the world. Singapore, after all, is famous (notorious in some circles) for banning the sale of chewing of gum since 1992. The town of Toowoomba in Queensland, Australia, provides a cautionary tale in this regard. In the grips of a serious drought, the city council proposed treating and reusing the town's wastewater. Rival groups soon sprang up to press the contentious debate on both sides of the issue. The Toowoomba Water Futures Project (with the motto "Keep our future flowing") faced off against the memorably named Citizens Against Drinking Sewage. Charges flew back and forth ("sewage sippers" was one of the more memorable epithets). Despite the longstanding drought, the proposal to drink treated sewage water was soundly defeated in a referendum, 62 percent to 38 percent. They ended up building a much more expensive pipeline.

Despite the experience of nearby Orange County, in the face of heated opposition, San Diego's city council voted in 1999 to halt its recycled water project. The local paper, the *San Diego Union-*

Tribune, ran an editorial stating that even though your golden retriever was comfortable drinking out of the toilet bowl, it didn't mean people should as well. There is something of the profane in drinking one's own waste.

The basic challenge to recycling wastewater, of course, is perception. Water users need to feel comfortable with the water coming out of their tap, and the idea of drinking some vestige of what was recently floating in a toilet bowl is simply hard for people to accept. Opponents say it will lead to a public health disaster. Never mind that the treated water can be made cleaner than water from the local reservoir. Never mind that we are drinking the same water that dinosaurs drank seventy million years ago and that has gone through the water cycle (and various species' gastrointestinal tracts) countless times since.

Water utilities are realizing they need to take a more indirect route than toilet-to-tap. Hence Orange County's underground pumping of its treated water. San Diego learned this lesson, too. It revisited recycled water again in 2007, this time in the midst of a drought. Called the Indirect Potable Reuse project, the proposed new plant would treat sewage water and send it to reservoirs and aquifers rather than directly into water mains. It was approved. Las Vegas, El Paso, and Tucson have similarly chosen to pump treated effluent into aquifers, recharging the groundwater and later pumping up for regular use.

Virtually anyone who thinks seriously about water shortages realizes how inefficient our current system is. Imagine if your next-door neighbor insisted on only using bottled water to flush his toilets, water his garden, or wash his cars. You'd think he was crazy. There is no rational excuse for using water clean enough to drink for washing down a driveway or watering your lawn. Yet we do just that every day. According to the American Water Works Association, the average American uses about seventy gallons of water a day. Most of our water, about 27 percent, simply goes down the drain flushing toilets. We use another 22 percent to wash clothes, and almost 20 percent for baths and showers. Once one adds in the water to wash dishes and run faucets and the water that leaks from pipes, the remaining "Other Domestic Uses" account for only 2 percent of total water use, and drinking water is an even smaller percentage than that.

Any way you measure it, the water we use for drinking and cooking is a tiny trickle of overall water consumption. We take well over 97 percent of the water that has been treated clean enough to drink and use it for purposes where the potability of the water is irrelevant. Why do we do this? And, more to the point, why don't we stop doing this?

The simple answer is that we do it because we can. Water is very cheap. It was cheap when our basic plumbing and water distribution systems were designed and laid out. And for most people, it's still cheap. In Durham, North Carolina, I pay less than ten dollars for every thousand gallons of water delivered to my house, and the national average is a good deal cheaper than that. While I am careful about not wasting water, the motive is not saving money.

We have seen the same dynamic with another basic commodity. Until very recently, gasoline was cheap, too. Cheap gas led to highway programs, far-flung suburbs, big cars, and sprawl. The difference between gas and water is that gas has gotten more expensive, with the result of more fuel-efficient vehicles and more thoughtful trip planning. In most places, by contrast, water is still so cheap that reengineering is not worth the cost, even when water scarcity is a real problem. Cheap water leads to inefficient use. Neither cheap gas nor cheap water is inherently wrong or immoral, but each is deeply problematic in a world of scarcity.

If water systems were being built today and deliberately designed to conserve drinking water, they would look very different. It is not necessary, of course, to put in place toilet-to-tap systems. It could just as easily be "toilet-to-hydrant" or "toilet-to-rose-bush." Indeed, that is increasingly the case around the country.

The basic idea is to segregate water supplies between potable and nonpotable sources, sometimes called gray water. Dual distribution systems—with one set of pipes for potable water and the other for gray water uses such as firefighting, lawn watering, etc.—are in place all over the country, with California, Texas, Arizona, and Florida in the lead. The state of Arizona even offers a tax credit for installation of a residential gray water system. Tucson, Arizona, has constructed more than one hundred sixty miles of pipes that carry the treated gray water to nine hundred sites, including schoolyards, road medians, cemeteries, and parks. In 2005, the system handled more than 4.4 billion gallons of gray water. Tucson's golf courses consume two-thirds of the recycled water, forced by law to switch from groundwater if gray water is available.

In Honolulu, Hawaii, the wastewater treatment plant generates two grades of nonpotable water. R-1 Water is intended for landscaping and agriculture. Golf courses, now able to purchase R-1 water for only twenty-five cents per thousand gallons, switched over from the more expensive groundwater for watering their greens and fairways. Water that has been treated by reverse osmosis (RO Water) is used to feed boilers and for processes that require high-purity water. As the project manager, Ken Windram, describes, the program has been successful: "When one of the industrial customers uses the RO water, the island saves 600,000 gallons a day of drinking water. With all the industrial users combined, we save about 2.5 million gallons a day of drinking water. We charge industrial users about $5 per thousand gallons for recycled water, yet they save between $2 and $7 per thousand gallons."

Beyond treated water, other gray water opportunities may be found in rainwater harvesting (capturing rainwater from roofs) or stormwater discharge (collecting rainwater that has flowed from streets and fields). If we can overcome the challenges of creating infrastructure, these sources can save energy (thereby reducing greenhouse gases), increase supplies of nonpotable water, and increase water security.

Beyond making more efficient use of the water we consume, a major opportunity for increasing freshwater supplies lies in plugging leaks. For the average American, a remarkable 13 percent of piped water is lost through leaking. And the problem is not simply at home faucets. Many of our water systems are in a shocking state of disrepair. The New York Times has reported that, across the nation, a major water pipe bursts every two minutes. In our nation's capital, a pipe bursts every day. Nor should this be surprising. Most of our nation's water systems were built decades ago. Some date back to the Civil War.

Buried beneath streets and fields, these pipes don't provoke a second thought from the average citizen until they burst and faucets run dry, yet these water mains are breaking down at an alarming rate. The EPA estimates that $335 billion will be needed simply to maintain the current water infrastructure over the next few decades, not to mention upgrading the system. While a rough estimate, we may be losing up to six billion gallons of water daily simply from leaking pipes. It costs about $200 per foot of replacement pipe, $1 million every mile, so they don't come cheap. New York City's Third Water Tunnel, currently scheduled for completion in 2020, will span more than sixty miles and meet the growing water demands of more than nine million area residents, but it comes with a six-billion-dollar price tag. Expensive, but what's the alternative?

To date, the primary option has been to bury our heads in the sand and do very little. We are starving our water system of funds, and have been doing so for years. Part of the reason is the invisibility of the water system, part is the lack of public understanding over how antiquated our infrastructure has become, and part is the belligerent refusal to pay for what the system really costs.

The obvious answer to inefficient water use and system maintenance is the same: raise water rates. When we have to pay more for something, whether gas or electricity, we either use less or do more with what we have. We drive less. We use more energy efficient appliances. We turn off the lights when leaving a room. The market signals make clear the benefits of efficiency, and we respond. And even with increased efficiency, raising water rates would still generate additional resources for needed infrastructure repairs and upgrades.

Raising water rates, though, seems almost as taboo in America as talk of raising taxes. Most people seem to assume that cheap water should be ours by right and that government, somehow, should find the means to pay for it on its own. We have taken the ready availability of water for granted in the past and intend to do so in the future.

To those in the water business, our unwillingness to make the proper level of investment is foolhardy. George Hawkins, the head of the District of Columbia Water and Sewer Authority, makes a telling comparison: "People pay more for their cell phones and cable television than for water. You can go a day without a phone or TV. You can't go a day without water." When he approached the District of Columbia's City Council to ask for a modest rate raise, though, he was raked over the coals. Jim Graham, a council member, proclaimed, "This rate hike is outrageous. Subway systems need repairs, and so do roads, but you don't see fares or tolls skyrocketing. Providing inexpensive, reliable water is a fundamental obligation of government. If they can't do that, they need to reform themselves, instead of just charging more." Graham was unhelpfully silent on how a water utility can reform itself to provide the money necessary for maintenance and upgrades on a decaying system.

This is not the case across the country, of course. Some cities have embraced the importance of conservation and water pricing in an era of scarcity. Las Vegas is perhaps the best example. In order to supply the opulent fountains and water shows that grace the Strip in a city with an average rainfall of four inches per year, the water is reused and expensive. Major corporations are starting to get the idea, as well. In June 2008, the CEO of the soft drink giant Coca-Cola stated that the company would become "water neutral." Every liter of water used to produce its drinks would be offset by water conservation and recycling programs. It's not clear how this will work in practice, but such a major commitment merits attention. Water is the company's most important raw material. In 2006, Coke used 290 billion liters of water to produce its beverages. The company was badly burned by protests in Kerala, India, charging that local wells had dried up because the company's operations had depleted the groundwater supplies. Even if Coke falls short of its goal, water conservation and recycling will necessarily remain major priorities. A report by the bank JP Morgan similarly concluded that water shortages pose threats that need to be addressed in corporate planning. As the lead author, Marc Levinson, made clear, "These are real business risks. This is not something far off in the future."

BEYOND TECHNOLOGIES THAT PRODUCE WATER, MOVE WATER, AND increase our efficiency of use, the last approach to consider for water provision is greater reliance on natural capital. New Yorkers love to brag about the quality of their tap water. In fact, they like to brag about a lot of things, but tap water is high on the list. New York City's water system provides over one billion gallons of drinking water to almost nine million New Yorkers every day. And it really is good tap water, often beating out bottled water in blind taste tests. The reason, though, is that it doesn't come from New York City. New York solved its drinking water problems in the early twentieth century through a massive engineering project, drawing water from the Catskill and Delaware watersheds located 125 miles north and west of the city and sending it through massive pipes to city reservoirs. In the late 1980s, however, New York City was forced to reassess its drinking water strategy. Congress passed an amendment to the Safe Drinking Water Act in 1986, requiring large municipalities taking their drinking water from surface water sources (i.e., reservoirs, rivers, lakes, and such) to pretreat the water prior to distribution in the water mains. When officials in New York City's Department of Environmental Protection did the calculations, they figured it was going to cost about six billion dollars to actually build a water treatment plant and hundreds of millions of dollars to operate it every year. The EPA said it would only cost three billion dollars to build, but this is still a big number. It is a lot of water for a lot of people.

New York was fretting over this cost when a clever city official named Al Appleton took a close look at the law and realized that there was a waiver provision. The law essentially said that if you could demonstrate to the EPA that there were other ways to provide safe drinking water, then you did not have to build the treatment plant. Appleton and some other folks started thinking, Since we're getting our water from the Catskills and Delaware watersheds, maybe we should think about how land management up there provides water quality in New York City and how we can influence their land management practices.

In 1905, recognizing the significance of the Catskills and Delaware watersheds to New York City's drinking water, the state assembly had granted New York City the power to regulate polluting activities in these areas. This created the unusual situation, to say the least, of a city with land use controls over communities more than a hundred miles away. In the early 1990s, acting on Appleton's strategy, the administration of Mayor David Dinkins announced new watershed rules for the Catskills and Delaware watersheds that would improve water quality, such as limits on the amount of paved surface on a property, buffers up to a thousand feet wide around reservoirs and up to five hundred feet from stream channels, and prohibitions on spreading manure within a hundred feet of a watercourse. Not surprisingly, the efforts of "rich city folk" in New York City to regulate, without prior consultation, how upstate farmers and landholders managed their properties were met with intense political opposition.

Faced with the concern of the EPA that New York City could not ensure catchment management would work, the governor of New York state stepped in and organized a stakeholder consultation process. Conducted over two years with more than a hundred fifty meetings, the group finally came up with a complex Memorandum of Agreement signed by sixty towns, ten villages, seven counties, and environmental groups that essentially exchanged payments from New York City for specific land management practices. One participant described the exhaustive process as similar to a "rolling Thanksgiving dinner with relatives you only want to see once a year."

The Memorandum of Agreement provided for $1.5 billion of spending commitments over ten years, funded by taxes on water bills (which New York City residents voted to allow) and municipal bonds. Of this, $250 million was targeted to acquisition of title and conservation easements in critical areas. $240 million was provided for "partnership programs." These ranged from new sewage treatment infrastructure, stormwater infrastructure to environmental education, and purchasing 125,000 acres around reservoirs.

The bottom line is that, for the cost at the time of a $600 million "green bond," New York City ensured that its water remained legal under the Safe Drinking Water Act. A major review by the EPA in 2002 persuaded the agency to extend the waiver treatment of surface waters for a further five years and then again in 2007. The expectation is they will waive them again in 2012.

The Catskills story is often held out as the poster child for an "ecosystem services" approach to providing clean water because it presents the core idea so neatly. New York City's managers needed to deliver clean water. They could get it one of two ways: through "built capital"—where they would build a treatment plant, engineer it, and run the water through it—or by investing in what you might call "natural capital"—where they could change the landscape practices where the water flowed to ensure the service of water purification. They found that if they invested in the natural capital rather than the built capital, they got a better deal, purely in financial terms. Obviously, there are a lot of other nature conservation benefits, in addition to the public education benefit of water users better understanding where their water comes from. Since the Catskills story was first made popular in the late 1990s, it has been held out as the prime example for why we should think differently about the provision of basic amenities.

There is a broader economic goal underpinning this approach. By making payments for ecosystem services, landowners' visions of value start to shift away from traditional commodity crops of agriculture and toward service provision. In addition to grain, corn, and timber, landowners currently may provide ecosystem services such as controlling floods, conserving nature, and cleaning water—but they do so for free. If they could be paid for some of these services, farmers would think differently and farms would look different—if a landowner is receiving multiple income streams, the land will be managed differently. Right now, farmlands are largely managed for monocultures. That is hardly surprising, since that's how farmers get paid. We have gotten very good at growing soy-beans because there is a ready market for them. One can imagine a world, though, where farmers are paid for more than the produce they bring to market. A greater focus on natural capital to ensure freshwater supplies—through landowners planting riparian buffers or maintaining vegetation in critical watersheds, for example—would lead to regular payments for these valuable services. If you can change the landowners' balance sheet, you can change the landscape.

The approach of paying for ecosystem services has worked not only in New York City but also around the globe. A 2010 study reported 216 payments and $9.2 billion in transactions for watershed services protecting 289 million hectares. Most of these programs were in Latin America, where water trust funds have become an important mechanism to conserve land and protect watersheds. The Quito water fund, for example, was created by the joint efforts of the municipal drinking water provider, the electrical utility, a local brewery, and a water bottling company. These partners have committed resources toward an eighty-year trust fund. The six-million-dollar fund's investment returns, supplemented by foreign aid from nongovernmental groups and development agencies, pay for conservation projects. These have ranged from strengthening protected areas and restoring degraded lands to supporting sustainable farming practices and reforestation. The primary goal in all these has been improved water quality, though there are significant additional benefits in terms of conservation and poverty alleviation. Quito's example is being followed in other Andean cities, including Lima, Cartagena, and Bogotá.

In Tanzania, CARE International has teamed with the World Wildlife Fund and other partners to create the Equitable Payment for Water Services program. Based in the Ruvu and Sigi river basins, the program aims to protect the primary water sources for the cities of Dar es Salaam and Tanga. To serve its four million residents and businesses, the Dar es Salaam Water and Sewerage Corporation has to spend roughly two million dollars every year treating water from the Ruvu River because of its high sediment load. Much as New

York City paid landowners in the Catskills to change their land management practices, the Tanzanian program pays upper watershed farmers to improve their soil conservation activities. In practice, this means reducing farmland expansion, logging, and mining. The public water utility (and Coca-Cola, which also contributes) benefits by avoiding the cost of treating water loaded with eroded soil. The farmers benefit by being compensated for the loss of income from forgoing traditional activities. The larger community benefits from the injected resources that contribute to poverty reduction. By 2008, more than four hundred fifty farmers were receiving payments.

BENJAMIN FRANKLIN IS REPUTED TO HAVE OBSERVED, "WHEN THE well's dry, we know the worth of water." This insight is as relevant today as it was in 1774. Cities that are thirsty and have the means will pay whatever it takes to obtain safe drinking water. A long line of entrepreneurs has already taken notice, hoping to profit from this undeniable demand. Whether money is to be made through pipelines, tankers, icebergs, desalination plants, treated sewage, LifeStraws, or some other innovative technology still on a drawing board remains to be seen. The clear message is that creative technologies and payment schemes for making, moving, and purifying water will only grow in importance in the coming decades.

ARE COMPANIES REALLY GOING TO MINE
WATER IN OUTER SPACE?

Any business venture funded by Google billionaires, an Academy Award–winning filmmaker, and the former chief software architect for Microsoft and run by a former NASA Mars mission manager passes the laugh test. So when this group announced in April 2012 that it was launching the company Planetary Resources to mine asteroids, it garnered a lot of media attention. The plan seems simple on its face—mine near-Earth asteroids for water and precious metals—and dauntingly complicated in practice.

Historically, the main actors in space ventures have been governments. Motivated in part by the Cold War, they were the only parties with the massive resources necessary to mobilize a space shot. This is all changing, for there are other private sector space ventures afoot. The founder of Amazon.com, Jeff Bezos, is financing Blue Origin, a company that plans to provide commercial space travel through reusable rockets. Richard Branson has launched Virgin Galactic, providing suborbital flights for space tourists.

Planetary Resources' business plan is based on four phases. The first will involve the launch of its Arkyd 100 series spacecraft. Loaded with telescopes and remote sensing technology, about six of these relatively cheap craft (a mere $10 million each) will piggyback on the planned launches of other satellites and come to rest in low orbit around the Earth. They will take a close look at asteroids, using spectroscopy and other tools to assess their likely composition. The Arkyd 200 series will be launched to a higher orbit and have its own propulsion system so it can further examine promising asteroids. The Arkyd 300 series will comprise a "robotic swarm" of robots that will approach specific asteroids from different angles and determine the final choices for mining sites. Saving the hardest for last, the fourth stage involves mining and transporting the materials to consumers, whether back to Earth or to a space station.

There are two major markets. The most obvious encompasses precious metals such as platinum, palladium, and iridium. Platinum is currently selling at $1,465 per ounce. Palladium comes in at a relative bargain of $600 per ounce. According to Planetary Resources, just one asteroid contains as much platinum, palladium, and other platinum-group precious metals than have been mined in human history. Simple math suggests the sales could be in the trillions of dollars. The problem, of course, is that if platinum and other precious metals do become more abundant because of asteroid mining, they will no longer be so precious and their price will drop. Even so, one could still expect a tidy profit. Getting the materials back to earth, though, is exceedingly difficult. And this makes mining water much more interesting.

There is plentiful water on Earth, of course, so where is the demand for outer space water? Planetary Resources has identified two moneymaking opportunities. The first is providing water for astronauts in space stations or manned missions. Lifting anything two hundred miles or more above the surface of the Earth requires a lot of propulsion, and that's expensive. It currently costs roughly $10,000 per pound of payload delivered into orbit. This means it costs $125,000 to provide drinking water for three astronauts on the space station. Using a local water source instead of transporting water into outer space is both cheaper and more efficient.

Another market for water lies in energy. Splitting molecules of water releases hydrogen and oxygen—two of the key sources for rocket propulsion. As with water, this could provide a much cheaper local fuel source than flying a mission's fuel from the Earth. One can imagine space vehicles filling up at "orbiting gas stations" before traveling beyond the earth's orbit to the universe and beyond.

There are plenty of criticisms one can make of Planetary Resources' venture, but thinking small is not one of them. As journalist Will Oremus has succinctly described, "This space-mining venture is either going to be a spectacular success or a spectacular failure. Either way, the emphasis will be on spectacular."

Afterword:
A Glass Half Empty/
A Glass Half Full

THE UNANIMOUS VOTE BY MCCLOUD'S DISTRICT COMMISSIONERS in 2003 to approve Nestlé's bottling operations came as a shock to many of the town's residents. Rather than settling the matter, however, the battle lines had just been drawn. A grassroots group, the McCloud Watershed Council, quickly formed to challenge the proposed million-square-foot plant. The council's stated goal was to look "for economic alternatives to Nestlé that bring living wage employment and long-term health to the community—without giving away the rights to our town's water for the next 100 years." If Nestlé's bottled water was going to become the new "Mother McCloud" for the community, replacing the historic industry support of timber, it was increasingly looking like this would be a shotgun marriage.

The first major counterattack was a legal challenge to the district commission's contract with Nestlé. This met with early success, and the contract was declared void in 2005 by a local judge. The decision was appealed by Nestlé and reversed by a California appellate court. The contract and its terms were back in place. First round to the McCloud Watershed Council, second round to Nestlé.

Meanwhile, as required by law, Nestlé was preparing an extensive Environmental Impact Review. When the review was submitted in 2007, more than four thousand public comments were filed. Opponents also lobbied at the state level, gaining the attention of Jerry Brown, the California attorney general at the time.

In a press release, Brown denounced the plant's impacts on climate change because of the oil needed to produce plastic water bottles and truck them across the United States. Going further, in a thinly veiled threat he stated that

> Nestlé will face swift legal challenge if it does not fully evaluate the environmental impact of diverting millions of gallons of spring water from the McCloud River into billions of plastic water bottles. . . . The suggested changes would require significant revision of the contract between Nestlé and the McCloud Community Services District, a new, formal project proposal, and circulation of a new Draft Environmental Impact Report.

In response to Brown's warning, Nestlé agreed to revise its environmental review and undertake studies of the proposed operation's impacts on the Squaw Valley Creek Watershed to establish baseline data. To avoid charges of bias, the study was directed by scientists from the University of California in coordination with the McCloud Watershed Council. Nestlé also convened a series of community conversations to facilitate discussion of the different viewpoints.

Realizing its original plans were no longer politically viable, in 2008 Nestlé made a major concession, proposing to reduce the size of the facility by two-thirds. Scaling back the project, however, did not quell the controversy. A year later, in September 2009, in a letter to the McCloud district board, Nestlé CEO Kim Jeffery wrote that "we have concluded that we no longer have a business need to build a new facility in McCloud and we are withdrawing our proposal to build a bottling facility in your community."

In its place, Nestlé planned to build a new fourteen-million-dollar facility in an industrial area of Sacramento. This would better serve the company's urban customers in Northern California, resulting in lower distribution costs and environmental impact. Nestlé planned to appraise the mill site it had purchased for the McCloud plant and, presumably, sell it to the highest bidder.

The fight was over.

After six years of contentious arguments and frustrating delays, Nestlé walked away from McCloud's glacier-fed springs. A local supporter, Doris Dragseth, was despondent. "The only thing we have to sell is water!" she lamented. "Now when [a potential water bottling company] sees the history, they are going to run." To Dragseth, McCloud seems fated to continue its slide into obscurity. Despite their best efforts, the community's elected leaders were unable to find a way for their drinking water to become an economic lifeblood for the town. Debra Anderson, an active member of the McCloud Watershed Council, saw things differently. She hailed Nestlé's change in plans as a victory for McCloud and other local communities.

Nestlé's search for spring waters continues. It has begun plans to open three other regional locations, including at Cascade Locks, a town forty miles east of Portland, Oregon. It may not be greeted warmly. Anderson reports that she is already receiving calls from concerned citizens in Cascade Locks, eager to learn strategies to thwart Nestlé's move to their community. The battle looks likely to be rejoined there.

While Nestlé's failure to build the bottling plant represented a real victory to some and defeat to others, in a larger sense it didn't really resolve anything. The market for bottled water is still going strong, as are the local fights against new plants. The battle in McCloud is over, but the war continues. The McCloud Watershed Council's activities have been mirrored by grassroots groups in other communities. In New England alone, opposition efforts have been led by H_2O for ME in Maine, Corporate Accountability International in Massachusetts, Save Our Groundwater in New Hampshire, and Water 1st in Vermont. The core issues of whether drinking water should be a commodity or a public good, and who gets access to the water, remain as divisive as ever.

Ironically, just four days after Nestlé's announcement, the McCloud District Council held a public hearing over a proposal to raise water rates. As with meetings over the Nestlé plant, the audience was packed and opinionated. A local business owner denounced the proposed increase, complaining that "people in this county are hurting all over. This smacks of the Boston Tea party . . . taxation without representation." The applause following his remarks showed he spoke for many who felt cheap drinking water to be theirs by right.

The story of drinking water is still being written.

Notes

Introduction: Mother McCloud

p. 15   the grocery store, the hotel: Michelle Conlin, "A Town Torn Apart by Nestlé; How a deal for a bottled water plant set off neighbor against neighbor in struggling McCloud, Calif.," *BusinessWeek*, Apr. 16, 2008, http://www.businessweek.com /magazine/content/08_15 /b4079042498703.htm.

p. 16   surpassing even soft drinks: Peter H. Gleick, *The World's Water* (Washington, D.C.: Island Press, 2012), 157.

p. 16   312 single–serve bottles: "Bottled Water," *Container Recycling Institute*, http://www.container-recycling.org/issues /bottledwater.htm; such as Perrier, Poland Spring: Bobby Caina Calvan, "Bottled-Water Deal Leaves Town Awash in Controversy," *Boston Globe*, June 26, 2005, http://www .boston.com/news/nation/articles/2005/06/26/bottled_wate r _deal_leaves_town_awash_in_controversy.

p. 17   and permitting fees: Conlin, "A Town Torn Apart."

p. 17   annual payments to the town: Eric Bailey, "Plan to Sell Water Roils Town," *Los Angeles Times*, Nov. 25, 2004, http://articles.latimes.com/2004/nov/25/local/me -mccloud25.

p. 17   "need the jobs": Conlin, "A Town Torn Apart."

p. 17   "Deal done": Erica Gies, "Nestlé's Thirst for Water Splits Small U.S. Town," *New York Times*, Mar. 19, 2008, http:/ /www.nytimes.com/2008/03/19/business/worldbusiness /19iht-rbognestle.html.

p. 18   "read like Nestlé's lawyers": Conlin, "A Town Torn Apart."

p. 18   "sell its birthright": Bailey, "Plan to Sell Water."

p. 18   "trout fishing streams": Gies, "Nestlé's Thirst for Water."

p. 18   "timber industry out of business": Bailey, "Plan to Sell Water."

p. 18   "privatize it, commodify": Robert Downes, "Ecotage: The Elusive Earth Liberation Front Strikes the Ice Mountain Bottling Plant," *Northern Express*, Oct. 9, 2003, http://www.northernexpress.com/editorial/features.asp?id=160.

p. 22   "blue is the new green": Adam Bluestein, "Blue is the New Green," *Inc.*, Oct. 1, 2008, http://www.inc.com/magazine/20081101/blue-is-the-new-green.html.

1: The Fountain of Youth

p. 25   "sagacious and diligent": Louise C. Slavicek, *Juan Ponce de León* (New York: Chelsea House Publishers, 2003), 52. Quoting Gonzalo Fernández de Oviedo, *Historia General y Natural de las Indias* (1535)

p. 25   the famed short story writer: The first few paragraphs of the quotation are excerpted. Washington Irving, *Voyages and Discoveries of the Companions of Columbus* (1835).

p. 25   Ponce de León set out with three ships: Francis Chapelle, *Wellsprings* (Piscataway, NJ: Rutgers University Press, 2005), 188.

p. 25   Ponce de León, 1474–1521: The sixteenth-century painting of Ponce de León can be found at Wikimedia, http://commons.wikimedia.org/wiki/File:Juan_Ponce_de_Le%C3%B3n.jpg.

p. 28   fourteen years after Ponce de León's death: Andrés Reséndez, *A Land So Strange: The Epic Journey of Cabez de Vaca* (New York: Basic Books, 2007), 264.

p. 28   to cure his sexual impotence: Oviedo, *Historia General y Natural.*

p. 29 the very oldest of recorded legends: J. F. Bierlein, *Parallel Myths* (New York: Ballantine Books, 1994), 200.

p. 30 "sweeter smelling than musk": Gary R. Varner, *The Mythic Forest, the Green Man and the Spirit of Nature* (New York: Algora Publishing, 2006), 138.

p. 30 da Vinci brought with him to Milan: John Mandeville, *The Travels of Sir John Mandeville*, trans. C.W.R.D. Moseley (London: Penguin Books, 1982), 9.

p. 30 a forest near the city of Polumbum, India: Ibid., 123.

p. 30 Cranach's vision of the Fountain: The painting can be found at Wikimedia, http://en.wikipedia.org/wiki/File :Lucas_Cranach_d._%C3%84._007.jpg.

p. 31 Odin gained eternal wisdom: John Carey, "Irish Parallels to the Myth of Odin's Eye," *Folklore* 94 (1983), 214.

p. 31 wisdom from swimming in the waters: Roy G. Willis, *World Mythology* (New York: Henry Holt and Company, 1993), 185.

p. 31 chickens drank from the magical puddle: Charles A.S. Williams, *Encyclopedia of Chinese Symbolism and Art Motives* (New York: Julian Press, 1960), 170.

p. 33 Jesus commanded his disciples: Matthew 13:16.

p. 34 drink is called Wai-ni-dula: Basil H. Thomson, "The Kalou-Vu (Ancestor-Gods) of the Fijians," *The Journal of the Anthropological Institute of Great Britain and Ireland* 24 (1895), 340.

p. 35 cannot drink ordinary water: A. E. Crawley, "Drinks, Drinking," *Encyclopedia of Religion and Ethics*, eds. James Hastings and John A. Selbie, vol. 9, (London: T&T Clark International, 2003), 76; this terminates the mourning: Ibid., 78.

p. 35 Chaco Indians of the American Southwest: Wilfred Barbrooke Grubb, *Among the Indians of the Paraguayan Chaco* (London: Charles Murray & Co., 1904), 44.

p. 35   taking his spirit to heaven: Terje Tvedt and Terje Oesti-gaard, eds., *A History of Water: The World of Water* (London: I. B. Tauris, 2006), xii.

p. 36   continuous use for 4,700 years: Gary R. Varner, *Sacred Wells: A Study in the History, Meaning, and Mythology of Holy Wells & Water* (New York: Algora Publishing, 2009), 9.

p. 36   evidence of religious worship at springs: Robert Miller, "Water Use in Syria and Palestine from the Neolithic to the Bronze Age," *World Archaeology* 11 (Feb. 1980), 331–333. C.E.N. Bromehead, "The Early History of Water Supply," *Geographical Journal* 99 (Mar. 1942), 142.

p. 36   examples compiled by a chronicler of sacred wells: Varner, *Sacred Wells*, 117–125.

p. 38   "ceremonies involving drinking from skulls": R. J. Stewart, *Celtic Gods, Celtic Goddesses* (London: Blandford Press, 1990), as quoted in Varner, *Sacred Wells*, 125.

p. 38   natural springs around the islands: William Drake Westervelt, *Legends of Old Honolulu* (Boston: Press of Geo. H. Ellis, 1915), 29.

p. 39   walking through the town's untended outskirts: The photograph can be found at Wikimedia, http://commons.wikimedia.org/wiki/File:Bernadette_Soubirous.jpg.

p. 40   finding her story credible: Jason Szabo, "Seeing is Believing: The Form and Substance of French Medical Debates over Lourdes," *Bulletin of the History of Medicine* 76 (2002), 203.

p. 40   the Sisters of Charity Convent: Ibid.

p. 40   greatest concentration of hotel rooms: Melissa Flower, "More than 130 Years after Vision, Lourdes Achieves Miracles," *Kingston Whig-Standard*, July 31, 1990, 1.

p. 41   Muggeridge derided the commerce: Malcolm Muggeridge, *Jesus Rediscovered* (New York: Doubleday & Company, 1969), 108.

p. 41   "this water may not be fit to drink": The photograph can be found at Wikimedia, http://commons.wikimedia.org /wiki/File:Lourdes_bidons_vierges_3.jpg.

p. 41   submerge up to their chins: Joseph P. Neville, "An 'Inside Story' about Lourdes," *New Oxford Review* 69 (Feb. 2002), 42.

p. 42   due to heavy consumption: "France rations Lourdes water," *Toronto Star*, Sept. 20, 1990, 23.

p. 42   officially "miraculous": "Miracles under the Microscope," *The Economist*, Apr. 22, 2000, 77.

p. 42   established these standards: Ibid.

p. 42   "must not result from medical treatment": Ibid.

p. 42   doctors making pilgrimage to the site: Ibid.; the case cannot be accounted for by medical: Sanctuaires Notre-Dame at Lourdes, http://www.lourdes-france.org.

p. 42   the number of documented Lourdes miracles: "The cures at Lourdes recognised as miraculous by the Church," Sanctuaires Notre-Dame at Lourdes, http://www.lourdes-france .org/upload/pdf/gb_guerisons.pdf.

p. 43   the international medical panel of doctors: Jamey Keaten, "Doctors call halt to certifying miracles," *Houston Chronicle*, Dec. 4, 2008, A14.

p. 43   a multivolume history of water: Tvedt and Oestigaard, *A History of Water*, x.

p. 43   "a secular deity in this post-romantic age": William Cronon, "Toward Reinventing Nature," in *Uncommon Ground*, ed. William Cronon (New York: W. W. Norton & Company, 1995), 36.

p. 44   "no clear evidence of benefit": Karen Bellenir, "Fact or Fiction? You Must Drink 8 Glasses of Water Daily," *Scientific American*, June 4, 2009.

p. 44   sixty-four ounces for a day's eating: Ibid.

p. 44   a kidney specialist at the National Institutes of Health: Benedict Carey, "Hard To Swallow," *Los Angeles Times*, Nov. 20, 2000.

p. 44   bottled water drinkers believe it improves: "Water Past Its Peak," *Marketing*, Aug. 17, 2011, 30.

p. 44   "no evidence that drinking": Judy Foreman, "The water fad has people soaking it up," *Boston Globe*, May 11, 1998, C1.

p. 44   "controlled by separate systems": Ibid.

2: Who Gets to Drink?

p. 47   go dormant and "turn off": See generally Luis P. Villarreal, "Are Viruses Alive?," *Scientific American*, Dec. 2004, 100.

p. 48   the United Nations passed a resolution: The Human Right to Water and Sanitation, A/64/L.63/Rev.1 (2010).

p. 48   "lack of access to clean water": Maude Barlow, "Access to Clean Water is Most Violated Human Right," *The Guardian*, July 21, 2010.

p. 48   "access to clean water for basic needs": Maude Barlow, "Blue Gold: The Global Water Crisis and the Commodification of the World's Water Supply," Council of Canadians (2001), http://www.canadians.org/water/publications/Blue_Gold.html.

p. 48   "the needs of the communities": "Water Privatization," Food & Water Watch, http://www.foodandwaterwatch.org/water/private-vs-public.

p. 49   settlements since the Neolithic time: Robert Miller, "Water Use in Syria and Palestine from the Neolithic to the Bronze Age," *World Archaeology* 11 (Feb. 1980), 331–333; Andrew Sherratt, "Water, Sail and Seasonality in Early Cereal Cultivation," *World Archaeology* 11 (Feb. 1980), 313–314.

p. 49   water storage sites have been found: Miller, "Water Use in Syria and Palestine," 335–336.

p. 49   reservoirs and plumbing have been identified: "Global Trends In Urban Water Supply And Waste Water Financing And Management," OECD, 2000.

p. 49   down the mountain slope: Jeff L. Brown, "Water Supply and Drainage at Macchu Picchu," WaterHistory.org,www .waterhistory.org/histories/machu.

p. 50   Jewish law regarding drinking water: Melanne Andromecca Civic, "A Comparative Analysis of the Israeli and Arab Water Law Traditions and Insights for Modern Water Sharing Agreement," *Denver Journal of International Law and Policy* 22 (1998), 437.

p. 50   "rivers and streams forming springs": Ibid., citing Dante A. Caponera, *Principles of Water Law and Administration* 22 (1992); Talmud Bavli Shabbat, 121b; Beitza, 391; Eiruvin, 46a and 48a; Tosephta Baba Qama, 6, 15.

p. 51   "just as thou refused the surplus": As quoted in Civic, "A Comparative Analysis of the Israeli and Arab Water Law Traditions," 442. As quoted in Dante Caponera, "Water Laws in Moslem Countries," U.N. Food and Agriculture Organization Development Paper No. 43 (Mar. 1954), 15–16.

p. 51   the Bedouin in the Negev: Aaron T. Wolf, "Indigenous Approaches to Water Conflict Negotiations and Implications for International Waters," *International Negotiation* 5 (2000), 357–363.

p. 51   "neither may be denied anyone": Ibid.

p. 51   described the system as "always ask": Deborah Rose, "Fresh Water Rights and Biophilia: Indigenous Australian Perspectives," *Dialogue* 23 (Mar. 2004), 37.

p. 51   "no one should be denied access": Pinimidzai Sithole, "Environmental Cultures of Development and Indigenous Knowledge: The Erosion of Traditional Boundaries in Conserving Wetlands in Rural Zimbabwe," IASCP 10th Biennial Conference (Aug. 2004).

p. 52   "You go to someone": Nontokozo Nemarundwe and Witness Kozanayi, "Institutional Arrangements for Water Resource Use: A Case Study from Southern Zimbabwe," *Journal of Southern African Studies* 29 (Mar. 2003), 202–204.

p. 52   upper castes maintain distinct water sources: Nandita Singh, "Water management traditions in Rural India: Valuing the Unvalued," 18th European Conference on Modern South Asian Studies (July 2004), available at http://www.sasnet.lu.se/EASASpapers/21Nanditaingh.pdf.

p. 52   public utilities are required to provide: Jim Rossi, "The Common Law 'Duty To Serve' and Protection of Consumers in an Age of Competitive Retail Public Utility Restructuring," *Vanderbilt Law Review* 51 (1998), 1233.

p. 52   treated as a fungible item for sale: Johannes M. Renger, "Institutional, Communal and Individual Ownership or Possession of Arable Land in Ancient Mesopotamia," *Chicago-Kent Law Review* 71 (1995), 269, 302.

p. 53   aqueducts play a critical part: A. Trevor Hodge, *Roman Aqueducts and Water Supply* (London: Gerald Duckworth & Co., 1992), 5.

p. 53   The famed Pont du Gard in France: The photograph can be found at Wikimedia, http://commons.wikimedia.org/wiki/File:Pontdugard.png.

p. 54   fountains, gardens, and even public toilets: In all, eleven aqueducts were constructed over approximately 550 years. O. F. Robinson, *Ancient Rome: City Planning and Administration* (London: Routledge, 1992), 98.

p. 54   the aqueducts forded rivers: Nelson Manfred Blake, *Water for the Cities: A History of the Urban Water Supply Problem in the United States* (Syracuse University Press, 1956), 14–15.

p. 54   prized water went to private uses: Evans, *Water Distribution in Ancient Rome*, 92 and 141.

p. 54   Excavations in Pompeii: Ibid., 11; "Watering Ancient Rome," *Nova* (Feb. 2000), available at http://www.pbs.org/wgbh/nova/lostempires/roman/watering2.html.

p. 54   the economics of Roman water supply: J. G. Landels, *Engineering in the Ancient World* (Berkeley, CA: University of California Press, 2002), 49. Hodge, *Roman Aqueducts*, 120:

"The *lacus* must have been as significant a social institution as the mediaeval village well, and it is small wonder that people of sensitivity, and sufficient financial means, preferred to pay for a private supply."

p. 54   40 percent of all the water delivered: Evans, *Water Distribution in Ancient Rome*, 141.

p. 54   pipes running from the main system: Landels, *Engineering in the Ancient World*, 34.

p. 55   jutting out from the sidewalk: The photograph can be found at Wikimedia, http://commons.wikimedia.org/wiki/File:Pompeii0069.jpg.

p. 55   daily water delivered to a Roman household: Evans, *Water Distribution in Ancient Rome*, 19.

p. 55   Piped delivery of water: Christer Bruun, *The Water Supply of Ancient Rome: A Study of Roman Imperial Administration* (Helsinki: Societas Scientarum Fennica, 1991), 77.

p. 55   to draw water illicitly: See Rabun Taylor, *Public Needs and Private Pleasures: Water Distribution, the Tiber River and the Urban Development of Ancient Rome* (Rome: L'Erma Di Bretschneider, 2000), 73–74.

p. 55   fine of 100,000 sesterces: Frontinus, quoting the *Lex Quinctia*, quoted in Taylor, *Public Needs and Private Pleasures*, 73

p. 55   construction was funded: Deane R. Blackman and Trevor A. Hodge, eds, *Frontinus' Legacy: Essays on Frontinus' De Aquis Urbis Romae* (Ann Arbor: Univ. of Michigan Press, 2001), 86; Evans, *Water Distribution in Ancient Rome*, 8.

p. 56   to cover the costs of system maintenance: Landels, *Engineering in the Ancient World*, 49; Evans, *Water Distribution in Ancient Rome*, 9.

p. 56   from ninety-one to almost six hundred: Malott, *Nomine Caesaris*, 6.

p. 56   historian Matthew Malott has written: Ibid., 5–6.

p. 57   San Marco church carries an inscription: Paolo Squatriti, *Water and Society in Early Medieval Italy, AD 400-1000* (Cambridge: Press Syndicate of the Univ. of Cambridge, 1998), 29–30.

p. 57   collected rainwater in cisterns: Michael C. Finnegan, "New York City's Watershed Agreement: A Lesson in Sharing Responsibility," *Pace Environmental Law Review* 14 (1997), 577, 586.

p. 58   cuts between Chambers and Canal: Charles H. Weidner, *Water for a City: A History of New York City's Problem from the Beginning to the Delaware System* (1974), 15.

p. 58   "many publique wells enclosed": As quoted in Gerard T. Koeppel, *Water for Gotham: A History* (Princeton: Princeton University Press, 2000), 21, citing Wayne Andrews, "A Glance at New York in 1697: The Travel Diary of Dr. Benjamin Bullivant," *New York Historical Society Quarterly* 40 (Jan. 1956), 55–73.

p. 59   the well water was so terrible: Koeppel, *Water for Gotham*, 27.

p. 59   "the worse this evil will be": Blake, *Water for the Cities*, 46.

p. 59   attractive landscaped gardens: Ibid., 13.

p. 60   "110 hogheads of 130 gallons each": Ibid., 13–14.

p. 60   how much money could be made: Ibid.

p. 60   to fund the public works: Images reprinted with permission from obsoletecurrency.blogspot.com.

p. 61   fled to escape the contagion: Blake, *Water for the Cities*, 5.

p. 62   "the corporation of the city Employ": Ibid., 3.

p. 62   powers that the Philadelphia City Council: Ibid., 47.

p. 63   Burr is on the left and Hamilton: The portraits can be found at Wikimedia, http://commons.wikimedia.org/wiki/File:Aaron_Burr.jpg, http://commons.wikimedia.org/wiki/File:Hamilton_small.jpg.

p. 64   provide free water for fighting fires: Blake, *Water for the Cities*, 50–51.

p. 64   the company would lose its charter: Ibid., 51.

p. 64   "any other monied transactions": Ibid., 50–51.

p. 65   the bare minimum to maintain its charter: Finnegan, "New York City's Watershed Agreement," 589.

p. 65   each additional fireplace: Blake, *Water for the Cities*, 59.

p. 65   "linen happily escapes the contamination": Ibid., 126.

p. 65   "the most outrageous insult": Ibid., 54.

p. 66   "less good water than the Dutch had bequeathed": Ibid., 101.

p. 66   a severe cholera epidemic: Ibid., 133.

p. 66   "washing the streets of the whole city": Ibid., 140.

p. 67   the Romans never built aqueducts for London: *London: The Greatest City: Medieval London*, at http://www.channel4.com/history/microsites/H/history/i-m/london2.html.

p. 67   owners of wharves and stairs: Text of the city ordinance is available at http://www.trytel.com/~tristan/towns/florilegium/community/cmfabr24.html.

p. 67   private commerce for water supply: "Water-Related Infrastructure in Medieval London," WaterHistory.org, http://www.waterhistory.org/histories/london/.

p. 68   "the confused state of the national currency": Blake, *Water for the Cities*, 165–166.

p. 68   a fifty-foot fountain: Elizabeth Royte, *Bottlemania* (New York: Bloomsbury, 2008), 97.

p. 68   their towns drowned: Finnegan, "New York City's Watershed Agreement," 14.

p. 69   so-called Croton Hydrants: Koeppel, *Water for Gotham*, 279.

p. 70   the father of medicine: Milton A. Lessler, "Lead and Lead Poisoning from Antiquity to Modern Times," *Ohio Journal of Science* 88 (1988), 78.

p. 70   "water conducted through earthen pipes": John Scarborough, "The Myth of Lead Poisoning among the Romans: An Essay Review," *Journal of the History of Medicine* 39 (1984), 469.

p. 71   "you could no more turn off": Hodge, "Vitruvius, Lead Pipes," 486.

p. 71   "hardens into a crust": "Lead Poisoning and Rome," http://penelope.uchicago.edu/~grout/encyclopaedia _romana/wine/leadpoisoning.html.

p. 71   by boiling the mixture: Nriagu, "Saturnine gout," 660.

p. 71   a diet with *sapa*: A. Mackie, A. Townshend, and H. A. Waldron, "Lead concentrations in bones from Roman York," *Journal of Archaeological Science* 2 (1975), 235.

3: Is It Safe to Drink the Water?

p. 72   From discussions with Chinese students, communal drinking fountains have become much less common, in large part because the population is increasingly concerned about drinking water quality. The communal fountain at Po Lin monastery has apparently been replaced with a standard mechanical drinking fountain since I visited in 2006.

p. 72   an article by a Lafayette College biology professor: "Dixie Cup Company History," http://academicmuseum.lafayette .edu/special/dixie/company.html.

p. 73   the dangers of common drinking cups: Ibid.

p. 74   plenty of minerals and bacteria: Royte, *Bottlemania*, 100–101.

p. 75   "Water, by its very nature": Chapelle, *Wellsprings*, 10.

p. 75   visitors to Paris that drinking the water: A. Lynn Martin, "The Baptism of Wine," *Gastronomica: The Journal of Food and Culture* 3 (2003), 21–22.

p. 75   international travelers suffer from diarrhea: "Travelers' Diarrhea," Centers for Disease Control and Prevention, last modified Nov. 21, 2006, http://www.cdc.gov/ncidod/dbmd /diseaseinfo/travelersdiarrhea_g.htm.

p. 77   "suggesting shrunken rawhide": W. J. McGee, "Desert Thirst as Disease," *Interstate Medical Journal* 13 (1906), 279, 283.

p. 77   springs and wells are found: C.E.N. Bromehead, "The Early History of Water Supply," *Geographical Journal* 99 (1942), 142.

p. 78   "Lack of good water": Royte, *Bottlemania*, 21.

p. 78   historian Karl Wittfogel: Karl Wittfogel, *Oriental Despotism: A Comparative Study of Total Power* (Vintage, 1957).

p. 78   "bad water is like poison": Joshua I. Barzilay, Winkler G. Weinberg, and J. William Eley, *The Water We Drink: Water Quality and Its Effects on Health* (1999), 10.

p. 78   disease killed eight times more: G. C. Cook, "Influence of Diarrhoeal Disease on Military and Naval Campaigns," *Journal of the Royal Society of Medicine* 94 (2001), 95.

p. 78   diarrhea and dysentery claimed: "Civil War Medicine: An Overview of Medicine," eHistory.com, http://ehistory.osu .edu/uscw/features/medicine/cwsurgeon/introduction.cfm.

p. 78   commanding the North African theater: Cook, "Influence of Diarrhoeal Disease," 97.

p. 79   "drink of the subaltern classes": Squatriti, *Water and Society in Early Medieval Italy*, 41.

p. 79   punished for drunkenness: Ibid., 38.

p. 79   "drink no water": Chapelle, *Wellsprings*, 102.

p. 79   "to drinke colde water": Ibid., 1.

p. 79   All quotes are from Chapelle, *Wellsprings*, 102, 1-2. 2.

p. 79   foiled the plot: Squatriti, *Water and Society in Early Medieval Italy*, 38.

p. 79   "all Europeans agreed on": Chapelle, *Wellsprings*, 102.

p. 80   The drink of choice in Egypt: Tom Standage, *A History of the World in Six Glasses* (New York: Walker, 2005), 104.

p. 80   constructed in Plymouth Plantation: Ibid., 105.

p. 80   Beer was routinely added: Chapelle, *Wellsprings*, 103.

p. 80   The mixtures elevated the status: Squatriti, *Water and Society in Early Medieval Italy*, 40.

p. 81   "high ground and hills": "Airs, Waters, Places," in *Hippocratic Writings*, trans. J. Chadwick and W. N. Mann (London: Penguin Classics, 1983), 148, 153.

p. 81   aqueducts to segregate drinking water: Evans, *Water Distribution in Ancient Rome*, 136–137, 140.

p. 81   drinking melted snow: Squatriti, *Water and Society in Early Medieval Italy*, 37.

p. 81   "so much filthe": Andrea Cast, "Women Drinking in Early Modern England" (unpublished PhD dissertation, University of Adelaide, 2001), 2, quoting Bullein, *The Gouernement of Healthe* (1558).

p. 81   "Flowing water is regarded safe": Eva-Marita Rinne, "'Seeing is Believing': Perceptions of Safe Water in Rural Yoruba," in *A History of Water: The World of Water*, eds. Terje Tvedt and Terje Oestigaard (London: I. B. Tauris, 2006), 269, 277, 281.

p. 82   a complex social hierarchy: Singh, "Water Management Traditions in Rural India."

p. 82   prepared with water by a non-Brahman: J. Abbott, *Keys of Power: A Study of Indian Ritual and Belief* (2003), 162.

p. 82   A drinking fountain on the county courthouse lawn: John Vachon, "A Drinking Fountain on the County Courthouse Lawn" (1938), http://www.loc.gov/rr/print/list/085_disc.html.

p. 84   the balance of four humors: Logan Clendening, *Source Book of Medical History* (Toronto: General Publishing, 1942), 39.

p. 84   slowing the flow of humors: Cast, "Women Drinking in Early Modern England," 1, quoting Bullein, *The Governement of Healthe* (1558).

p. 84   phlegmatic in the upper left: The drawing can be found at Wikimedia, http://upload.wikimedia.org/wikipedia/commons /thumb/e/ea/Lavater1.jpg/220px-Lavater1.jpg.

p. 85   the agent of disease: Nancy Tomes, *The Gospel of Germs: Men, Women, and the Microbe in American Life* (Cambridge: Harvard Univ. Press, 1998), 3.

p. 85   get sick from drinking certain types: Robert D. Morris, *The Blue Death: Disease, Disaster and the Water We Drink* (New York: HarperCollins, 2007) 32.

p. 86   tanneries, slaughterhouses, cemeteries: Ibid.

p. 86   other waste from streets: "What Was Life Like in Medieval London?," Museum of London, http://www.museumoflondon .org.uk/Explore-online/Pocket-histories/Medieval-life.

p. 86   a fire near a waterhole: Deborah Rose, "Fresh Water Rights and Biophilia: Indigenous Australian Perspectives," *Dialogue* (Mar. 2004), 35, 37.

p. 86   "washing clothes near the drinking water": Rinne, "'Seeing Is Believing,'" 280–281.

p. 86   her well covered with a rock: Barzilay, Weinberg, and Eley, *The Water We Drink*, 8.

p. 87   "excrementation of the Metropolis": Gleick, *The World's Water*, 129.

p. 87   Houses of Parliament bearable: "Parliament and the Thames," UK Parliament, http://www.parliament.uk /parliamentary_publications_and_archives/parliamentary _archives/archives_parliament_and_the_thames.cfm.

p. 87   "increasing industrialization, urbanization": Martin, "The Baptism of Wine," 21–22.

p. 87   typhoid had killed more than 50,000: Michael C. Finnegan, "New York City's Watershed Agreement," 577, 590.

p. 88   John Snow, 1813–1858: The photograph can be found at Wikimedia, http://upload.wikimedia.org/wikipedia /commons/c/cc/John_Snow.jpg.

p. 88   the first royal to give birth under anesthesia: Morris, *The Blue Death*, 55.

p. 88   distillation apparatus in his lodgings: Ibid., 36.

p. 89   a report written by Snow in 1855: John Snow, "Report on the Cholera Outbreak in the Parish of St. James, Westminster, During the Autumn of 1854" (1855), 100, http:/ /collections.nlm.nih.gov/pageturner/viewer.html?PID=nlm :nlmuid-34721190R-bk.

p. 89   remove the pump handle at Broad Street: This story is related in Chapelle, *Wellsprings*, 81–82.

p. 90   boasted a pump handle as its symbol: Morris, *The Blue Death*, 86; Chapelle, *Wellsprings*, 82.

p. 90   John Snow's map of cholera: Snow, "Report on the Cholera Outbreak," 100.

p. 91   the same germs reproduce: Tomes, *The Gospel of Germs*, 33.

p. 91   "Foul effluvia": Morris, *The Blue Death*, 41–42.

p. 91   a cesspit directly adjacent: Chapelle, *Wellsprings*, 83.

p. 91   the most effective politician: Morris, *The Blue Death*, 44.

p. 91   attention to drainage, clean drinking water: The photograph of Chadwick can be found at Wikimedia, http://en .wikipedia.org/wiki/File:SirEdwinChadwick.jpg.

p. 92   Report of the Sanitary Condition: Edwin Chadwick, *Report on the Sanitary Condition of the Labouring Population of Great Britain, 1842*, ed. M. W. Flinn (Edinburgh University Press, 1965).

p. 93   "habitual avidity for sensual gratifications": Morris, *The Blue Death*, 50.

p. 93   calls for improved sanitation: Julia Twigg, "The Vegetarian Movement in England, 1847–1981: A Study of the Structure of its Ideology" (unpublished PhD dissertation, London School of Economics, University of London, 1981), http://www.ivu.org/history/thesis/medicine.html.

p. 94   sanitary reform as the "Will of God": Strang, *The Meaning of Water*, 30.

p. 94   the miasmatic theory of disease: Morris, *The Blue Death*, 46.

p. 94   designed to drain rain from the streets: Ibid., 48–49, 51–52.

p. 94   a shocking seventeen years old: Marq de Villiers, *Water: The Fate of Our Most Precious Resource* (Boston: Houghton Mifflin, 2000), 104–105.

p. 95   similar stories for Chicago, Philadelphia: See, e.g., *History of Public Works in the United States, 1776–1976*, ed. Ellis Armstrong (Washington, D.C.: American Public Works Association, 1976), 399.

p. 95   "animal food at their tables": Blake, *Water for the Cities*, 9.

p. 95   fresh from designing the water system: This story is recounted in Morris, *The Blue Death*, 137–138.

p. 95   reversed the flow: Robert Glennon, *Unquenchable: America's Water Crisis and What to Do About It* (Washington, DC: Island Press, 2009), 209.

p. 96   too many potential intervening factors: Missouri v. Illinois, 200 U.S. 496 (1906).

p. 96   jewels in England's colonial crown: This story is recounted in Gleick, *The World's Water*, 129.

p. 97   fever still claimed thousands: Chapelle, *Wellsprings*, 181.

p. 98   Sanskrit writings from approximately 2000 BC: Kathy Jesperson, "Search for Clean Water Continues," *On Tap*, Summer 1996, 6, http://www.nesc.wvu.edu/ndwc/pdf/OT/OTs96.pdf.

p. 98   the range of treatment technologies: Ibid.

p. 98   the common practice was light boiling: Cast, "Women Drinking in Early Modern England," 2.

p. 98   purifying water by passing it: "History of Drinking Water

Systems," Department of Engineering, Mercer University (2005), http://egrweb.mercer.edu/eve406/eve406rom/documents/History-Water.pdf; Baker, *The Quest for Pure Water*, 19, 118.

p. 98   first municipal plant was not built: "History of Drinking Water Systems," 2.

p. 99   tombs of the Egyptian pharaohs: M. N. Baker, *The Quest for Pure Water* (Denver: American Waste Water Association, 1948), 2.

p. 100   "water did not cause typhoid": Joel A. Tarr & T. F. Josie, "Critical Decisions in Pittsburgh Water and Wastewater Treatment," in *A History of Water: The World of Water*, eds. Terje Tvedt and Terje Oestigaard (London: I. B. Tauris, 2006), 206.

p. 100   adoption of chlorinated water: Patrick Gurian and Joel A. Tarr, "The First Federal Drinking Water Quality Standards and Their Evolution: A History from 1914 to 1974," in *Improving Regulation: Cases in Environment, Health, and Safety*, eds. Paul S. Fischbeck and R. Scott Farrow (Washington, DC: Resources for the Future, 2001), 43, 53.

p. 100   more than five thousand water treatment systems: Chapelle, *Wellsprings*, 15.

p. 100   the bottled water sector collapsed: Ibid.

p. 101   any other technological advance: Ibid.

p. 101   "horses and other animals refuse": Joseph Race, *Chlorination of Water* (1918), 63.

p. 101   "delivered to Jersey City pure": The Mayor and Aldermen of Jersey City v. Jersey City Water Supply Company 79 N.J. Ct of Chancery Reports 212, 214 (July 11, 1911). See also Race, *Chlorination of Water*, 12.

p. 101   "as pure as mountain spring water" Morris, *The Blue Death*, 161.

p. 102   fortified cities fell: Raymond P. Dougherty, "Sennacherib and the Walled Cities of Judah," *Journal of Biblical Literature* 49, no. 2 (1930), 160, 162-63.

p. 102   "Millo in the city of David": 2 Chronicles 32:5.

p. 103   the dark, winding 533-meter path: Amos Frumkin and Aryeh Shimron, "Tunnel Engineering in the Iron Age: Geoarchaeology of the Siloam Tunnel, Jerusalem," *Journal of Archaeological Science* 33 (2006), 227–28.

p. 103   "I imposed my yoke": Dougherty, "Sennacherib and the Walled Cities of Judah," 162.

p. 104   leasing official mugs: *London: The Greatest City*; "The Great Conduit," Florilegium Urbanum, http://www.trytel .com/~tristan/towns/florilegium/community/cmfabr24.html; Roger D. Hansen, "Water-Related Infrastructure in Medieval London," WaterHistory.org, http://www.waterhistory .org/histories/london/london.pdf.

p. 104   contracted with their local monasteries: "The Great Conduit."

p. 104   "a glass of water fit to drink": As quoted in Peter Gleick, *Bottled and Sold* (Washington, DC: Island Press, 2010), 4.

p. 104   a philanthropic society: Howard Malchow, "Free Water: The Public Drinking Fountain Movement and Victorian London," *London Journal* 4 (1978), 181, 184–188.

p. 105   a venture dedicated to the common good: "The Metropolitan Drinking Fountain and Cattle Trough Association," DrinkingFountains.org, http://www.drinkingfountains.org /Attachments%28PDF%29/DFA%20HIstory.pdf.

p. 106   commemoration of the drinking fountain: Lithograph from *Illustrated London News*, Apr. 30, 1859.

p. 107   the grandeur of the civic edifice: The photograph can be found at Wikimedia, http://commons.wikimedia.org/wiki /File:Worcester_Cross_drinking_fountain,_Kidderminster _-_DSCF0918.jpg.

p. 108   about one pipe break a day: Charles Duhigg, "Saving U.S.

Water and Sewer Systems Would Be Costly," *New York Times*, Mar. 14, 2010.

p. 109   thirty-six million gallons per day: Ken Belson, "Plumber's Job on a Giant's Scale: Fixing New York's Drinking Straw," *New York Times*, Nov. 22, 2008, http://www.nytimes.com /2008/11/23/nyregion/23tunnel.html.

p. 109   the lead soldering used to join: "What's on Tap," National Resources Defense Council, June 2003, http://www.nrdc .org/water/drinking/uscities/contents.asp.

p. 109   breaks in water and sewer lines: Glennon, *Unquenchable*, 211.

p. 109   we need $335 billion: Duhigg, "Saving U.S. Water and Sewer Systems," *New York Times*, Mar. 14, 2010.

p. 110   waterborne parasites, viruses: Ibid.

p. 110   about nine hundred deaths: Glennon, *Unquenchable*, 66.

p. 110   This history is based on the research of the architectural historian, Giorgio Gionighian. Giorgio Gionighian, *Building a Renaissance Double House in Venice*, 8 ARQ 299 (nos. 3/4, 2004). See also Giorigio Gianighian, *L'Acqua di Venezia: Dal medioevo all'acquedotto e oltre*, Ananke 134 (2010).

p. 112   Illustrazioni di G. Del Pedros © tratte da *Venezia come* di G. Gianighian e P. Pavanini, Ambier & Keller editors, Venezia 2010. Reproduced with publisher's permission.

4: Death in Small Doses

p. 113   analysis of his hair suggests arsenic: "Napoleon poison theory revived," *CNN World*, June 1, 2001, http://articles .cnn.com/2001-06-01/world/napoleon.poisoning_1_pascal -kintz-ben-weider-hair-samples?_s =PM:WORLD.

p. 114   to remedy this public health problem: Allan H. Smith et al., "Contamination of Drinking-Water by Arsenic in Bangladesh: a Public Health Emergency," *Bulletin of the World Health Organization* 78 (2000), 1093; A. Mushtaque and R. Chowdhury, "Arsenic Crisis in Bangladesh," *Scientific American* (Aug. 2004), 86, 90.

p. 114 "more than 10 million tubewells": Ibid.

p. 115 concentrations below 50 parts: This history is recounted in Cass R. Sunstein, "The Arithmetic of Arsenic," *Georgetown Law Journal* 90 (2002), 2255.

p. 115 one drop of arsenic in fifty drums: Charles Duhigg, "That Tap Water is Legal but may be Unhealthy," *New York Times*, Dec. 17, 2009.

p. 115 "but you didn't vote for this": As quoted in Sunstein, "The Arithmetic of Arsenic," 2255.

p. 117 "the groundwater can kill you": Email from Alex Pfaff, Professor, Sanford Institute for Public Policy, Duke University, to author (Sept. 26, 2007).

p. 117 the harm from microbial diseases: Ibid. Moreover, many of the traditional ponds used as water sources have since been polluted or converted into aquaculture.

p. 117 "arsenic-contaminated tube-well water": Ben Crow and Farhana Sultana, "Gender, Class, and Access to Water: Three Cases in a Poor and Crowded Delta," *Society and Natural Resources* 15 (2002), 709, 718.

p. 117 "Tubewells had fitted nicely": Mushtaque and Chowdhury, "Arsenic Crisis in Bangladesh," 90.

p. 118 ten versus fifty seconds: Zane Satterfield, "What Does Ppm or Ppb Mean?," National Environmental Services Center at West Virginia University, http://www.nesc.wvu.edu/ndwc/articles/ot/fa04/q&a.pdf.

p. 118 additional capacity in the water treatment plant: Jason K. Burnett and Robert W. Hahn, "A Costly Benefit," *Regulation* (Fall 2001), 44.

p. 118 estimates ranging from six lives saved: Sunstein, "The Arithmetic of Arsenic," 2258. "Today, the maximum contaminant level for arsenic is ten parts per billion, and more than fifty-six million Americans drink water that exceeds this level." Royte, *Bottlemania*, 121.

p. 119   "range below 50 parts per billion": Sunstein, "The Arithmetic of Arsenic," 2258.

p. 119   bladder, colon, and rectal cancer: John D. Graham and Jonathan Baert Wiener, "Confronting Risk Tradeoffs," in *Risk Versus Risk: Tradeoffs in Protecting Health and the Environment*, eds. John D. Graham and Jonathan Baert Wiener (Cambridge: Harvard University Press, 1995), 15; Morris, *The Blue Death*, 168–177.

p. 119   younger versus older victims: Susan W. Putnam and Jonathan Baert Wiener, "Seeking Safe Drinking Water," in *Ibid*. 124–125.

p. 119   Interfere with the endocrine system: "Endocrine Disruptors/ PPCPs," American Water Works Association, http://www .awwa.org/Resources/topicspecific.cfm?ItemNumber =3647&navItemNumber=1580; "New Findings on the Timing of Sexual Maturity," Our Stolen Future, http://www .ourstolenfuture.org/NewScience/reproduction/Puberty /puberty.htm.

p. 120   behavior of certain wildlife: "IPCS Global Assessment of EDCs," World Health Organization, http://www.who.int /ipcs/publications/en/ch1.pdf.

p. 120   impact on human populations: J. H. Kim, "Removal of Endocrine Disruptors Using Homogeneous Metal Catalyst Combined with Nanofiltration Membrane," *Water Science and Technology* 51 (2005), 381.

p. 120   other persistent organic pollutants: Jerome Nriagu, "Pollutants and Health of Communities in the Great Lakes Basin," http://www.miseagrant.umich.edu/downloads /research/papers/GLCOMM.pdf.

p. 120   ten times higher than the level: "Endocrine Disruptors," Birth Defect Research for Children, http://www .birthdefects.org/research/factsheets/fact%20EDCs.pdf.

p. 121   widely used for controlling mosquitoes: Heidi J. Auman et al, "PCBS, DDE, DDT, and TCDD-EQ in Two Species of Island, Midway Atoll, North Pacific Ocean," *Environmental Toxicology and Chemistry* 16 (1997), 498.

p. 121   so-called intersex fish: "Intersex Fish Found in Susquehanna River, Delmarva Lakes," Chesapeake Bay Program, Nov. 17, 2010, http://www.chesapeakebay.net/news_intersexfish10.aspx?menuitem=54704.

p. 121   Florida's Lake Apopka: "Endocrine Disruptors on the Gulf Coast," Regional Perspectives in Environmental Science, http://www.mhhe.com/biosci/pae/environmentalscience/casestudies/case7.mhtml.

p. 121   pharmaceuticals and personal care products: See, e.g., Julie Gerberding, "Pharmaceuticals and Personal Care Products (PPCPs) in Drinking Water," DrinkTap.org, http://www.drinktap.org/consumerdnn/Home/WaterInformation/WaterQuality/PharmaceuticalsPPCPs/tabid/73/Default.aspx; Abby C. Collier, "Pharmaceutical Contaminants in Pota Water: Potential Concerns for Pregnant Women and Children," *EcoHealth* 4 (2007), 164, 170.

p. 121   80 percent of the streams: Jennifer Waters, "Water shortages," *CQ Researcher* 20 (June 18, 2010), 529.

p. 121   study of private wells: Glennon, *Unquenchable*, 71.

p. 121   fifty-six pharmaceuticals or their by-products: Jeff Donn, Martha Mendoza, and Justin Pritchard, "Pharmaceuticals lurking in U.S. drinking water," MSNBC.com., Mar. 10, 2008.

p. 122   steroids and antibiotics near cattle feedlots: "Antibiotics Used for Growth in Food Animals Making their Way into Waterways," *Science Daily*, Oct. 25, 2004.

p. 122   New York, Houston, Chicago: Donn, Mendoza, and Pritchard, "Pharmaceuticals lurking in U.S. drinking water."

p. 122   "exposed to other people's drugs": Ibid.

p. 122   "might pose a risk to water safety": "Meeting report: pharmaceuticals in water," *Environmental Health Perspectives*, July 2010, 1016.

p. 122   pharmaceutical traces in drinking water: Jennifer Waters, "Water Shortages," 529.

p. 122   "emergent contaminants": Glennon, *Unquenchable*, 168.

p. 123   "the doses are so small": Ibid.

p. 123   twenty Olympic-size swimming pools: "Priest Point Park Sediment Study Shows Very Low Dioxin Levels," Washington Department of Ecology, Mar. 24, 2011, http://www.ecy.wa.gov/news/2011/091.html.

p. 124   synthetic compounds in the environment: Royte, *Bottlemania*, 127–129.

p. 124   ultraviolet light, reverse osmosis: Glennon, *Unquenchable*, 169.

p. 125   extend to private well water: Glennon, Ibid., 71.

p. 125   not a single chemical: This section is drawn from a series of articles in the *New York Times* by Charles Duhigg, "That Tap Water is Legal but May be Unhealthy" *New York Times*, Dec. 16, 2009. The contaminants are listed at http://water.epa.gov/drink/contaminants/basicinformation/index.cfm.

p. 125   violated key provisions: Charles Duhigg, "Millions in U.S. Drink Dirty Water, Records Show," *New York Times*, Dec. 8, 2009.

p. 126   "the level of enforcement activity": Ibid.

p. 126   "dumping poisons into streams": Ibid.

p. 127   bacteria, nitrates, and phosphates: Charles Duhigg, "Health Ills Abound as Farm Runoff Fouls," *New York Times*, Sept. 17, 2009.

p. 127   Fracking diagram. http://www.epa.gov/hfstudy/pdfs/overview-fact-sheet.pdf.

p. 128   national gas from overseas: Marianne Lavelle, "Natural as stirs Hope and Fear in Pennsylvania," *National Geographic*, Oct. 13, 2010.

p. 128   fracking could satisfy the nation's need: Abrahm Lustgarten, "Scientific Study Links Flammable Drinking Water to Fracking," ProPublica, http://www.propublica.org/article/scientific-study-links-flammable-drinking-water-to-fracking.

p. 128   Any ray of hope here: Ibid.

p. 129   methane seepage in water wells: Letter to Cabot Oil & Gas Corporation, available at ProPublica, http://s3.amazonaws.com/propublica/assets/methane/pdep_nov_cabot_090227.pdf.

p. 129   "lifted clear off the ground": Abrahm Lustgarten, "Officials in Three States Pin Water Woes on Gas Drilling," ProPublica, Apr. 26, 2009.

p. 129   natural gas drilling boom: See http://www.gaslandthemovie.com/about-the-film.

p. 130   distant drinking water sources: Bryan Walsh, "Another Fracking Mess for the Shale-Gas Industry," *Time*, May 9, 2011.

p. 130   had the CEO himself drunk the fluid: Catherine Tsai, "Halliburton Executive Drinks Fracking Fluid At Conference," *Huffington Post*, Aug. 22, 2011, http://www.huffingtonpost.com/2011/08/22/halliburton-executive-drinks-fracking-fluid_n_933621.html.

p. 130-1 exempted fracking from coverage: Abrahm Lustgarten, "Natural Gas Drilling: What We Don't Know," ProPublica, http://www.propublica.org/article/natural-gas-drilling-what-we-dont-know-1231.

p. 131   the "Halliburton Loophole": Editorial, "The Halliburton Loophole," *New York Times*, Nov. 2, 2009, http://www.nytimes.com/2009/11/03/opinion/03tue3.html.

p. 131   West Virginia has one inspector: Ibid.

DRINKING WATER

p. 131   a 1 in 3,333 chance: Morris, *The Blue Death*, 162.

p. 133   anthropologist Eva-Marita Rinne: Rinne, "'Seeing is Believing,'" 278.

p. 134   more valuable than diamonds: See, e.g., Michael V. White, "Doctoring Adam Smith: The Fable of the Diamonds and Water Paradox," *History of Political Economy* 34 (2002), 659.

p. 134   drinking from the nearby red well: Nava Ashraf et al., "Can Higher Prices Stimulate Product Use? Evidence from a Field Experiment in Zambia" (National Bureau of Economic Research, working paper no. 13247, 2007), http://www.nber.org/papers/w13247.pdf.

p. 135   does not provide cause for alarm: "Where are PPCPs found in the environment?," Environmental Protection Agency, http://epa.gov/ppcp/faq.html#ifthereareindeed.

p. 136   additional 25 percent worried: Charles Fishman, *The Big Thirst: The Secret Life and Turbulent Future of Water* (New York: Free Press 2011), 174.

p. 136   standards for bottled water: See "Bottled Water: Pure Drink or Pure Hype?," Natural Resources Defense Council (1999), http://www.nrdc.org/water/drinking/bw/bwinx.asp.

p. 138   the Sacramento radio station: "Radio Station Fires 10 After Deadly Contest," CBS5.com, Jan. 16, 2007, http://cbs5.com/watercooler/water.contest.water.2.278829.html.

p. 138   cause of death was determined: "Doctors: Marathoner Died from Too Much Water," TheBostonChannel.com, Aug. 13, 2002, http://www.thebostonchannel.com/newscenter5/1610699/detail.html.

p. 138   on the day of the race: Steve Nearman, "Too Much of a Good Thing," *Washington Times*, Oct. 24, 2003.

p. 139   and even death: Coco Ballantyne, "Strange but True: Drinking Too Much Water Can Kill," *Scientific American*, June 21, 2007.

p. 139   As Paracelsus famously expounded: W. Norman Aldridge, *Mechanisms and Concepts in Toxicology* (Taylor & Francis: London, 1996), 137.

5: Blue Terror

p. 140   break-in at the town's water tower: Tom Arrandale, "Hydro Defense," *Newsday* (Apr. 2007), 50.

p. 142   poisonous hellebore roots: Gleick, *The World's Water.*

p. 142   diseased animal carcasses: James A. Romano, Brian J. Lukey, and Harry Salem, eds., *Chemical Warfare Agents: Chemistry, Pharmacology, Toxicology, and Therapeutics* (Boca Raton: CRC press, 2007), 53.

p. 142   allegedly introduced cholera strains: Ibid.

p. 142   cherry laurel water: "Security and Water," Water Encyclopedia: Science and Issues, http://www.waterencyclopedia .com/Re-St/Security-and-Water.html.

p. 142   the strategic position they occupy: J. E. Hoover, "Water Supply Facilities and National Defense," *Journal of the American Water Works Association* 33, no. 11 (1941), 1861.

p. 142   facility in Fort Detrick: "Chemical and Biological Terrorism: The Threat According to the Open Literature," Canadian Security Intelligence Service, http://www.csis-scrs.gc .ca/pblctns/thr/cbtrrrsm02-eng.asp.

p. 142   a plot by the white supremacist group: "Covenant Sword and Arm of the Lord (CSA)," National Consortium for the Study of Terrorism and Responses to Terrorism, http://www.start.umd.edu/start/data_collections/tops /terrorist_organization_profile.asp?id=3226.

p. 142   a tunnel under the U.S. embassy: Andrew J. Whelton et al., "The Cyanic Threat to Potable Water," American Water Works Association (AWWA) Annual Conference and Exposition Proceedings (June 15–19, 2003), 1.

p. 142   soldiers in Afghanistan: "Water Unsecured: Public Drinking Water is Vulnerable to Terrorist Attack," The Public Citizen (Oct. 2004), 101.

p. 142-3 "threats against municipal water systems": Peter S. Beering, "Threats on Tap: Understanding the Terrorist Threat to Water," *Journal of Water Resources Planning and Management* 128, no. 3 (2002), 163.

p. 143 A classified 2012 U.S. intelligence assessment: Karen De-Young, "Water shortages increasingly will offer new weapons for states, terror groups," *Washington Post*, Mar. 22, 2012.

p. 144 a modern water system: GAO, Drinking Water Experts' Views on How Future Federal Funding Can Best Be Spent to Improve Security (October 2003), http://www .globalsecurity.org/security/library/report/gao/d0429.pdf.

p. 144 75,000 dams: John B. Stephenson, "Drinking Water: Experts' Views on How Federal Funding Can Best Be Spent to Improve Security," United States Government Accountability Office (Sept. 30, 2004), 4.

p. 144 two million miles of pipe: Benjamin H. Grumbles, "Statement of Benjamin H. Grumbles Acting Assistant Administrator for Water U.S. Environmental Protection Agency before the Subcommittee on Environment and Hazardous Materials Energy and Commerce Committee" (Sept. 30, 2004), 9.

p. 144 160,000 drinking water facilities: Government Accounting Office, Drinking Water: Experts' Views on How Federal Funding Can Best Be Spent To Improve Security 5 (2004, GAO-04-1098T).

p. 144 bird droppings in the town's water tank: "Occurrence and Monitoring Document for the Final Ground Water Rule," Environmental Protection Agency (Oct. 2006), 2–6, http://www.epa.gov/ogwdw/disinfection/gwr/pdfs /support_gwr_occurrence-monitoring.pdf; Robert M. Clark and Rofl A Deininger, "Protecting the Nation's Critical Infrastructure: The Vulnerability of U.S. Water Supply

Systems," *Journal of Contingencies and Crisis Management* 8 (June 2000), 78.

p. 146 assessed as possible or probable weapons: Clark and Deininger, "Protecting the Nation's Critical Infrastructure," 73.

p. 146 bioengineered agents: Mark Wheelis and Malcolm Dando, "New Technology and Future Developments in Biological Warfare," United Nations Institute for Disarmament Research, http://www.unidir.org/pdf/articles/pdf-art115.pdf.

p. 146 known generally as SCADA systems: Yacov Y. Haimes, "Strategic Responses to Risks of Terrorism to Water Sources," *Journal of Water Resources Planning and Management* 128 (Nov./Dec. 2002), 384.

p. 146 encouraging football viewers: Sam McManis, "Super Bowl XXI: Notebook: 'Experts' of the Media Pick Giants to Win It," *Los Angeles Times*, Jan. 25, 1987, http://articles.latimes.com/1987-01-25/sports/sp-5854_1_mark-bavaro.

p. 146 all sprinted to relieve themselves: Linda Yates, "Down the Tubes," *Peace Magazine*, Oct.–Dec. 2008, http://peacemagazine.org/archive/v24n4p19.htm. But see Snopes.com dismissing this as a Super Bowl Legend, http://www.snopes.com/sports/football/superbowl.asp.

p. 147 noises to prevent birds: "2008 Watershed Protection Plan Update," Massachusetts Department of Conservation and Recreation, http://www.mass.gov/dcr/watersupply/watershed/documents/2008dcrwppv2cwachusett.pdf.

p. 148 reservoir with cyanide: Brad Poole, "Keeping Our Water Safe; Tucson Water has Spent $3M to Boost Security Since 9/11," *Tucson Citizen*, Sept. 6, 2005, 1A.

p. 148 microfiltration or ultrafiltration: Clark and Deininger, "Protecting the Nation's Critical Infrastructure," 75.

p. 148 focused on airborne contaminants: Ibid.

p. 149 the Government Accountability Office: "Drinking Water: Experts' Views on How Future Federal Funding Can Best

Be Spent to Improve Security," U.S. Government Accountability Office, Oct. 31, 2003, http://www.gao.gov /products/GAO-04-29.

p. 149   this slug of infected water: P. Aarne Vesilind, "Engineering and the Threat of Terrorism," *Journal of Professional Issues in Engineering Education and Practice*, Apr. 2003, 70–71.

p. 150   flowed out of faucets around: "Case Histories of Selected Backflow Incidents," NoBackFlow.com, http://www .nobackflow.com/casehist.htm.

p. 150   gallons of fire-retardant foam: Yochi J. Dreazen, "Reservoirs May Be Safe, but House Pipes Can be Used to Push Toxins into a Neighborhood," *Wall Street Journal*, Dec. 27, 2001, A14.

p. 150   "attempt to create a backflow": Ibid.

p. 151   a lock of blond hair looping: "Buster Backflow," American Backflow Prevention Association, http://abpa.org/buster _backflow.htm. Page 3 from the Buster Backflow© Comic Book #1 used with permission of the American Backflow Prevention Association, ABPA.org.

p. 152   a drum of toxic chemicals: Dreazen, "Reservoirs May Be Safe," A14.

p. 152   President Clinton issued: Haimes, "Strategic Responses to Risks of Terrorism to Water Sources," 383.

p. 152   following the attacks of 9/11: "Instructions to Assist Community Water Systems in Complying with the Public Health Security and Bioterrorism Preparedness and Response Act of 2002," Office of Water EPA 810-B-02-001, http://www.epa.gov/safewater/watersecurity/pubs /util-inst.pdf.

p. 153   security, law enforcement: Grumbles, "Statement of Benjamin H. Grumbles," 7.

p. 153   patrols of Chicago's intake sites: Gleick, *The World's Water*.

p. 153   tripling the dedicated police force: Arrandale, "Hydro Defense," 50. See also "State, City Announce Landmark Agreement to Safeguard New York City Drinking Water," New York City Environmental Protection, http://www.nyc.gov/html/dep/html/press_releases/11-11pr.shtml.

p. 154   with sodium hypochlorite: "Water Unsecured," 106.

p. 154   trout, he said: Arrandale, "Hydro Defense," 50.

p. 155   detected sediments disturbed: Ibid.

p. 155   "vigilant in protecting our water systems": Jennifer Smith, "Protecting the Water Supply; City Gets Federal Funds to Install Alert System for Drinking Water in Case of Terror Attack, Contamination," Newsday, Apr. 25, 2008, A22.

p. 156   "perceived as key targets": "Terrorism and Security Issues Facing the Water Infrastructure Sector," Congressional Research Service (2003), 2.

p. 156   of this amount, $113 million: "Water Unsecured," The Public Citizen, 103.

p. 156   seems like a lot of money: Ibid.

p. 156   the size of Dallas: "Protecting our Water: Drinking Water Security in America After 9/11," American Water Works Association, http://fortressteam.com/resources/watersecurity.pdf.

p. 156   improved lighting, locks: Ibid.

p. 157   anti-asteroid laser cannon: Brandon Keim, "How to Defend Earth Against an Asteroid Strike," Wired Science, Mar. 27, 2009, http://www.wired.com/wiredscience/2009/03/planetdefense.

p. 159   did not weaken teeth but: "The Story of Fluoridation," National Institute of Dental and Craniofacial Research, Mar. 25, 2011, http://www.nidcr.nih.gov/OralHealth/Topics/Fluoride/TheStoryofFluoridation.htm.

p. 160   fluoridated their water: "Water fluoridation statistics for 2006," Division of Oral Health, National Center for Chronic Disease Prevention and Health Promotion, Sept. 1, 2008.

p. 159   this public health intervention: See, e.g., Marian S. Mc-Donagh, Penny F. Whiting, and Paul M. Wilson et al., "Systematic review of water fluoridation," BMJ 321 (Oct. 7, 2000), 855–859.

p. 160   Ten Great Public Health Achievements: "Ten Great Public Health Achievements," Morbidity and Mortality Weekly Report 48, no. 2 (Apr. 2, 1999), 241–243, http://cdc.gov/mmwr/preview/mmwrhtml/00056796.htm.

p. 160   the anti-Communist Keep America Committee: An image of the flyer can be found at Wikimedia, http://commons.wikimedia.org/wiki/File:Unholy_three.png.

6: Bigger Than Soft Drinks

p. 161   sending eighteen people to the hospital: Luis Zaragoza and Claudia Zequeira, "UCF in hot water with fans," Orlando Sentinel, Sept. 18, 2007.

p. 162   "will not be offering free water": "UCF Officials Apologize For Water Problems, Will Offer Free Bottles Next Game," WKMG, Sept. 17, 2007.

p. 162   Weird Al Yankovic: Peter H. Gleick, "Celebrities and Bottled Water: Spoiled, Misinformed, or Just Plain Weird," Huffington Post, Sept. 3, 2010, http://www.huffingtonpost.com/peter-h-gleick/celebrities-and-bottled-w_b_705534.html.

p. 163   painting by Velázquez: An image of the painting can be found at Wikimedia, http://commons.wikimedia.org/wiki/File:15_El_Aguador_de_Sevilla_%28Wellington_Museum,_Apsley_House,_Londres,_1623%29.jpg.

p. 164   drinking at St. Maelrubha's Well: Varner, Sacred Wells, 117.

p. 165   known in Roman times as the Hot Town: Stanley Young and Melba Levick, Beautiful Spas and Hot Springs of California (San Francisco: Chronicle Books LLC, 2003), 8.

p. 165   "lay in a supply at home and cannot drink": P. E. LaMoreaux and J. T. Tanner, eds., *Springs and Bottled Waters of the World* (New York: Springer-Verlag Berlin Heidelberg, 2001), 114.

p. 165   "to liberate the genius": Ibid.,109.

p. 167   "destination for pilgrims": Varner Op. Cit., 142.

p. 167   "on the other days let him eat meat": Ibid., 140.

p. 168   its own ceramics works: Stephen J. Davis, "Pilgrimage and the Cult of Saint Thecla," *Pilgrimage and Holy Space in Late Antique Egypt* 134 (1998), 303; Peter Grossman, "The Pilgrimage Center of Abu Mina," *Pilgrimage and Holy Space in Late Antique Egypt* 134 (1998), 281.

p. 168   A sketch of water bottles: Henri Leclercq, *Dictionnaire d'Archeologie Chretienne et de Liturgie* (Paris: Letouzey et Ané, 1903), 383.

p. 169   breaking up kidney stones: Lamoreaux and Tanner, *Springs and Bottled Waters of the World*, 107.

p. 169   a peculiar stately promenade: Christopher Anstey and Annick Cossic, *The New Bath Guide* (Richmond hill: Broadcast Books, 2009), 111.

p. 170   passed decrees in 1781: Lamoreaux and Tanner, *Springs and Bottled Waters of the World*, 114.

p. 171   as ambassador to France: Arthur Von Wiesenberger, *The Pocket Guide to Bottled Water* (Chicago: Contemporary Books, 1991), 16.

p. 171   Vichy bottles were popular: Eric Thomas Jennings, *Curing the Colonizers: Hydrotherapy, Climatology, and French Colonial Spas* (Durham: Duke University Press, 2006), 207.

p. 171   Appollinaris became a favorite: Maureen P. Green and Timothy Green, *The Best Bottled Waters in the World* (New York: Simon & Schuster, 1986), 69.

p. 171   his cherished Badoit water: Ibid., 10.

p. 172   former mayor of Vergèze: Ibid.

p. 172   chose to keep the Perrier name: Barry Fox, "Secrets of the Source," *New Scientist*, Nov. 19, 1988, 47.

p. 172   Perrier when mixing whisky: Chapelle, *Wellsprings*, 15.

p. 172   "battles stomach problems": Daniela Brignone, *Ferrarelle: A Sparkling Italian Story* (Schirmer Mosel: Widenmayerstr [Munich] 2001), 46.

p. 173   Germany more than 300 brands: Dooley Worth, "The Tasting of Waters," *Sarasota Herald-Tribune*, June 2, 2002, 68.

p. 173   introduction of chlorine: Harlan Bengtson, "Water Chlorination History—The mid-1800s through the early 1900s," Bright Hub, http://www.brighthub.com/engineering/civil /articles/77511.aspx>; Chapelle, *Wellsprings*, 15.

p. 173   "in their lawn mower": "Bottled Water: A river of money," MSN Money, http://articles.moneycentral.msn.com/Investing /Extra/BottledWaterARiverOfMoney.aspx.

p. 174   largest advertising budget ever: Ibid.

p. 174   runners crossed the line: Nina Etkin, *Foods of Association: Biocultural Perspectives on Foods and Beverages That Mediate Sociability* (Tucson: University of Arizona Press, 2009), 189.

p. 174   more than three-hundred-fold: Paul Copley, *Marketing Communications Management: Concepts and Theories, Cases and Practices* (Burlington, MA: Elsevier Butterworth-Heinmann, 2004), 320.

p. 174   synonymous with bottled water: "Perrier Water," Encyclopedia for Cooks (2012), http://www.practicallyedible.com /edible.nsf/pages/perrierwater.

p. 174   "an exercise and fitness orientation": Wendy Weinstein, "Water, Water Everywhere," *Marketing Management* 3 (1994), 4.

p. 175   confirmed benzene levels: George James, "Perrier Recalls Its Water in U.S. After Benzene Is Found in Bottles," *New York Times*, Feb. 10, 1990.

p. 175   ".off market shelves for eleven weeks: Michael White, *A Short Course in International Marketing Blunders* (Petaluma, CA: World Trade Press, 2002), 18.

p. 175   the trendy Lutèce restaurant: James, "Perrier Recalls Its Water."

p. 176   closely trailed by Danone: "The Global Bottled Water Market by Volume," *Global Water Intelligence* 8, no. 7 (July 2007), http://www.globalwaterintel.com/archive/8/7/analysis /chart-of-the-month.html.

p. 176   opening about 1,500 bottles: Royte, *Bottlemania*, 42.

p. 176   fastest-growing drinks segment: Datamonitor, *Global Bottled Water: Industry Profile* (2004), 7.

p. 176   That figure has grown thirtyfold: Gleick, *The World's Water*, 5.

p. 176   American drinks thirty gallons: Erik Olson, "Bottled Water: Pure Drink or Pure Hype?," Natural Resources Defense Council, Apr. 1999, http://www.nrdc.org/water /drinking/bw/chap2.asp; Gleick, *The World's Water*, 6.

p. 176   rarely or never drink tap: Annie Shuppy, "H_2O U.," *Chronicle of Higher Education*, Nov. 3, 2006.

p. 177   "every restaurant should be offering it": William Orilio, "The Bottled Water Phenomenon," eHotelier.com, http://ehotelier.com/hospitality-news/item.php?id=A514 _0_11_0_M.

p. 177   "just nipping at you all the time": Weinstein, "Water, Water Everywhere."

p. 177   the brain behind Pet Refresh: Pet Refresh, http://petrefresh .com/press.htm.

p. 177   may be laughing all the way: Mihi Ahn, "Dogs lapping up specially bottled water," *Arizona Daily Star*, May 2, 2004.

p. 178   "the price of wine, milk": Olson, "Bottled Water," quoting Gustave Leven, Chairman of the Board of Perrier, France.

p. 178   Coke and Pepsi take tap water: Gleick, *The World's Water*, 80.

p. 179   snowcapped peaks closest to Ayer: Olson, "Bottled Water."

p. 179   Pepsi agreed to change: "Aquafina Labels To Show Source: Tap Water," CBS MoneyWatch, http://www.cbsnews.com /stories/2007/07/27/business/main3105021.shtml. Prior to the change, the label stated, "Bottled at the source P.W.S.," where consumers were supposed to understand that the acronym stood for "Public Water System."

p. 179   "Nestlé isn't saying": Gleick, *The World's Water*.

p. 180   "what the bottled water industry did": "The Story of Bottled Water," Food & Water Watch, http://www. foodandwaterwatch.org/water/bottled.

p. 180   convenience, style, taste: See, e.g., Olson, "Bottled Water"; Robert E. Hurd, *Consumer Attitude Survey on Water Quality Issues* (Denver, CO: American Water Works Association, 1993), 19.

p. 180   does not leach into the liquid: Gleick, *The World's Water*, 91.

p. 180   It revolutionized our industry: "Aqua Awards," *Beverage Industry* 90 (Nov. 1999), quoting Kim Jeffery.

p. 181   "ice bruises the bubbles": "Water, Water Everywhere," *Time*, May 20, 1985.

p. 181   "the no-beverages section": Bob Condor, "Flooding the Market: Bottled Water to Be No. 2 U.S. Drink," *Chicago Tribune*, Apr. 6, 2003, Q-9.

p. 181   "the nexus of pop-culture glamour": Anna Lenzer, "Spin the Bottle," *Mother Jones* (Sept.–Oct. 2009), 34.

p. 181   designing a water carafe: Gleick, *The World's Water*, 147.

p. 181   provide counsel to diners: Brian C. Howard, "Message in a Bottle," *E–The Environment Magazine* (Sept.–Oct. 2003), http://www.emagazine.com/view/?1125.

p. 181   "a sharp spritz": Arthur von Wiesenberger, H_2O: *The Guide to Quality Bottled Water* (Chicago: Contemporary Books, 1978), 11.

p. 182   ABC's 20/20: Tom Standage, "Bad to the Last Drop," *New York Times*, Aug. 1, 2005; John Stossel, "Is Bottled Water Better Than Tap?," ABC 20/20, http://abcnews.go.com /2020/Health/story?id=728070&page=1; Gleick, *The World's Water*, 80; "GMA: Water Taste Test," Good Morning America, http://abcnews.go.com/GMA/story?id=126984 &page=1.

p. 182   attributed the rise in tooth cavities: Juliet Eilperin, "Filtered and bottled water consumption could increase tooth decay risk," *Washington Post*, Jan. 17, 2011.

p. 183   "relegated to showers": As quoted in Gleick, *The World's Water*, 1.

p. 183   seventeen gallons more soft drinks: Ibid., 12–13.

p. 183   regulated as a food product: Sally Squires, "Is Bottled Water Worth the Price?," *Washington Post*, Jan. 22, 1986, Health Section 14.

p. 183   manufacturers must remove or reduce: Gleick, *The World's Water*, 43.

p. 183   water never enters into interstate commerce: Olson, "Bottled Water."

p. 183   Ten states do not regulate: Gleick, *The World's Water*, 37.

p. 183   only one-quarter of one person: "Money Down the Drain? A Review of Bottled Water in Massachusetts," Massachusetts Senate Committee on Post Audit and Oversight (2000), 7.

p. 184   forty-three states fund one or fewer: Howard, "Message in a Bottle."

p. 184   more than 330,000 times: "Drinking Water," NYC Environmental Protection, http://nyc.gov/html/dep/html /drinking_water/index.shtml.

p. 184   if fines are ever levied: "Money Down the Drain."

p. 184   "specific source, mineral composition": Gleick, *The World's Water*, 59.

p. 184 Cleveland with the local tap: Howard, "Message in a Bottle."

p. 185 "purity can be misguided": Standage, "Bad to the Last Drop."

p. 185 bottles contained arsenic: Olson, "Bottled Water."

p. 185 arsenic, benzene, chloroform: "Bottled Water and Vended Water: Are Consumers Getting Their Money's Worth?," Office of Research, California Legislature Assembly (1985), 2.

p. 185 Kansas Department of Health: Howard, "Message in a Bottle."

p. 186 discarded daily in trash cans: "Bottled Water," *Container Recycling Institute*, http://www.container-recycling.org /facts/plastic/bottledwater.htm.

p. 186 water bottles in its trash: Howard, "Message in a Bottle."

p. 186 "better for the environment": "Pepsico's Aquafina Launches the Eco-Fina Bottle, the Lightest Weight Bottle in the Market," Pepsico, http://www.pepsico .com/PressRelease/pepsicos-aquafina-launches-the -eco-fina-bottle-the-lightest-weight-bottle-in- the03252009.html.

p. 186 overall recycling rate for plastic: Gleick, *The World's Water*, 97.

p. 186 "16 percent of PET water bottles": Howard, "Message in a Bottle."

p. 186 the sixth state to do so: Gleick, *The World's Water*, 101.

p. 187 a lot more greenhouse gas emissions: Maureen Clancy, "Bottled water can be a poor environmental choice," *San Diego Union-Tribune*, Aug. 20, 2007.

p. 187 website lists a series of initiatives: Fiji Water Newsroom, http://www.fijiwater.co.uk/Newsstand.aspx.

p. 187 "Greenwashes of the Year": Heidi Spiegelbaum, "The Greenwash Brigade," American Public Media Marketplace, http://www.marketplace.org/topics/sustainability/greenwash-brigade/fiji-water-numbers.

p. 187 American Nuns similarly voiced: Gleick, *The World's Water*, 140.

p. 188 Del Posto in New York and Poggio: Marian Burros, "Fighting the Tide, a Few Restaurants Tilt to Tap Water," *New York Times*, May 30, 2007.

p. 188 "the greatest marketing scam": Royte, *Bottlemania*, 149.

p. 188 water filter and reusable container: Rick Rouan, "Water experiences a bottleneck in sales," *Beverage Industry* (Oct. 2010), 12; Glennon, *Unquenchable*, 48.

p. 189 install fifty water fountains: "UCF To Install Water Fountains In New Stadium," WESH, Sept. 18, 2007, http://www.wesh.com/news/14143574/detail.html?rss=orl&psp=news.

p. 190 trendiest restaurants: Florence Fabricant, "In a Drought, Putting a Spin on the Bottle," *New York Times*, Apr. 3, 2002.

p. 190 Atlanta restaurants did the same: Catherine Cobb, "Drought Drives Water Conservation Efforts in Southeast," *Nation's Restaurant News*, Nov. 4, 2007. Many of the restaurants only served tap water upon request.

7: Need Versus Greed

p. 192 Cochabamba's residents lack access: Erik B. Bluemel, "The Implications of Formulating a Human Right to Water," *Ecology Law Quarterly* 31 (2004), 957, 965.

p. 192 up to ten times more: Elizabeth Peredo Beltran, "Water, Privatization and Conflict: Women from the Cochabamba Valley," *Global Issue Papers* 4 (Apr. 2004), 13; William Finnegan, "Leasing the Rain," *The New Yorker*, Apr. 8, 2002, 43.

p. 193 declared the property of the state: Maria McFarland

Sanchez-Moreno and Tracy Higgins, "Special Report: No Recourse: Transnational Corporations and the Protection of Economic, Social, and Cultural Rights in Bolivia," *Fordham International Law Journal* 27 (2004), 1663, 1761.

p. 193   "a fundamental human right": The Cochabamba Declaration (2000), available at http://www.citizen.org/cmep /article_redirect.cfm?ID=10304.

p. 194   "recognized as an economic good": The Dublin Statement on Water and Sustainable Development (1992), available at http://www.wmo.int/pages/prog/hwrp/documents/english/icwedece.html.

p. 195   sub-Saharan Africa: "Keeping sanitation in the international spotlight," *The Lancet* 371 (Mar. 29, 2008), 1045.

p. 195   illnesses caused by contaminated water: "Water Facts," Water.org, http://water.org/water-crisis/water-facts/water.

p. 195   the death of one child: Morris, *The Blue Death*, 264.

p. 195   every dollar spent to improve sanitation: J. Bartram et al., "Focusing on improved water and sanitation for health," *The Lancet* 365 (2005), 810.

p. 195   within a fifteen-minute walk: John Thompson et al., "Waiting at the Tap: Changes in Urban Water Use in East Africa Over Three Decades," *Environment & Urbanization* 12 (2000), 37, 48.

p. 196   170 million people have to walk: Fishman, *The Big Thirst*, 240.

p. 196   put a human face on the situation: Aylito's story is adapted from Tina Rosenberg, "The Burden of Thirst," *National Geographic*, Apr. 2010.

p. 197   A group of Indian girls stopping: The photograph, by Tom Maisey, can be found at Wikimedia, http://commons .wikimedia.org/wiki/File:Girls_carrying_water_in_India.jpg.

p. 198   greatest threat facing their citizens: Personal communication with William Reilly, former EPA Administrator (Sept. 21, 2005).

p. 198   the term "water deprivation": Ben Crow, "Water: Gender and Material Inequalities in the Global South" (Center for Global, International, & Regional Studies, University of California, Santa Cruz, working paper no. 2001-5, 2001), 3, http://repositories.cdlib.org/cgi/viewcontent.cgi?article =1000&context=cgirs.

p. 198   "poverty is, quite literally, de-civilizing": Fishman, *The Big Thirst*, 246.

p. 199   95 percent of water systems: Glennon, *Unquenchable*, 248.

p. 200   growing at an annual 6 percent: Gleick, *The World's Water*, 45.

p. 200   privatized across the globe: Finnegan, "Leasing the Rain."

p. 200   infrastructure to public/private partnerships: Gleick, *The World's Water*, 48.

p. 201   have been renegotiated: J. Luis Guasch, Jean-Jacques Laffont, and Stephane Straub, "Renegotiation of Concession Contracts in Latin America" (ESE Discussion Papers, Edinburgh School of Economics, University of Edinburgh, 2004), 103, http://ideas.repec.org/p/edn/esedps/103.html.

p. 210   "full cost recovery": Bakker, "Archipelagos and Networks," 2.

p. 202   water provision and sewer lines expanded: Sebastian Galiani et al., "Water for Life: The Impact of the Privatization of Water Services on Child Mortality," *Journal of Political Economy* 113 (Feb. 2005), 83.

p. 202   one of the authors concluded: Ernesto Schargrodsky, "Water and Human Well Being Executive Session" (VIU, San Servelo, July 20, 2009), http://www.hks.harvard.edu /var/ezp_site/storage/fckeditor/file/pdfs/centers-programs /centers/cid/ssp/docs/events/workshops/2009/water /Schargrodsky_Infrastructure_disc_090720.pdf.

p. 203   "he forgot to lay the pipes": Glennon, *Unquenchable*, 247.

p. 203   to privatization in Argentina: Ibid.

p. 203   "cutting off poor Argentines": "Buenos Aires: Collapse of the Privatization Deal," Food & Water Watch, http://www .foodandwaterwatch.org/global/latin-america/argentina /buenos-aires-collapse-of-the-privatization-deal.

p. 204   "rate hikes, cut-offs": Maude Barlow and Tony Clarke, "The Struggle For Latin America's Water," North American Congress on Latin America.

p. 204   human right to water: Gleick, *Unquenchable*, 206 (table listing "international documents, treaties, declarations, and standards recognizing the right to water and related forms of health and human development").

p. 204   "accessible and affordable water": General Comment No. 15 (2002), The right to water (arts. 11 and 12 of the International Covenant on Economic, Social and Cultural Rights), http://www.unhchr.ch/tbs/doc.nsf/0 /a5458d1d1bbd713fc1256cc400389e94.

p. 204   seven to fourteen gallons a day: Peter Gleick has suggested the basic minimum for drinking, cooking, bathing and sanitation should be 13 gallons a day. Glennon, *Unquenchable*, 229.

p. 205   "what corporations and investors want": The Council of Canadians, http://www.canadians.org.

p. 205   resolution in 2010 declaring: The Human Right to Water and Sanitation, A/64/L.63/Rev.1 (2010).

p. 206   "from one of charity or commodity": Erik B. Bluemel, "The Implications of Formulating a Human Right to Water," *Ecology Law Quarterly* 31 (2004), 957, 973.

p. 206   at least fifteen national constitutions: "Right to Water: Moving towards a global consensus?," World Water Council, http://www.worldwaterforum5.org/fileadmin/wwc/Programs /Right_to_Water/Pdf_doct/Story_RTW_CD_March07 _compressed.pdf.

p. 206 "in any civilised society": Chameli Singh v. State of U.P., Indian Supreme Court (1996) 2SCC549:(AIR 1996 SC 1051).

p. 207 list went on and on: S.K. Garg v. State of U.P. and Ors., May 28, 1998.

p. 207 stopping the burial of bodies: M.C Mehta v. Union of India (1988) 1 SCC 471.

p. 208 "large numbers due to dehydration": S.K. Garg v. State of U.P. and Ors.

p. 208 17 percent of Indians do not have access: Amy Yee, "Liter by Liter, Indians Get Cleaner Water," *New York Times*, Mar. 21, 2012.

p. 208 entitlement of twenty-five liters: Alix-Gowlland Gualtieri, "South Africa's Water Law and Policy Framework: Implications for the Right to Water" (IELRC Working Paper, 2007), 1, 4, http://www.ielrc.org/content/w0703.pdf.

p. 209 municipalities have installed prepaid meters: Mazibuko, Case CCT 39/09 at 7.

p. 209 lower court said the practice: Mazibuko and Others v. City of Johannesburg and Others (Centre on Housing Rights and Evictions as amicus curiae) [2008] 4 All SA 471 (W).

p. 209 "to realise the achievement of the right": Mazibuko, Case CCT 39/09 at 25.

p. 209 more than eight million South Africans: "In the matter between: Lindiwe Mazibuko and Others and the City of Johannesburg and Others," Constitutional Court of South Africa, Case CCT 39/09, 2 (2009).

p. 210 "to receive it from the hydrants": Jeffrey A. Kroessler, "Water for the City," *The Old Croton Aqueduct: Rural Resources Meet Urban Needs* (Yonkers, NY: Hudson River Museum of Westchester, 1992), 14.

p. 211 of water from rain barrels: Finnegan, "Leasing the Rain," 47–51.

p. 213   from 0.01 to 0.05 cents: "Preventing Diarrheal Disease in Developing Countries: Proven Household Water Treatment Options, "Centers for Disease Control and Prevention," Nov. 2010.

p. 213   technique has been disseminated: Daniele S. Lantagne et al., "Household water treatment and safe storage options in developing countries: A review of current implementation practices," Woodrow Wilson Center Navigating Peace Initiative.

p. 213   130 million sachets: "Safe Drinking Water," P&G Health Sciences Institute, http://www.pghsi.com/pghsi/safewater.

p. 214   "is warranted on the basis": Thomas Clasen et al., "Interventions to improve water quality for preventing diarrhoea: systematic review and meta-analysis," *BMJ* 334 (Mar. 12, 2007), http://www.bmj.com/content/334/7597/782.

p. 214   review of POU field studies: Lorna Fewtrell et al., "Water, sanitation, and hygiene interventions to reduce diarrhoea in less developed countries: a systematic review and meta-analysis," *Lancet Infectious Diseases* 5(2005), 42, 48.

p. 215   those who purchase the kits: Nava Ashraf, James Berry, and Jesse M. Shaprio, "Can Higher Prices Stimulate Product Use? Evidence from a Field Experiment in Zambia," *American Economic Review* 100 (2010), 2383.

p. 215   "willing to pay for water quantity": Alix Peterson, Michael Kremer, and Robyn Meeks, "Water and Human Well Being: Report of an Executive Session on the Grand Challenges of a Sustainability Transition, San Servolo Island, Venice, Italy: July 20-21, 2009" (CID Working Paper No. 188, Center for International Development Working Paper, Cambridge, MA: Harvard University, Nov. 2009).

p. 215   this level of use is no small achievement: Daniele S. Lantagne et al., "Household water treatment and safe storage options in developing countries."

p. 215   "You're a professor?": The quotations in this section are from a talk Scott Harrison gave at Duke's Nicholas School of the Environment on April 27, 2009.

p. 217   Scott Harrison, the founder: The photograph, provided by the Silicon Prairie News, can be found at Wikimedia, http://commons.wikimedia.org/wiki/File:Scott_Harrison _2010.jpg.

p. 220   cities around the globe hosted events: Amanda Rose, "Twestival Raises Over $250K and Counting," http:/ /mashable.com/2009/02/18/twestival-results.

p. 221   and the teaser headline: "Hot Bachelors," People, June 30, 2008, 99.

p. 223   the exercise of a human faculty: <http://dowsers.org/dows-ing/about-asd/history-of-dowsing>.

p. 223   the famed skeptic" <http://www.randi.org/encyclopedia /dowsing.html>.

8: Finding Water for the Twenty-First Century

p. 225   "a shocking plot to sell": "H$_2$0," Canadian Broadcasting Corporation, http://www.cbc.ca/h2o/index.html.

p. 226   past fifty years to transport: See Adam Dicke, "Bulk Water Transfers," Water Is Life, http://academic.evergreen.edu /g/grossmaz/DICKEAC.

p. 226   the water to Asian markets: Lynette Kalsnes, "Great Lakes Face Increasing Pressure for Water from World, Own Back-yard," WBEZ95.1, June 21, 2011, http://www.wbez.org /frontandcenter/2011-06-21/great-lakes-face-increasing -pressure-water-world-own-backyard-88159.

p. 226   "Once the tap is turned on": Maude Barlow, "The Glob-alization of Water," Global Water Issues, http://www .enviroalternatives.com/waterglobal.html.

p. 227   "fair is fair, and Great Lakes": "Barricading the Great Lakes," Los Angeles Times, Feb. 13, 1985.

p. 227   level has fallen to the lowest: Glennon, *Unquenchable*, 98.

p. 227   "no interest in feeding": "Canada's water isn't for sale," *Montreal Gazette*, July 22, 2001, A18.

p. 227   "will allow elites to assure": Martin O'Malley and Angela Mulholland, "Canada's Water," CBC News Online, http://www.portaec.net/library/ocean/water/canadas_water.html.

p. 228   the plot of the H_2O television series: Steve Maich, "America Is Thirsty," *Maclean's*, Dec. 28, 2005, 26–30.

p. 228   Toronto withdraws 1.7 billion liters: "Toronto Water at a Glance," Toronto.ca, http://www.toronto.ca/water/glance.htm.

p. 228   shipping channel that flows: Robert Loeffler, "The Great Lakes Water Drain," *Earth Watch Ohio*, http://www.ecowatch.org/pubs/febmar08/great_lakes_drain.htm.

p. 228   "crops that are then shipped": Maich, "America Is Thirsty," 8.

p. 228   "the economic climate in northern Ontario": Aaron Freeman, "Blue Gold: The Political Economy of Water Trading in Canada," *Multinational Monitor*, Apr. 1, 1999.

p. 229   in containers of twenty liters: Noah Hall, "Capping the Bottle on Uncertainty: Closing the Information Loophole in the Great Lakes–St. Lawrence River Basin Water Resources Compact," *Case Western Law Review* 60 (2010), 1211.

p. 230   "no one can use it": Fishman, *The Big Thirst*, 85.

p. 230   "better cheap politics than water": Ibid.

p. 231   the twenty-first century's equivalent: Marc Champion, "Water Hogs on the Ski Slopes," *Wall Street Journal*, Jan. 24, 2008.

p. 231   six ships per month: "Thirsty Barcelona Gets Water Shipments," Sky News, http://news.sky.com/home/sky-news-archive/article/1315908.

p. 231   "a drive-through hamburger": Brian McAndrew, "There's minimal legislation to stop the export of Canada's greater natural resource—Water up for grabs," *The Guelph Mercury*, Sept. 25, 1999.

p. 232   but Pickens believes time: Susan Berfield, "T. Boone Pickens Thinks Water is the New Oil—And He's Betting $100 Million that He's Right," *Bloomberg Business Week*, June 12, 2008.

p. 232   proposals to tow icebergs: Thomas K. Grose, "Just Thaw and Serve," *Time*, May 29, 2011.

p. 232   they already push icebergs: Michael Ryan, "Iceberg Wrangler," *Smithsonian*, Feb. 2003.

p. 232   poles and the equatorial regions: "Water from Icebergs," National Oceanographic and Atmospheric Administration, http://oceanexplorer.noaa.gov/edu/learning/player /lesson12/l12la1.html.

p. 232   "the purest water": Grose, "Just Thaw and Serve."

p. 233   "underappreciated, mispriced": Sarah O'Connor, "Traders seek a fresh well in world of commodities," *Financial Times*, July 24, 2008.

p. 233   Otto Spork perpetrated fraud: OSC finds, *Financial Post*, http://business.financialpost.com/2011/05/18/otto-spork -perpetrated-fraud-osc-finds/.

p. 234   twelve thousand desalination plants: "Thirsty? How 'Bout a Cool, Refreshing Cup of Seawater?," U.S. Geological Survey, http://ga.water.usgs.gov/edu/drinkseawater.html.

p. 234   such widespread adoption: Susanna Eden, Tim W. Glass, and Valerie Herman, "Desalination in Arizona—A Growing Component of the State's Future Water Supply Portfolio," Water Research Center, College of Agriculture and Life Sciences at the University of Arizona, http://ag .arizona.edu/azwater/arroyo/Arroyo_2011.pdf.

p. 234   ten times more expensive: Adam Bluestein, "Blue Is the New Green." "The cost of producing 1 cubic meter (264 gallons) of desalinated water ranges from about $1 to $1.50, compared with 10 cents to 20 cents to obtain water from a reservoir or well. (Average U.S. daily household use is about 350 gallons.)"

p. 234   450 million liters a day: "Shoaiba, Saudi Arabia," Water-Technology.net, http://www.water-technology.net/projects /shoaiba-desalination.

p. 235   Navy aircraft carrier: Tom Harris, "How Aircraft Carriers Work," How Stuff Works, Aug. 29, 2002, http://science .howstuffworks.com/aircraft-carrier.htm.

p. 235   in a reverse osmosis plant: Glennon, Unquenchable, 155.

p. 235   capitalists clearly think: Bluestein, "Blue Is the New Green."

p. 236   projects that desalinated water: Glennon, Unquenchable, 153.

p. 237   capillary condensation: John Roach, "Water Harvested from Diesel Exhaust," Cosmic Log on MSNBC.com, Apr. 26, 2011, http://cosmiclog.msnbc.msn.com/_news/2011/04/06 /6419789-water-harvested-from-diesel-exhaust. For more information about capillary action, see "Capillary Action," U.S. Geological Survey, http://ga.water.usgs.gov /edu/capillaryaction .html. The site explains capillary action through a simple science experiment with water and celery.

p. 237   one gallon of diesel fuel: Roach, "Water Harvested from Diesel Exhaust," 42.

p. 237   the LifeStraw is: Mike Hanlon, "The LifeStraw Makes Dirty Water Clean," Gizmag.com, http://www.gizmag.com /go/4418.

p. 238   to drink from puddles: "Revolutionary 'LifeStraw' to assist during floods," ABC News (Australia), May 6, 2011, http://www.abc.net.au/news/2011-05-06/revolutionary-lifestraw-to-assist-during-floods/2706866.

p. 238   as WaterMill produces: Bryn Nelson, "Turning Air Into Water? Gadget Does Just That," Frontiers on MSNBC

.com, Dec. 8, 2008, http://www.msnbc.ms.com/id /28003681 /ns/technology_and_science-innovation.

p. 238 billboards in poor, rural areas: Andrew Chambers, "Africa's not-so-magic roundabout, *Guardian*, Nov. 24, 2009, http://www.guardian.co.uk/commentisfree/2009/nov/24 /africa-charity-water-pumps-roundabouts.

p. 239 struggling to spin it: Freschi, "Some NGOs CAN adjust to Failure."

p. 239 astronauts aboard: Seth Borenstein, "Astronauts Sample Recycled Urine, Sweat," *Virginian Pilot-Ledger Star*, May 24, 2009, N6.

p. 239 transport the heavy liquid: "International Space Station," NASA, Nov. 17, 2008, http://www.nasa.gov/mission_pages /station/behindscenes/waterrecycler.html.

p. 240 no matter how crystalline the water: Fishman, *The Big Thirst*, 157.

p. 240 recycling wastewater has become: Kathy Chu, "From toilets to tap: How we get tap water from sewage," *USA Today*, Mar. 3, 2011.

p. 241 "better to be self-reliant": Ibid.

p. 241 more expensive pipeline: Fishman, *The Big Thirst*, 154-165.

p. 242 your golden retriever: Maureen Cavanaugh and Gloria Penner, "Political Analysis: The Legacy of Toilet to Tap," KPBS, Aug. 4, 2010, http://www.kpbs.org/news/2010/aug /04/political-analysis-legacy-toilet-tap.

p. 242 plant would treat sewage water: Tom Arrandale, "Flushing Away Fears: Toilets-to-Tap Water Recycling Gets Past the Yuck Factor," *Governing*, May 2008, http://www.sandiego .gov/water/waterreuse/pdf/flushingawayfears.pdf.

p. 242 wash dishes and run faucets: "Water Use Statistics," DrinkTap.org, http://www.drinktap.org/consumerdnn /Home /WaterInformation/Conservation/WaterUseStatistics/tabid /85/Default.aspx.

p. 244   gallons of gray water: Glennon, *Unquenchable*, 164.

p. 244   "charge industrial users": Caigan Mackenzie, "Wastewater Reuse Conserves Water and Protects Waterways," National Environmental Services Center, Winter 2005, http://www .nesc.wvu.edu/ndwc/articles/OT/WI05/reuse.pdf.

p. 244   13 percent of piped water is lost: "Water Use Statistics."

p. 244   a major water pipe bursts: Charles Duhigg, "Toxic Waters: Saving U.S. Water and Sewer Systems Would Be Costly," *New York Times*, Mar. 14, 2010.

p. 245   simply from leaking pipes: Bluestein, "Blue Is the New Green."

p. 245   costs about $200 per foot: Fishman, *The Big Thirst*, 109.

p. 245   will span more than sixty miles: "New York Third Water Tunnel," Wonders of the World Databank, http://www.pbs .org/wgbh/buildingbig/wonder/structure/ny_third_water.html.

p. 246   "can't go a day without water": Charles Duhigg, "Saving U.S. Water and Sewer Systems Would Be Costly," *New York Times*, Mar. 14, 2010.

p. 246   "water neutral": Ling Woo Liu, "Water Pressure," *Time*, June 12, 2008.

p. 246   badly burned by protests: Ibid.

p. 248   "rolling Thanksgiving dinner": Gretchen Daily and Katherine Ellison, *The New Economy of Nature* (Washington, D.C.: Island Press), 74.

p. 249   new sewage treatment infrastructure: Michael Finnegan, "New York City's Watershed Agreement: A Lesson in Sharing Responsibility," *Pace Environmental Law Review* 14:626, 1997.

p. 250   study reported 216 payments: Tracy Stanton et al., *The State of Watershed Payments: An Emerging Marketplace* (Washington, D.C.: Ecosystem Marketplace, 2010), xi.

p. 250   Quito water fund: This case study is adapted from Stanton, *The State of Watershed Payments*, 18.

p. 250 Ruvu and Sigi River basins: This case study is adapted from Stanton, *The State of Watershed Payments*, 34.

p. 251 "When the well's dry": Glennon, *Unquenchable*, 16.

p. 253 platinum, palladium: "US firm plans to mine asteroids for minerals, water," *Agence France-Presse*, Apr. 25, 2012.

p. 253 delivered into orbit: Gregg Easterbrook, "Giving NASA a Real Mission," *Harvard Business Review*, May 3, 2012.

p. 254 "emphasis will be on spectacular": Will Oremus, "Deep Space Mine," Slate.com, May 11, 2012.

Afterword: A Glass Half Empty/A Glass Half Full

p. 255 "the rights to our town's water": McCloud Watershed Council, http://www.mccloudwatershedcouncil.org/about-us.

p. 256 "a new Draft Environmental Impact Report": "Atty. Gen. Brown Warns Nestlé of Legal Challenge to Water Bottling Plant," Office of the Attorney General, July 29, 2008, http://ag.ca.gov/newsalerts/print_release.php?id=1591.

p. 256 "we are withdrawing our proposal ": "Nestlé Waters North America Withdraws McCloud Project Proposal," Nestlé Waters, Sept. 10, 2009, http://www.press.nestle-watersna .com/press/Nestle-Waters-North-America-Withdraws -McCloud-Project-Proposal.htm.

p. 257 "they are going to run": Charlie Unkefer, "McCloud meeting marks the end of the Nestlé era," *Mount Shasta Herald*, Sept. 15, 2009.

p. 257 including at Cascade Locks: Andre Meunier, "Nestlé eyes Columbia Gorge spring to bottle water," *Oregonian*, June 12, 2009.

p. 257 Save Our Groundwater: Glennon, *Unquenchable*, 45.

p. 258 "taxation without representation": Unkefer, "McCloud meeting marks the end of the Nestlé era."

Index